Web
Page

Visual QuickProject Guide Collection

by Elizabeth Castro, Nolan Hester, and David Morris

Peachpit
Press

Web Page Visual QuickProject Guide Collection

Elizabeth Castro, Nolan Hester, and David Morris

Peachpit Press

1249 Eighth Street
Berkeley, CA 94710
510/524-2178
800/283-9444
510/524-2221 (fax)

Find us on the Web at: www.peachpit.com
To report errors, please send a note to errata@peachpit.com

Peachpit Press is a division of Pearson Education

Copyright © 2006 by Peachpit Press

Note: This edition is a collection of these three books, also published by Peachpit Press:

Creating a Web Page with HTML: Visual QuickProject Guide (ISBN 0-321-27847-X)
Copyright © 2005 by Elizabeth Castro.

Creating a Web Page in Dreamweaver: Visual Quick Project Guide (0-321-27843-7)
Copyright © 2005 by Nolan Hester

Creating a Web Site with Flash: Visual QuickProject Guide (0-321-32125-1)
Copyright © 2005 by David Morris

Notice of Rights

All rights reserved. No part of this book may be reproduced or transmitted in any form by any means, electronic, mechanical, photocopying, recording, or otherwise, without the prior written permission of the publisher. For information on getting permission for reprints and excerpts, contact permissions@peachpit.com.

Notice of Liability

The information in this book is distributed on an "As Is" basis without warranty. While every precaution has been taken in the preparation of the book, neither the author nor Peachpit Press shall have any liability to any person or entity with respect to any loss or damage caused or alleged to be caused directly or indirectly by the instructions contained in this book or by the computer software and hardware products described in it.

Trademarks

Visual QuickProject Guide is a registered trademark of Peachpit Press, a division of Pearson Education. All other trademarks are the property of their respective owners.

Many of the designations used by manufacturers and sellers to distinguish their products are claimed as trademarks. Where those designations appear in this book, and Peachpit Press was aware of a trademark claim, the designations appear as requested by the owner of the trademark. All other product names and services identified throughout this book are used in editorial fashion only and for the benefit of such companies with no intention of infringement of the trademark. No such use, or the use of any trade name, is intended to convey endorsement or other affiliation with this book.

ISBN 0-321-37465-7

9 8 7 6 5 4 3 2 1

Printed and bound in the United States of America

A Note About This Collection

Thank you for purchasing the Web Page Visual QuickProject Guide Collection. By combining three books into one, you save money and learn just what you need to get the job done.

Creating a Web Page with HTML: Visual QuickProject Guide is the first book in this combined volume, with the index for the book following immediately after the text. This is followed by Creating a Web Page in Dreamweaver: Visual QuickProject Guide and Creating a Web Site with Flash: Visual QuickProject Guide, with their respective indexes following immediately after each book, as well.

Each of these titles has a companion Web site where you can find project files and updates.

Creating a Web Page with HTML: Visual QuickProject Guide
Companion Web site at www.cookwood.com/htmlvqj gives you the complete project files for the book, including the image files and intermediate pages created throughout the project, as well as a complete list of HTML elements, CSS properties, color codes, and more.

Creating a Web Page in Dreamweaver: Visual QuickProject Guide
Companion Web site at www.waywest.net/dwvqj gives you the example files used in the book, including the images. You'll also find extra tips on working with Dreamweaver.

Creating a Web Site with Flash: Visual QuickProject Guide
Companion Web site at www.peachpit.com/vqj/flash gives you project files and updates. In the Support Files section of the site, you'll find all of the files you need to complete the project in the book. You can also download the intermediate files created in each chapter and the files that make up the final project site.

Full-color projects from the folks who bring you Visual QuickStart Guides...

Visual QuickProject

Creating a Web Page

with HTML

ELIZABETH CASTRO

creating
a web page
with html

Visual QuickProject Guide

by Elizabeth Castro

Peachpit
Press

Visual QuickProject Guide
Creating a Web Page with HTML
Elizabeth Castro

Peachpit Press
1249 Eighth Street
Berkeley, CA 94710
510/524-2178
800/283-9444
510/524-2221 (fax)

Find us on the World Wide Web at: www.peachpit.com
To report errors, please send a note to errata@peachpit.com
Peachpit Press is a division of Pearson Education

Copyright © 2005 by Elizabeth Castro

Cover design: The Visual Group with Aren Howell
Cover production: Aren Howell
Interior design: Elizabeth Castro
Cover photo credit: Digital Vision

Notice of Rights
All rights reserved. No part of this book may be reproduced or transmitted in any form by any means, electronic, mechanical, photocopying, recording, or otherwise, without the prior written permission of the publisher. For information on getting permission for reprints and excerpts, contact permissions@peachpit.com.

Notice of Liability
The information in this book is distributed on an "As Is" basis, without warranty. While every precaution has been taken in the preparation of the book, neither the author nor Peachpit Press shall have any liability to any person or entity with respect to any loss or damage caused or alleged to be caused directly or indirectly by the instructions contained in this book or by the computer software and hardware products described in it.

Trademarks
Visual QuickProject Guide is a registered trademark of Peachpit Press, a division of Pearson Education.

All other trademarks are the property of their respective owners.

Throughout this book, trademarks are used. Rather than put a trademark symbol with every occurrence of a trademarked name, we state that we are using the names in an editorial fashion only and to the benefit of the trademark owner with no intention of infringement of the trademark. No such use, or the use of any trade name, is intended to convey endorsement or other affiliation with this book.

ISBN 0-321-27847-X

Printed and bound in the United States of America

For Miquel and Rosa,
who got me started in this business
—and in Barcelona.

Special Thanks to...

Miquel Bada and Dimas Cabré, who lent me their offices, computers, and Internet connections when I was away from mine,

Margaret Christie, who looked through early drafts with a beginner's eyes,

Lisa Brazieal and Connie Jeung-Mills at Peachpit Press, who helped shepherd this book through production,

Nancy Davis, my amazing editor at Peachpit Press, who continues to ask just the right questions and offer just the right answers,

and Kissy Matthewson, who didn't want to learn so much about HTML, and thus inspired this book.

contents

contents

introduction

The Visual QuickProject Guide that you hold in your hands
offers a unique way to learn about new technologies. Instead of
drowning you in theoretical possibilities and lengthy explanations,
this Visual QuickProject Guide uses big, color illustrations coupled
with clear, concise step-by-step instructions to show you how to
complete one specific project in a matter of hours.

Our project in this book is to create a beautiful web site using
HTML and CSS, the two fundamental and standard technologies
used in web design today. Our web site showcases a collection of
beautiful photographs and postcards, but since the project covers
all the basic techniques, you'll be able to use what you learn to
create your own web sites—perhaps to show off your vacation
pictures from Egypt, share reading lists with your book group, or
keep track of your team's soccer game schedule.

Why should you write your own HTML and CSS instead of using
web page software like FrontPage or Dreamweaver? First, you
can create HTML and CSS with the free text editor that came with
your computer; no other investment is required. Second, HTML
and CSS are simple and straightforward and easier to learn than
a big software program. In addition, you'll have complete control
over how your page looks and works. Finally, you'll be able to
use the most standard and up-to-date versions of HTML and CSS,
without waiting for—or paying for—software upgrades.

what you'll create

On the home page, create a transparent GIF image with beautiful text for a logo.

Use a background image that adds to the feel of your page (but doesn't distract from the content).

Create a navigation bar to give your page a distinctive look and make it easy for visitors to navigate your site.

Create links to other pages on your site.

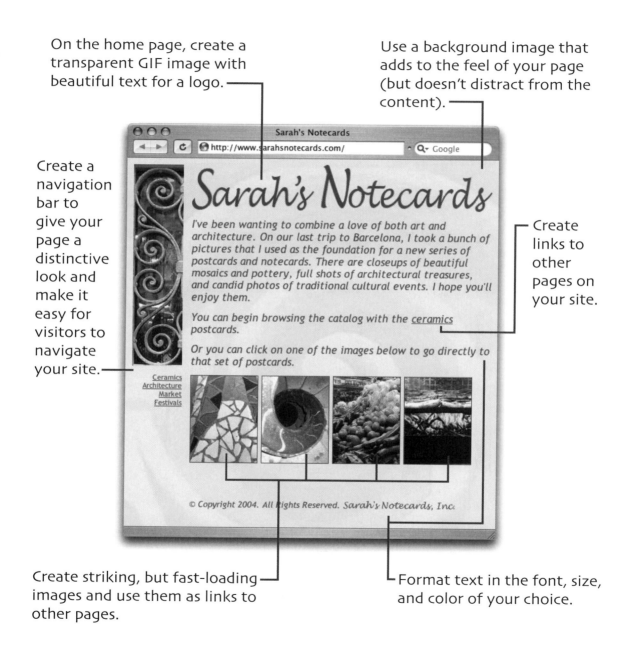

Create striking, but fast-loading images and use them as links to other pages.

Format text in the font, size, and color of your choice.

On the inner page, use headers to divide the information into hierarchical sections.

Format text to your liking.

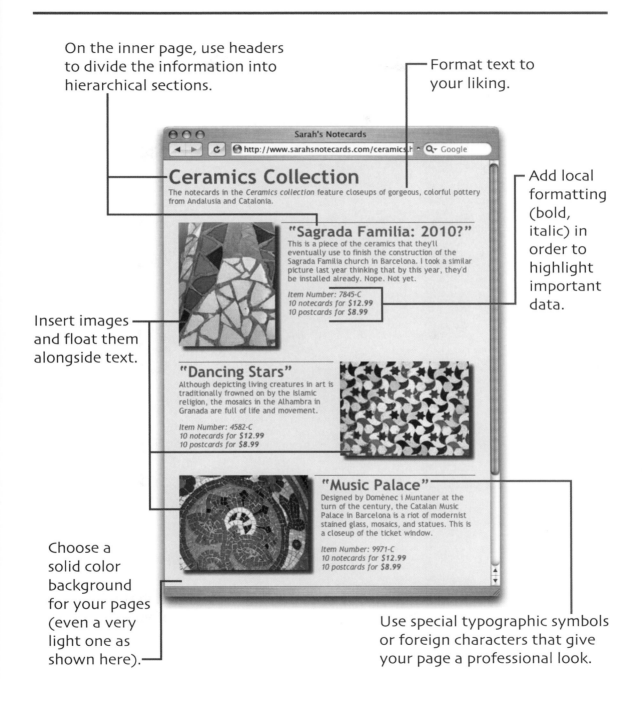

Add local formatting (bold, italic) in order to highlight important data.

Insert images and float them alongside text.

Choose a solid color background for your pages (even a very light one as shown here).

Use special typographic symbols or foreign characters that give your page a professional look.

how this book works

The title of each section explains what is covered on that page.

In this book, you'll create two HTML files (ceramics.html in Chapter 1 and index.html in Chapter 2). The code that you'll need to type in for the HTML files will be displayed on an orange background.

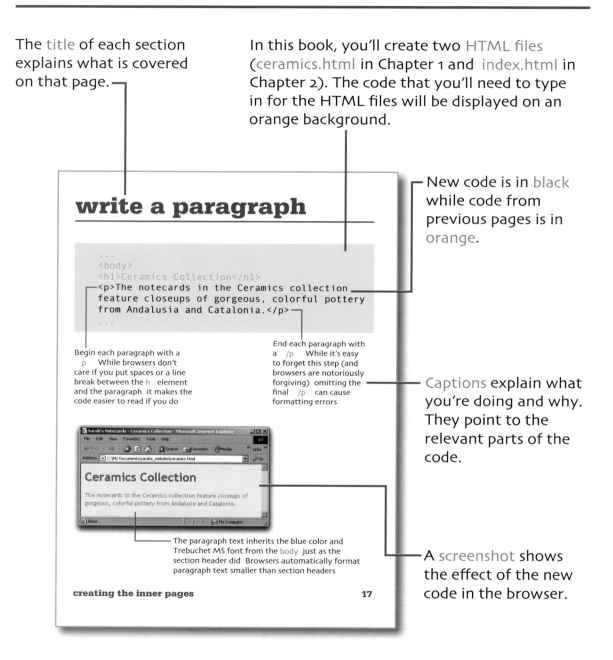

New code is in black while code from previous pages is in orange.

write a paragraph

```
. . .
<body>
<h1>Ceramics Collection</h1>
<p>The notecards in the Ceramics collection
feature closeups of gorgeous, colorful pottery
from Andalusia and Catalonia.</p>
. . .
```

Begin each paragraph with a p While browsers don't care if you put spaces or a line break between the h element and the paragraph it makes the code easier to read if you do

End each paragraph with a /p While it's easy to forget this step (and browsers are notoriously forgiving) omitting the final /p can cause formatting errors

Captions explain what you're doing and why. They point to the relevant parts of the code.

The paragraph text inherits the blue color and Trebuchet MS font from the body just as the section header did Browsers automatically format paragraph text smaller than section headers

A screenshot shows the effect of the new code in the browser.

creating the inner pages 17

introduction

You'll create two CSS style sheets that will contain formatting information for the HTML files (sarahs_styles.css in Chapter 1 and home.css in Chapter 2). The CSS code is shown on a green background. Again, new code is shown in black; existing code is a darker shade of green than its background.

An ellipsis (...) indicates that there is more code in this document and that it was explained on an earlier page.

Names of HTML elements, CSS properties, file names, and other important concepts are shown in orange.

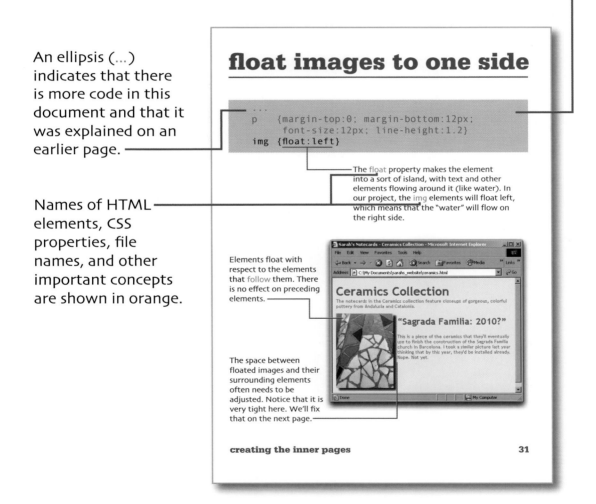

float images to one side

```
...
p    {margin-top:0; margin-bottom:12px;
      font-size:12px; line-height:1.2}
img  {float:left}
```

The float property makes the element into a sort of island, with text and other elements flowing around it (like water). In our project, the img elements will float left, which means that the "water" will flow on the right side.

Elements float with respect to the elements that follow them. There is no effect on preceding elements.

Ceramics Collection
The notecards in the Ceramics collection feature closeups of gorgeous, colorful pottery from Andalusia and Catalonia.

"Sagrada Familia: 2010?"
This is a piece of the ceramics that they'll eventually use to finish the construction of the Sagrada Familia church in Barcelona. I took a similar picture last year thinking that by this year, they'd be installed already. Nope. Not yet.

The space between floated images and their surrounding elements often needs to be adjusted. Notice that it is very tight here. We'll fix that on the next page.

creating the inner pages   **31**

how this book works

The extra bits section at the end of each chapter contains additional tips and tricks that you might like to know—but that aren't absolutely necessary for creating the web page.

The heading for each group of tips matches the section title. (The colors are just for decoration and have no hidden meaning.)

write a title

extra bits

save as html p. 6
- In fact in this book you'll be writing XHTML which is the most current most standard version of HTML The extension is still html
- Don't choose the Save in HTML or Save for Web formats in Micro soft Word They are designed for converting a Word document into HTML not for saving a document already written in HTML
- Once you save a document with the html extension double click ing it will often open your brows er not the text editor In order to edit the page either open it from inside your text editor (using File Open) or right click it on the desktop and choose Open with [your text editor]

start the web page p. 7
- Officially, web pages should begin with a DOCTYPE declaration which describes the version of HTML being used For example:

  !DOCTYPE html PUBLIC " // W C//DTD XHTML Transi tional//EN"

  "http://www w org/TR/xhtml / DTD/xhtml transitional dtd"

  html xmlns "http://www w org/ /xhtml"

  But it's not the end of the world if you just start with html

write a title p. 9
- The title of your web page is one of the key factors in getting it ranked on a search engine like Google. Use specific words in your title that reflect the content of your page

color the background p. 13
- An element's background is trans parent by default That means that if it is on top of another ele ment you'll see the other ele ment's background color shining through
- The part of a style rule that de scribes the elements that will be affected by the rule is called the selector It can be as simple as an element's name as in the example here (body) or it can be more complex in order to select only certain elements that satisfy given criteria We'll see some more com plicated selectors in Chapter

Next to the heading there's a page number that also shows which section the tips belong to.

48

creating the inner pages

the web site

You can find this book's companion web site at http://www.cookwood.com/htmlvqj/

Be sure to visit the extras section, where you'll find a complete list of HTML elements, CSS properties, color codes, and much more.

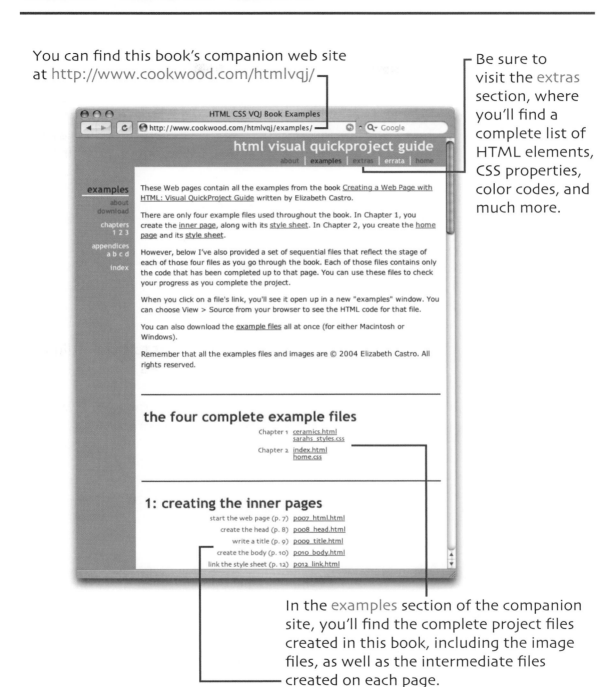

In the examples section of the companion site, you'll find the complete project files created in this book, including the image files, as well as the intermediate files created on each page.

useful tools

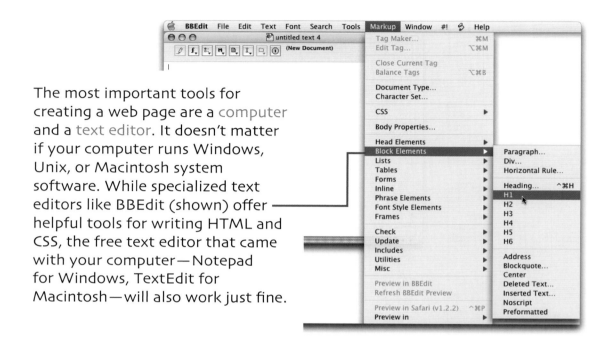

The most important tools for creating a web page are a computer and a text editor. It doesn't matter if your computer runs Windows, Unix, or Macintosh system software. While specialized text editors like BBEdit (shown) offer helpful tools for writing HTML and CSS, the free text editor that came with your computer—Notepad for Windows, TextEdit for Macintosh—will also work just fine.

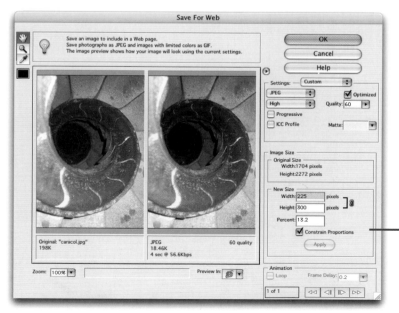

An image editor is useful for retouching and resizing photographs and graphic images for your web site. Many digital cameras and scanners come bundled with some kind of image editor, like Adobe Photoshop Elements, shown here.

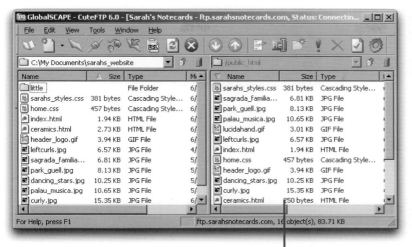

Once you've finished writing your web site you'll need to upload it to your web host to make it available on the Internet. While some web hosts let you do this through a browser, an FTP program, like Cute FTP (shown) makes transferring the files much easier.

And, of course, you'll want to use one or more browsers, like Internet Explorer (shown), Opera, and Safari, in order to test your pages and make sure they look the way they should. Explorer and Safari are both free. Opera has both a free and a paid version.

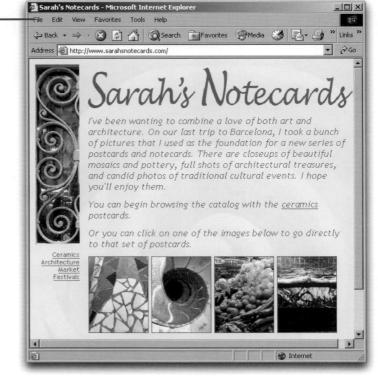

the next step

While this Visual QuickProject Guide will you give you an excellent foundation in HTML (actually XHTML) and CSS, I have to confess that there's a lot more to learn: tables, frames, forms, multimedia, and much more. If you're curious, check out my complete reference: HTML for the World Wide Web, with XHTML and CSS, Fifth Edition: Visual QuickStart Guide, also published by Peachpit Press.

The HTML VQS features clear examples, concise, step-by-step instructions, hundreds of illustrations, and lots of helpful tips. It covers every aspect of HTML (XHTML) and CSS in detail. It is the number one bestselling guide to HTML.

1. creating the inner pages

Sarah's Notecards – Ceramics Collection

file:///Users/liz/Documents/sarahs_website ^ Q Google

Ceramics Collection

The notecards in the *Ceramics collection* feature closeups of gorgeous, colorful pottery from Andalusia and Catalonia.

"Sagrada Familia: 2010?"

This is a piece of the ceramics that they'll eventually use to finish the construction of the Sagrada Familia church in Barcelona. I took a similar picture last year thinking that by this year, they'd be installed already. Nope. Not yet.

Item Number: 7845-C
10 notecards for $12.99
10 postcards for $8.99

"Dancing Stars"

Although depicting living creatures in art is traditionally frowned on by the Islamic religion, the mosaics in the Alhambra in Granada are full of life and movement.

Item Number: 4582-C
10 notecards for $12.99
10 postcards for $8.99

"Music Palace"

Designed by Domènec i Muntaner at the turn of the century, the Catalan Music Palace in Barcelona is a riot of modernist stained glass, mosaics, and statues. This is a closeup of the ticket window.

Item Number: 9971-C
10 notecards for $12.99
10 postcards for $8.99

The project that we'll complete in this book is a web site with two kinds of pages: inner pages that contain details and photos about the postcard collections that we sell, and one main, or home page which links to each of those individual pages. Because it's simpler, we'll start in this chapter by creating one of the inner pages, as shown at left. We'll create the home page in Chapter 2.

what we'll do

1 First, on pages 4–10, we'll get set up by creating a text file for the web page itself (ceramics.html). We'll then create its basic structure and give it a title.

3 On pages 14 –18, we'll create the level 1 header and the first paragraph and select a font and color for both.

5 On pages 27–31, we'll move on to creating the level 2 headers and the additional text. We'll adjust the size of the new content and then float the image to its left.

7 On pages 35–38, we'll then add the item and price information with manual line breaks and local formatting.

9 On pages 42–47, we'll finally move on to adding the three other postcards on this page, and then we'll classify them so that every other one floats to the right.

http://www.sarahsnotec

Ceramics Collecti
The notecards in the *Ceramics collection* featu
Andalusia and Catalonia.

"Sagra
This is a piece
finish the con
Barcelona. I t
year, they'd b

Item Number:
10 notecards j
10 postcards f

"Dancing Stars"
Although depicting living creatures in art is
frowned on by the Islamic religion, the mosa
Alhambra in Granada are full of life and mov

Item Number: 4582-C
10 notecards for $12.99
10 postcards for $8.99

"Park Guell Bench"
Antoni Gaudi's bench in the Park Guell overl

creating the inner pages

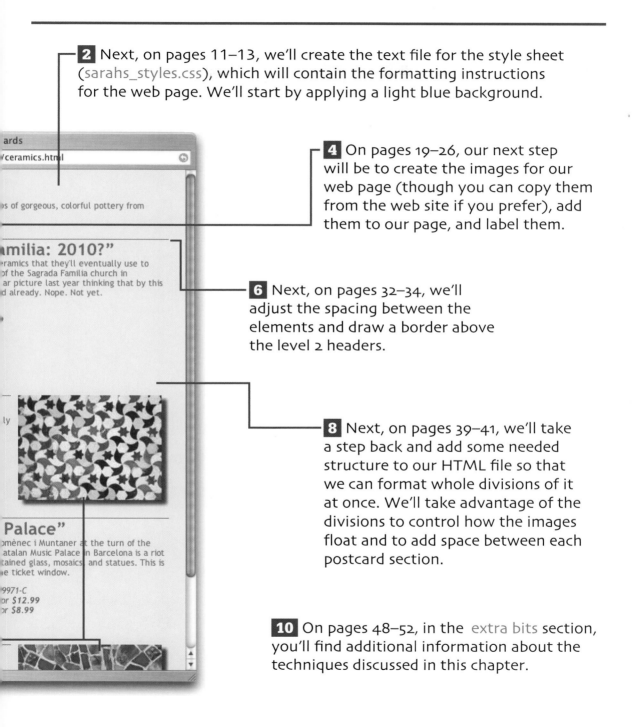

2 Next, on pages 11–13, we'll create the text file for the style sheet (sarahs_styles.css), which will contain the formatting instructions for the web page. We'll start by applying a light blue background.

4 On pages 19–26, our next step will be to create the images for our web page (though you can copy them from the web site if you prefer), add them to our page, and label them.

6 Next, on pages 32–34, we'll adjust the spacing between the elements and draw a border above the level 2 headers.

8 Next, on pages 39–41, we'll take a step back and add some needed structure to our HTML file so that we can format whole divisions of it at once. We'll take advantage of the divisions to control how the images float and to add space between each postcard section.

10 On pages 48–52, in the extra bits section, you'll find additional information about the techniques discussed in this chapter.

create a folder

In the Windows Explorer (as shown here) or in the Mac's Finder, choose File > New > Folder to create the folder in which you'll organize all the files in your web site. This simple, but extremely important, step will take all the pain out of creating links and inserting images later on.

Call the folder sarahs_website, with all lowercase letters. Never include spaces or any punctuation besides the underscore. (This is Mac OS X but the Windows desktop is pretty similar looking.)

sarahs_website

creating the inner pages

open a new html file

A web page is nothing more than a simple text file. To start yours, choose File > New from your preferred text editor. You can use a dedicated text editor like Bare Bones Software's BBEdit (for Mac) or UltraEdit (for Windows) or a word processor like Word or WordPerfect.

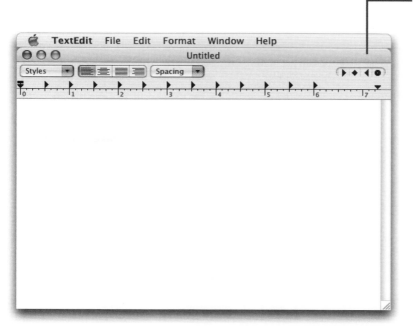

Here is a new, empty text document in TextEdit for Macintosh. You can use the text editor or word processor that you're most comfortable with (or that's the cheapest).

creating the inner pages

save as html

Before you start writing your web page, save it in the proper format by choosing File > Save As from your text editor or word processor.

It's absolutely essential that you pay attention to where you save your files. In this example, we'll save everything in the sarahs_website folder we created earlier.

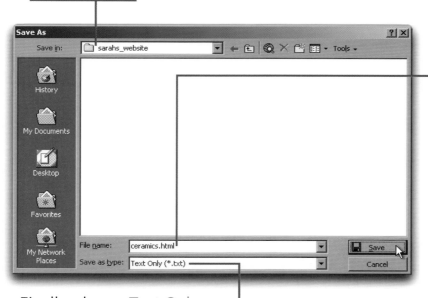

Name the file ceramics.html. In general, use all lowercase letters for your file names. Never include punctuation or spaces besides the underscore. Add the .html extension to all web page files.

Finally, choose Text Only (sometimes called "Plain Text") as the format for your web page files.

start the web page

The < html > tag is the first bit of HTML code that you should type in the ceramics.html web page file that you created on the previous page. After leaving space for the contents of your web page, type the closing </html> tag.

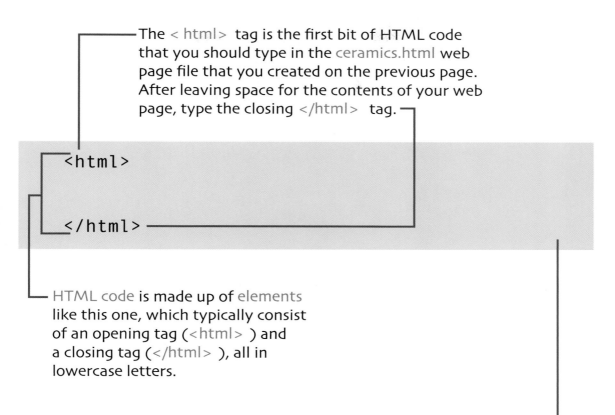

```
<html>



</html>
```

HTML code is made up of elements like this one, which typically consist of an opening tag (<html>) and a closing tag (</html>), all in lowercase letters.

In this book, the HTML code (which in this chapter is the contents of the ceramics.html file) will appear with a light orange background as shown here. The tags being discussed on a particular page will be shown in black while the existing tags (already explained on previous pages) will be shown in a slightly darker orange.

create the head

The < head > tag should go just after the initial < html > tag. The head section contains information about the page, including the title, style and scripts, author, and more.

```
<html>
<head>


</head>

</html>
```

The closing </head> tag separates the information of the head section from the contents of the body section (which contains the visible part of your web page, and which we'll create on page 10).

write a title

The title of your page goes inside opening and closing title tags within the head section of your web page file. It doesn't matter if the code spans more than one line.

```
<html>
<head>
<title>Sarah's Notecards - Ceramics Collection
</title>

</head>
...
```

In this book, the ellipsis (...) indicates that there is more code than can fit in the illustration.

The title is displayed in the browser's window bar (often with the browser's name).

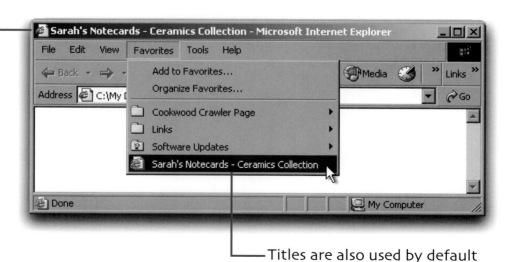

Titles are also used by default to identify pages saved as favorites or bookmarks.

create the body

Again, the ellipsis (...) indicates that some of the code has been omitted from the illustration.

```
. . .
</head>
<body>


</body>
</html>
```

The body section contains the parts of your web page that visitors will see: text, images, links, and more. It begins directly after the closing `</head>` tag and ends right before the final `</html>` tag.

create the style sheet

1 A style sheet is a separate text file that contains the formatting instructions for your web page. To create one, choose File > New from your preferred text editor.

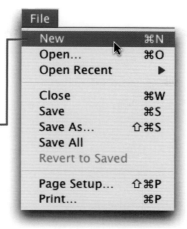

2 Next, choose File > Save As to give the style sheet the proper name and extension.

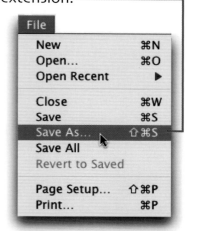

3 Use sarahs_styles.css for the name of the style sheet. In general, use all lowercase letters with no punctuation or spaces except the underscore, and always add the .css extension.

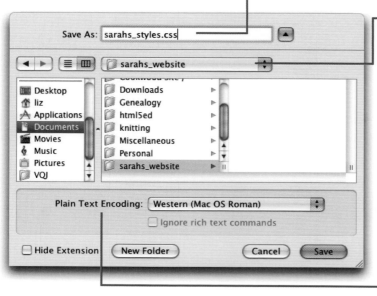

4 Again, pay attention to where you save your files. For this project, we'll store everything in the sarahs_website folder to facilitate linking the documents later.

5 Be sure to save the style sheet in Plain Text or Text Only format. Accept the default encoding.

link the style sheet

The link tag can be placed anywhere between the opening and closing head tags (in the HTML file).

In this book, you'll learn how to create CSS or Cascading Style Sheets. While there are other style sheet languages, CSS is the standard.

```
<head>
<title>Sarah's Notecards - Ceramics Collection
</title>
<link rel="stylesheet" type="text/css"
href="sarahs_styles.css" />
</head>
```

Be sure to type the style sheet's file name exactly as you saved it on the previous page. As long as it is located in the same folder as the HTML file that uses it, you don't need to add any additional path information.

Because the link element is self-contained—that is, there is no separate opening or closing tag but rather one single unit—you must include the forward slash (/) before the final greater-than sign (>).

color the background

The actual formatting instructions consist of a property (background) and value (#EDF2FF , which is the CSS way to specify the blue I wanted) separated by a colon (:). You can find a table of CSS properties and values in Appendix B. You'll find a color chart in Appendix C.

This will be the first line of the sarahs_styles.css style sheet that we created on page 11.

```
body {background: #EDF2FF}
```

A style rule begins with the name of the element(s) that you are formatting (body, in this case) and is followed by curly brackets ({ }) that contain the details about how the element should be styled.

In this book, the code for style sheets (which in this chapter is the contents of the sarahs_styles.css file) will be shown with a green background. The new code being discussed will be shown in black while existing fragments will be shown in a darker green.

Save both the CSS and the HTML files and then open the web page with a browser to see the blue background.

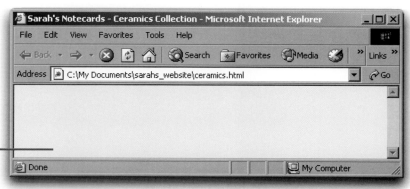

add a section header

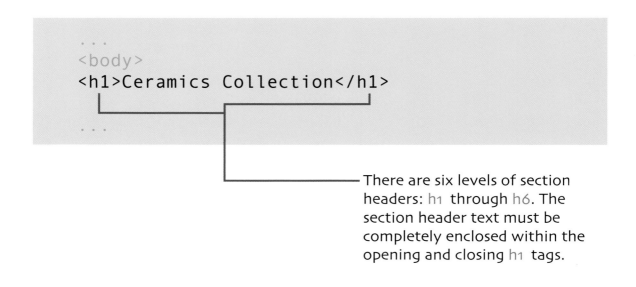

```
. . .
<body>
<h1>Ceramics Collection</h1>
. . .
```

There are six levels of section headers: h1 through h6. The section header text must be completely enclosed within the opening and closing h1 tags.

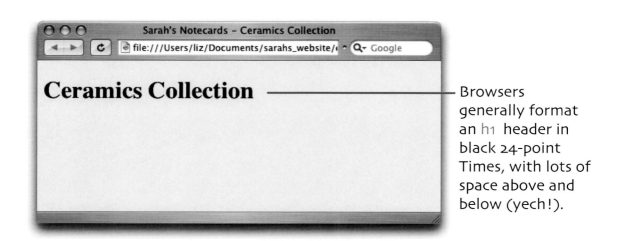

Browsers generally format an h1 header in black 24-point Times, with lots of space above and below (yech!).

choose fonts

Each style rule may have as many property-value pairs as needed. Separate each one from the next with a semicolon (;).

Enclose multi-word font names in quotes (").

Separate font choices with commas (,).

```
body {background: #EDF2FF;
      font-family: "Trebuchet MS", Arial,
         Helvetica, sans-serif}
```

Some properties (like font-family) are inherited. This means that they affect not only the element to which they are applied (body) but also the elements contained in that element (h1). Appendix B explains which properties are inherited.

The font-family property lets you specify the preferred fonts for displaying a given element. If the first font is not available on your visitor's computer, the second font will be attempted, and so on. You can also specify a generic font style (like sans-serif) in case the visitor has none of the preferred fonts installed.

After saving the CSS file and refreshing the browser, you can see the new font (in this case, the visitor's computer did have Trebuchet MS, a pretty common font, installed). We'll work on the color and spacing shortly.

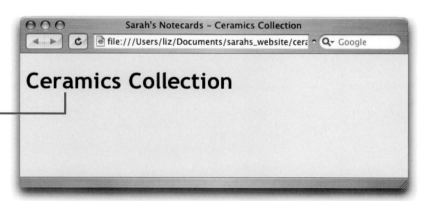

creating the inner pages

change text color

```
body {background: #EDF2FF;
      font-family: "Trebuchet MS", Arial,
      Helvetica, sans-serif;
      color: #4D65A0}
```

The color property controls the "foreground" color of an element. It's principally used to change text color. You'll find a list of allowed color names, as well as a selection of colors and their codes, in Appendix C.

Text on a web page looks best when there's enough contrast between it and the background. You don't want to make your visitors have to strain to read your page.

Sarah's Notecards - Ceramics Collection - Microsoft Internet Explorer

File   Edit   View   Favorites   Tools   Help

Back   Search   Favorites   Links

Address   C:\My Documents\sarahs_website\ceramics.html   Go

Ceramics Collection

Done   My Computer

write a paragraph

```
. . .
<body>
<h1>Ceramics Collection</h1>
<p>The notecards in the Ceramics collection
feature closeups of gorgeous, colorful pottery
from Andalusia and Catalonia.</p>
. . .
```

Begin each paragraph with a `<p>` . While browsers don't care if you put spaces or a line break between the h1 element and the paragraph, it makes the code easier to read if you do.

End each paragraph with a `</p>` . While it's easy to forget this step (and browsers are notoriously forgiving), omitting the final `</p>` can cause formatting errors.

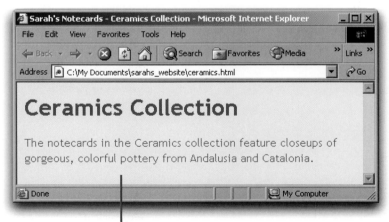

The paragraph text inherits the blue color and Trebuchet MS font from the body, just as the section header did. Browsers automatically format paragraph text smaller than section headers.

adjust spacing

```
body {background: #EDF2FF;
      font-family: "Trebuchet MS", Arial,
      Helvetica, sans-serif;
      color: #4D65A0}
h1  {margin:0}
p   {margin-top:0; margin-bottom:12px}
```

The margin property controls how much space is added between elements. Most browsers automatically add margin space to headers and paragraphs. To keep the header section next to the paragraph that follows it, set margins for both elements to 0 (zero).

To keep a certain amount of space between paragraphs, set the bottom margin to 12 pixels, as shown. Make sure there is no space between the 12 and the px.

The section header looks much better closer to the paragraph. Note that the body still has a bit of margin which is keeping the h1 and p elements from butting up next to the browser window itself.

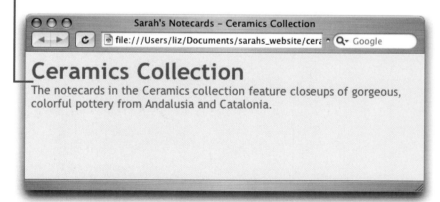

Sarah's Notecards – Ceramics Collection

file:///Users/liz/Documents/sarahs_website/cera

Q▾ Google

Ceramics Collection

The notecards in the Ceramics collection feature closeups of gorgeous, colorful pottery from Andalusia and Catalonia.

create a web image

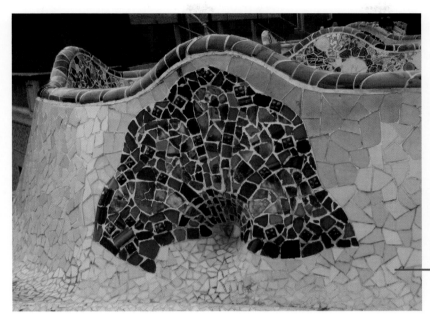

Here is the original photo, taken with a Canon G2 digital camera, at 2272 by 1704 pixels. The photo has an overall bluish tint and it seems like it could be cropped better. It's also huge, weighing in at 11Mb, which would take an awful long time to load.

The final image, which has been cropped and resized, had its levels adjusted, and saved as a compressed JPEG. It now takes up only 14.5K. There are many good image editors, including Adobe Photoshop Elements and JASC's Paint Shop Pro, which both retail for $99 but often come included free with digital cameras and scanners.

crop an image

1 Select the cropping tool. (This is Photoshop Elements but most image editors work in a similar way.)

2 If you want, set the desired final size in pixels. This saves you the job of resizing it manually later on.

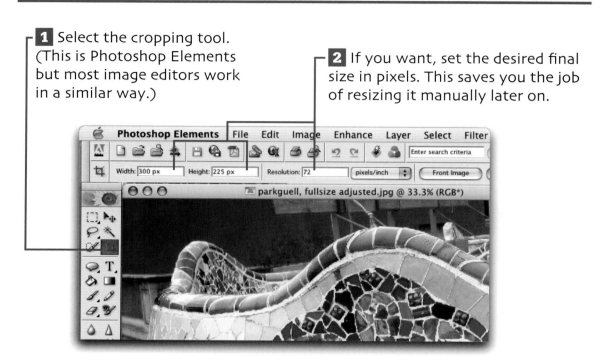

3 Position the cropping frame until the highlighted part covers just the portion of the image that you want to keep. Then double-click inside to crop (or choose Image > Crop).

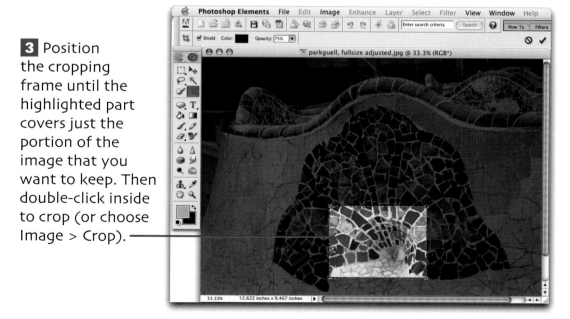

creating the inner pages

adjust levels

1 The original image is dark and lifeless.

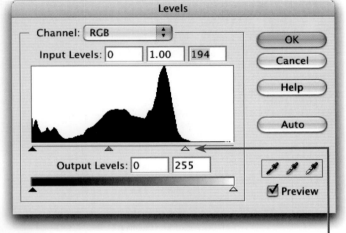

2 In the Levels box (Command - L), drag the white triangle leftward towards the foot of the mountain to increase the tonal range of the highlights. You can also drag the black triangle rightward toward the mountain (to adjust the shadows). Here it's not necessary.

3 The image is brighter and better balanced. The effect is even more pronounced (and important) on screen, i.e., in a web browser.

resize an image

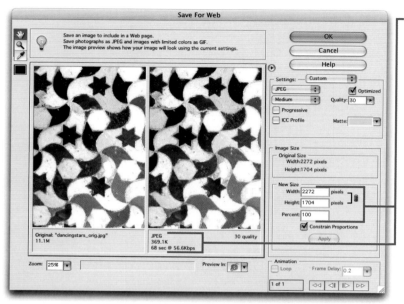

Many digital cameras and scanners create images that are simply too big for a web page. This one measures 2272 pixels across, almost four times as big as an average page. And it takes up 369K, which will take more than a minute to download.

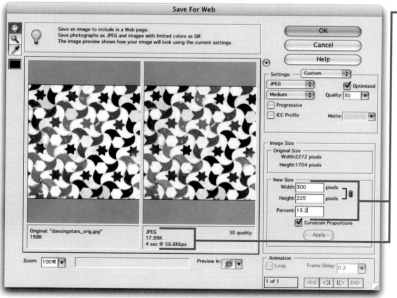

In Photoshop Elements, choose File > Save for Web and then use the Image Size area to resize your image. Choose a size keeping in mind that an average web page measures around 600 pixels wide, and that the bigger the image, the longer it will take to download. Here I've reduced the image to 300 pixels wide and it now only takes 4 seconds to download.

format photos as jpeg

The JPEG format is the most efficient compression system for photographs. ——

The Quality of the JPEG compression is directly related to the final size of the image. However, you can often trade a small amount of quality for a considerable amount of reduced download time. ——

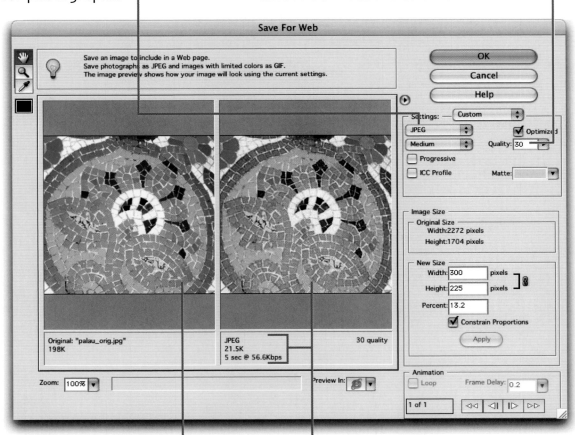

In Photoshop Elements' Save For Web dialog box, you can compare the compressed version with the original in order to determine a quality that's high enough to look pretty and low enough to ensure an acceptable download time.

organize the photos

Once you click OK in the Save For Web dialog box, you'll be able to give your image a name. Remember to use all lowercase letters and no spaces or punctuation except the underscore.

Pay attention to where you save your images. It's easiest if you put them in the same folder as your other web files.

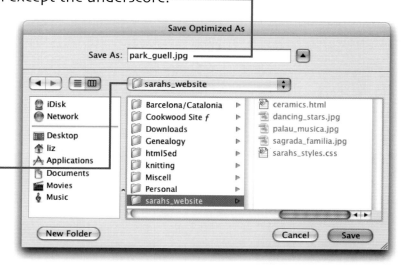

When you've finished preparing your images, check again to make sure they're in the same folder as your HTML document. It will make linking the images much easier.

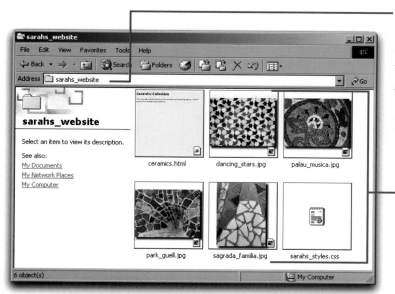

creating the inner pages

add photos to page

The img element is for adding photos to the page. Specify the image's file name and location with the src attribute. As long as the image is in the same folder as the HTML file, you don't need to add any extra path information.

The text in the alt attribute will appear if the image fails to load. It is also helpful to the vision impaired.

```
. . .
<p>The notecards in the Ceramics collection
feature closeups of gorgeous, colorful pottery
from Andalusia and Catalonia.</p>
<img src="sagrada_familia.jpg" alt="Future
Sagrada Familia Ceramics" width="160"
height="210" />
. . .
```

Type in the height and width of the image in pixels or as a percentage of the browser window.

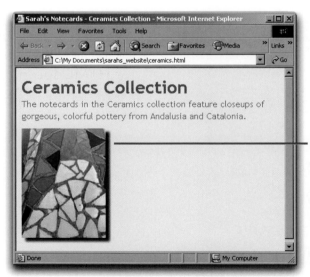

By default, an image appears directly after the code that precedes it. Since the preceding element was a paragraph, this image starts on its own line. Images, can, however, appear within a line.

label a photo

```
. . .
<img src="sagrada_familia.jpg" alt="Future
Sagrada Familia Ceramics" width="160"
height="210" title="Sagrada Familia: 2010?,
10 notecards for $12.99, 10 postcards for
$8.99" />
. . .
```

To create a label, insert a title attribute within the img element (it doesn't matter where). Be sure to enclose the label text in quotation marks.

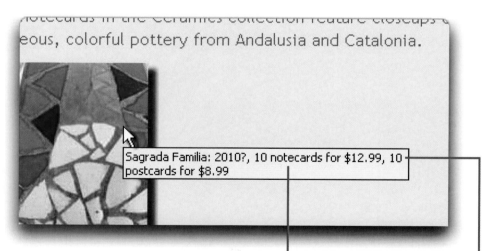

A label appears when your visitor points at the image with their mouse. Labels automatically disappear within a few seconds (and thus should be short enough to be read in that amount of time).

You can fix that nasty line break with a non-breaking space ( ). See extra bits on page 50.

add a subheader

```
. . .
<img src="sagrada_familia.jpg" alt="Future
Sagrada Familia Ceramics" width="160"
height="210" title="Sagrada Familia: 2010?,
10 notecards for $12.99, 10 postcards for
$8.99" />
<h2>Sagrada Familia: 2010?</h2>
. . .
```

There are six levels of header, from h1 to h6. Don't forget the matching closing tag.

Headers automatically start on a new line.

Browsers automatically format headers bigger and bolder than surrounding text with each subsequent level smaller than the preceding one. The font and color that we applied to the entire body (on pages 15–16) override the browser's defaults.

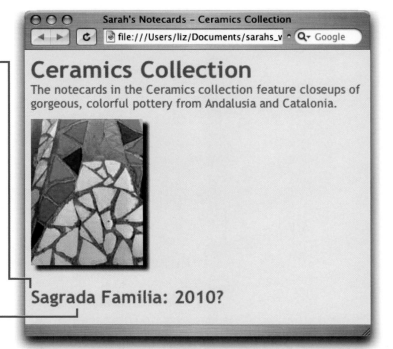

use special characters

```
. . .
<h2>&ldquo;Sagrada Familia: 2010?&rdquo;</h2>
. . .
```

The code for a special character, called a reference, starts with an ampersand (&), which is followed by the character's name or number (ldquo), and is then finished off with a semicolon (;).

ldquo and rdquo stand for "left double quotes" and "right double quotes" respectively.

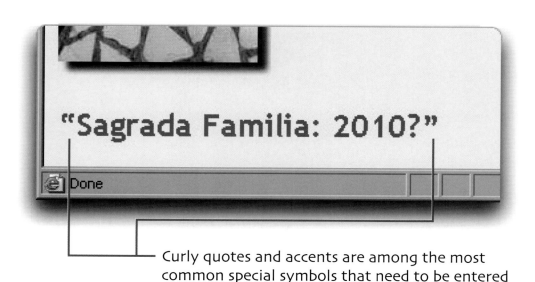

"Sagrada Familia: 2010?"

Done

Curly quotes and accents are among the most common special symbols that need to be entered with character references. They help give your page a professional look. If you type them in directly, they are not displayed properly. You can find a list of special characters and their corresponding references in Appendix D.

add more text

```
. . .
<h2>&ldquo;Sagrada Familia: 2010?&rdquo;</h2>
<p>This is a piece of the ceramics that
they'll eventually use to finish the
construction of the Sagrada Familia church
in Barcelona. I took a similar picture last
year thinking that by this year, they'd be
installed already. Nope. Not yet.</p>
. . .
```

Begin each paragraph with a `<p>` .

End each paragraph with a `</p>` .

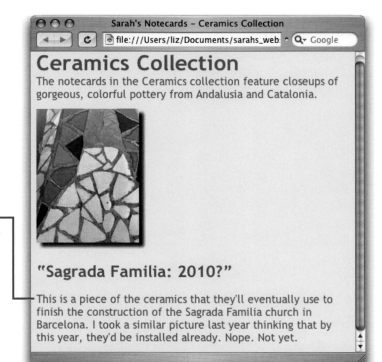

A new paragraph starts on its own line below the header. It has the same formatting as the first paragraph we entered.

change font size

There must be a semicolon between every property-value pair!

```
...
h1    {margin: 0}
p     {margin-top:0; margin-bottom:12px;
       font-size:12px; line-height:1.2}
```

The font-size property can be specified in several ways, with pixels being the most common and best supported unit. Make sure there's no space between the number and the px.

Specifying the line-height gives you control over the amount of space between lines. Here, for example, there will be 14.4px (1.2 times the font size of 12px) between each line of paragraph text.

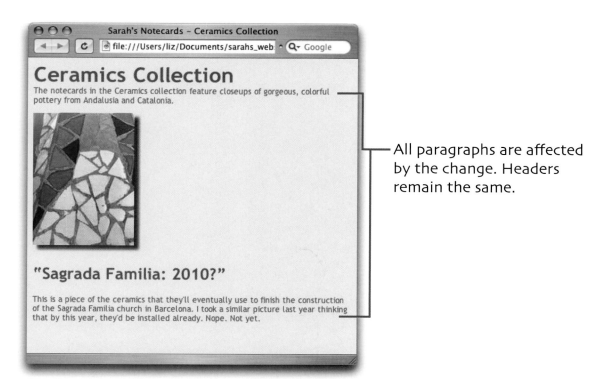

All paragraphs are affected by the change. Headers remain the same.

float images to one side

```
. . .
p    {margin-top:0; margin-bottom:12px;
      font-size:12px; line-height:1.2}
img  {float:left}
```

The float property makes the element into a sort of island, with text and other elements flowing around it (like water). In our project, the img elements will float left, which means that the "water" will flow on the right side.

Elements float with respect to the elements that follow them. There is no effect on preceding elements.

The space between floated images and their surrounding elements often needs to be adjusted. Notice that it is very tight here. We'll fix that on the next page.

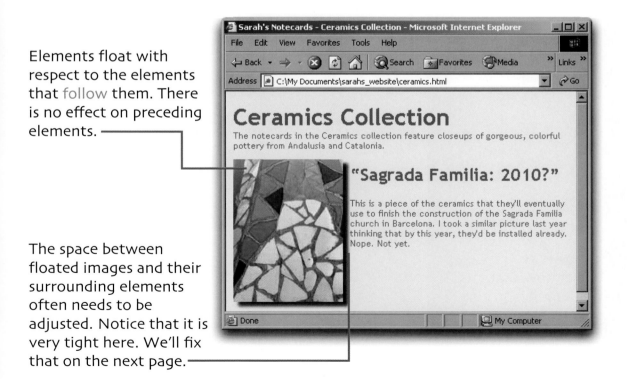

creating the inner pages

31

pad the images

```
. . .
p    {margin-top:0; margin-bottom:12px;
      font-size:12px; line-height:1.2}
img  {float:left; padding-right:10px}
```

We'll add a 10-pixel-wide pad (a beach for our island) to the right side of the floating images to keep the surrounding elements from touching. Padding may also be applied to the top, bottom, or left, or to all sides (by leaving out the direction).

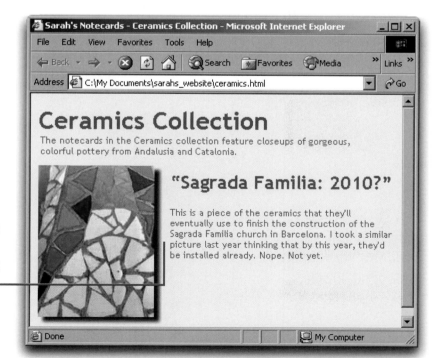

The text looks much better now that it is not jammed up next to the photo.

reuse styles

```
. . .
h1, h2    {margin: 0}
p         {margin-top:0; margin-bottom:12px;
           font-size:12px; line-height:1.2}
img       {float:left; padding-right:10px}
```

We applied a margin of 0 to the level 1 headers back on page 18 to remove the default space that most browsers apply around headers. To apply this style to level 2 headers as well, simply type a comma (,) and h2 after the original h1.

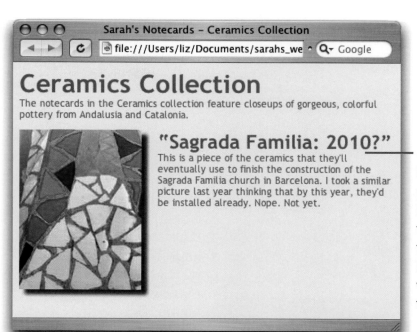

I'm not sure why browsers habitually put so much space between a header and the paragraph that follows it. But it sure looks better now that we've gotten rid of the extra space.

draw a border

```
. . .
h1, h2      {margin: 0}
h2          {border-top: 1px solid #4D65A0}
p           {margin-top:0; margin-bottom:12px;
             font-size:12px; line-height:1.2}
. . .
```

Since we only want the level 2 headers to have the border, we make a new rule just for h2. Its properties will be added to previous rules that apply to h2 (and would override them if they conflicted—which here they do not).

A border has three parts: width (1px), style (solid), and color (#4D65A0). You'll find a list of border properties in Appendix B. You'll find a list of color codes in Appendix C.

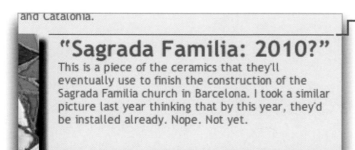

and Catalonia.

"Sagrada Familia: 2010?"

This is a piece of the ceramics that they'll eventually use to finish the construction of the Sagrada Familia church in Barcelona. I took a similar picture last year thinking that by this year, they'd be installed already. Nope. Not yet.

A solid blue, 1-pixel border will now appear at the top of each level 2 header. Borders are drawn on the outside edge of any padding that has been applied and on the inside edge of the element's margin.

classify paragraphs

```
  . . .
<p>This is a piece of the ceramics that
they'll eventually use to finish the
construction of the Sagrada Familia church
in Barcelona. I took a similar picture last
year thinking that by this year, they'd be
installed already. Nope. Not yet.</p>
<p class="sales_info">Item Number: 7845-C</p>
  . . .
```

We'll create a new kind of paragraph for the postcards' sales information. We label these paragraphs as such by adding the class attribute. On the next page, we'll be able to add formatting to only the paragraphs labeled with this class.

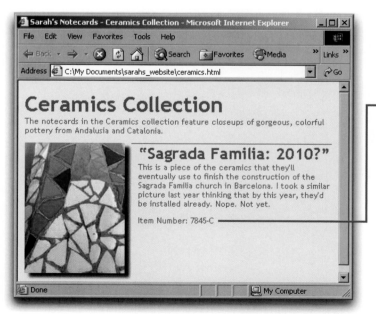

The sales_info paragraph starts out with the same formatting as all other paragraphs. We'll add to it on the next page.

apply italics to a class

```
. . .
p {margin-top: 0; margin-bottom: 12px;
    font-size: 12px; line-height:1.2}
p.sales_info {font-style: italic}
. . .
```

The period (.) here means that this style rule applies only to p elements with a class attribute of sales_info.

The font-style property specifies whether text should be displayed as italic, oblique, or normal.

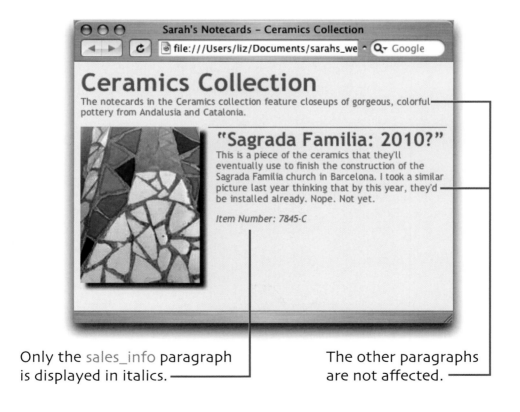

Only the sales_info paragraph is displayed in italics.

The other paragraphs are not affected.

creating the inner pages

add line breaks

```
    . . .
    <p class="sales_info">Item Number: 7845-C
    <br />10 notecards for $12.99
    <br />10 postcards for $8.99

    </p>
    . . .
```

Insert < br /> where each line break should occur. There should be a space between the br and the forward slash (/).

It doesn't matter if you type the HTML code on separate lines or not. I have done that here to make the code easier to read, but it is not required.

You might want to insert line breaks in short lists of things or in lines of poetry.

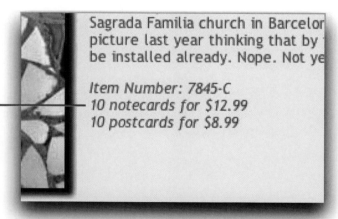

Sagrada Familia church in Barcelor
picture last year thinking that by
be installed already. Nope. Not ye

Item Number: 7845-C
10 notecards for $12.99
10 postcards for $8.99

add local formatting

Add `<i>` at the beginning and `</i>` at the end of text to display a small amount of text in italics. (For large amounts, use font-style, described on page 36.)

```
...
<p>The notecards in the <i>Ceramics collec-
tion</i> feature closeups of gorgeous, color-
ful pottery from Andalusia and Catalonia.</p>
...
<p class="sales_info">Item Number: 7845-C
<br />10 notecards for <b>$12.99</b>
<br />10 postcards for <b>$8.99</b>
...
```

Add `<b>` at the beginning and `</b>` at the end to make a small amount of text bold. (For large amounts, use font-weight, described on page 72.)

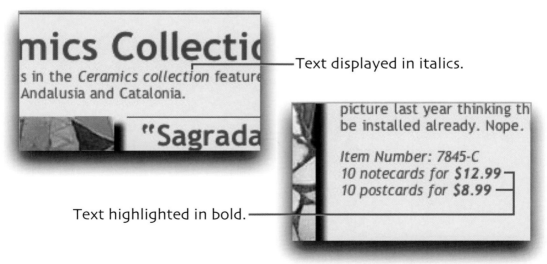

Text displayed in italics.

Text highlighted in bold.

add structure

We can divide the web page into its structural elements (introduction, information about postcards, etc.) with div elements, and then format those divisions as a unit (as shown on pages 40–41).

Label each division with an appropriate value for the class attribute (e.g., intro and postcard).

```
. . .
<div class="intro"><h1>Ceramics Collection
</h1>
<p>The notecards in the <i>Ceramics collec-
tion</i> feature closeups of gorgeous, color-
ful pottery from Andalusia and Catalonia.</p>
</div>

<div class="postcard">
<img src="sagrada_familia.jpg" alt="Sagrada
Familia Ceramics" width="160" height="210"
title= "Sagrada Familia: 2010?, 10 notecards
for $12.99, 10 postcards for $8.99" />

<h2>&ldquo;Sagrada Familia: 2010?&rdquo;</h2>
<p>This is a piece of the ceramics that ...
Nope. Not yet.</p>

<p class="sales_info">Item Number: 7845-C
<br />10 notecards for <b>$12.99</b>
<br />10 postcards for <b>$8.99</b>
</p>
</div>
. . .
```

creating the inner pages

pad a division

Once we have created and labeled the divisions of our web page, we can apply styles to an entire division. Here we add 15 pixels of padding around all four sides of each postcard division.

```
. . .
body  {background: #EDF2FF;
        font-family: "Trebuchet MS", Arial,
        Helvetica, sans-serif; color: #4D65A0}
div.postcard {padding:15px}
h1, h2 {margin: 0}
. . .
```

Remember, the period means "apply this style to only the div elements whose class is postcard".

The postcard division (but not the intro division) now has 15 pixels of padding on all sides to help set it off from the other parts of the web page.

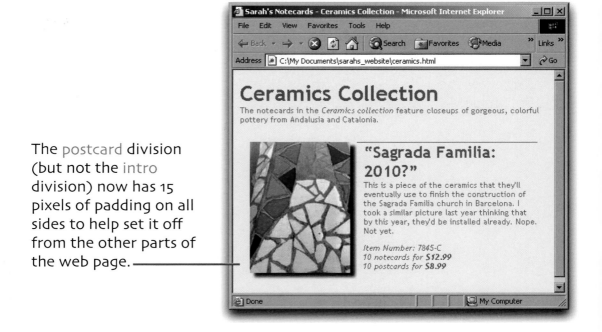

creating the inner pages

clear floats

Set the clear property for div elements to both so that a new postcard division (which we'll add on pages 42–43) won't start until both the left and right sides are free of floating elements—that is, until we get past the picture of the previous postcard.

```
. . .
body  {background: #EDF2FF;
       font-family: "Trebuchet MS", Arial,
       Helvetica, sans-serif; color: #4D65A0}
div {clear:both}
div.postcard {padding:15px}
h1, h2 {margin: 0}
. . .
```

The next division will start after the floating image.

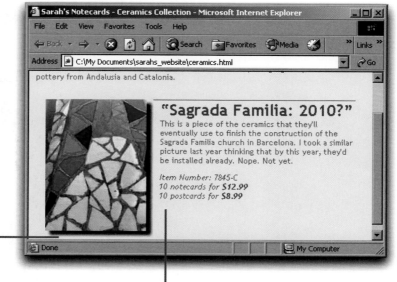

Without the clear property, the next elements would start directly after the preceding element (10 postcards for $8.99).

add another postcard

The new division has precisely the same elements as the previous one: an image with a title followed by a level 2 header, a paragraph, and finally, the sales information.

```
. . .
<p class="sales_info">Ref: 7845-C
<br />10 notecards for <b>$12.99</b>
<br />10 postcards for <b>$8.99</b>
</p>
</div>
<div class="postcard">
<img src="dancing_stars.jpg" alt="Dancing
Stars at the Alhambra" width="210"
height="160" title="Alhambra Stars, 10
notecards for $12.99, 10 postcards for
$8.99" />
<h2>&ldquo;Dancing Stars&rdquo;</h2>
<p>Although depicting living creatures in art
is traditionally frowned on by the Islamic
religion, the mosaics in the Alhambra in
Granada are full of life and movement.
</p>

<p class="sales_info">Item Number: 4582-C
<br />10 notecards for <b>$12.99</b>
<br />10 postcards for <b>$8.99</b>
</p>
</div>
```

The beauty of CSS is that the new elements are automatically formatted just like their existing counterparts.

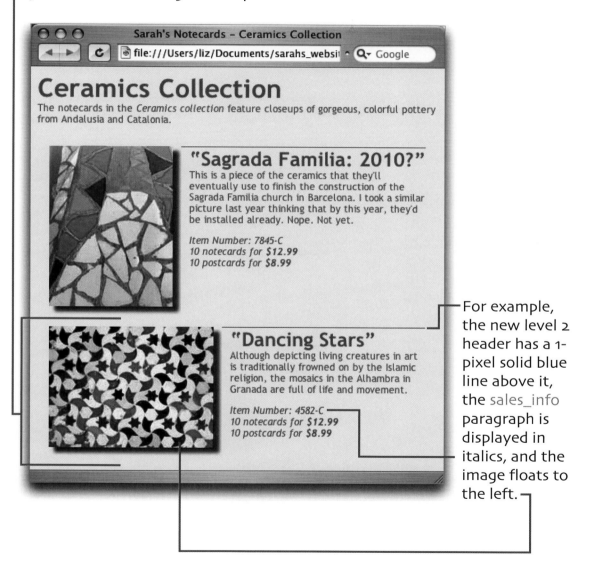

For example, the new level 2 header has a 1-pixel solid blue line above it, the sales_info paragraph is displayed in italics, and the image floats to the left.

float images to right

```
. . .
<div class="postcard">
<img src="sagrada_familia.jpg" class="odd"
alt="Sagrada Familia Ceramics" width="160"
height="210" title= "Sagrada Familia: 2010?,
10 notecards for $12.99, 10 postcards for
$8.99" />

. . .
<div class="postcard">
<img src="dancing_stars.jpg" class="even"
alt="Dancing Stars at the Alhambra"
width="210" height="160" title="Alhambra
Stars, 10 notecards for $12.99, 10 postcards
for $8.99" />
. . .
```

1 To float every other image to the right, we first need to divide the images into two classes: the odd ones and the even ones.

```
. . .
img.odd {float:left;padding-right:10px}
img.even {float:right;padding-left:10px}
. . .
```

2 Next, we make the existing img style rule apply only to the img elements whose class is odd.

3 Finally, we add a second style rule to float the even images to the right (with padding on the left).

The first image continues to float to the left as before.

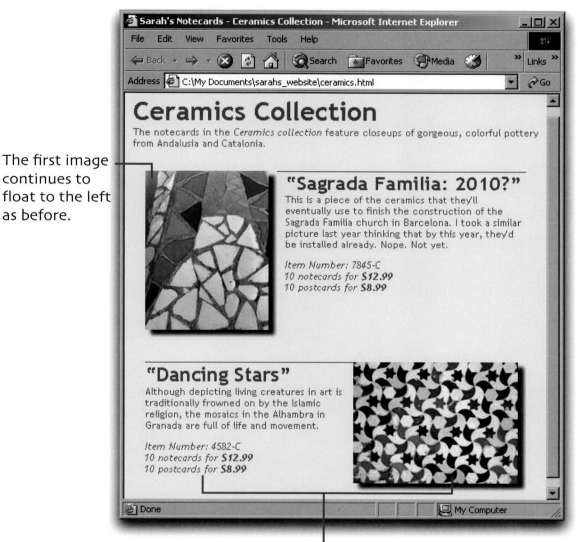

The even image "island" now floats to the right while its "water" flows to the left. We needed to put the padding on the left to separate the image from the descriptive text.

mimic shadow

```
. . .
img.odd {float:left;padding-right:10px}
img.even {float:right;padding-left:10px;
          background:#EDF2FF}
. . .
```

We'll change the even images' background color to the same light blue as the body's background.

The drop shadow makes it look as if there is a space between the first image and the blue line even though they're right next to one another.

The color of the padding comes from an element's background—which by default is transparent. By setting the image's background—and thus its padding—to the same light blue as the body's background, we cover up 10 pixels of the blue line and create the same effect that the shadow creates in the upper image.

finish inner page

Finish the inner page by adding the necessary HTML code to create the last two postcard divisions. (You can find the example files online, if you prefer. See page xiii.)

extra bits

save as html p. 6

- In fact, in this book, you'll be writing XHTML, which is the most current, most standard version of HTML. The extension is still .html.

- Don't choose the Save as Web Page command in Microsoft Word. It is designed for converting a Word document into HTML, not for saving a document already written in HTML.

- Once you save a document with the .html extension, double-clicking it will often open your browser, not the text editor. In order to edit the page, either open it from inside your text editor (using File > Open) or right-click it on the desktop, and choose Open with [your text editor].

start the web page p. 7

- Officially, web pages should begin with a DOCTYPE declaration, which describes the version of HTML being used. For example:

  <!DOCTYPE html PUBLIC "-//
  W3C//DTD XHTML 1.0 Transi -
  tional//EN"

  "http://www.w3.org/TR/xhtml1/
  DTD/xhtml1-transitional.dtd">

  <html xmlns="http://www.
  w3.org/1999/xhtml">

  But it's not the end of the world if you just start with <html> .

write a title p. 9

- The title of your web page is one of the key factors in getting it ranked on a search engine like Google. Use specific words in your title that reflect the content of your page.

color the background p. 13

- An element's background is transparent by default. That means that if it is on top of another element, you'll see the other element's background shining through.

- The part of a style rule that describes the elements that will be affected by the rule is called the selector. It can be as simple as an element's name as in the example here (body), or it can be more complex in order to select only certain elements that satisfy given criteria. We'll see some more complicated selectors in Chapter 2.

creating the inner pages

choose fonts p. 15

- The following fonts come with the standard installation of Internet Explorer for Windows and are thus likely to be installed on your visitor's computer: Andale Mono, Arial Black, Comic Sans MS, Georgia, Impact, Trebuchet MS, Verdana and Webdings. For more information, see http://www. microsoft.com/typography/fonts/ default.aspx.

- There is a font property which acts as a shortcut for specifying not only the font-family, but also the font-size, line-height, font-weight, font-style, and font-variant. For details, see Appendix B, CSS Reference.

- An element that is inside another element is called a child element. The outer element is called a parent element.

adjust spacing p. 18

- The margin is the amount of space around the outer edge of an element, beyond the padding and the border (which are discussed on pages 32 and 34, respectively). It is colorless.

- If you use one value, as in margin:0, it is applied to all four sides equally.

- If you use two values, as in margin: 5px 0, the first is used for the top and bottom and the second is used for the right and left.

- With three values, as in margin: 10px 5px 4px, the first is used for the top, the second for the right and left and the third for the bottom.

- If you use four values, as in margin: 10px 2px 5px 8px, they are applied to the top, right, bottom, and left, in clockwise order.

- You can add the margin to one particular side of the element by using margin-top, margin-bottom, margin-right, or margin-left instead of just margin. In that case, of course, just one value is required.

create a web image p. 19

- The techniques described on pages 19–23 are designed to be illustra - tive, not exhaustive—since there are many different image editors on the market. The most impor- tant thing to learn is that photos almost always need to be cropped or resized, adjusted, and com- pressed. You may need to consult your image editor's manual or help screens to figure out the exact steps it requires.

extra bits

format photos as jpeg p. 23

- When an image is compressed with JPEG, some details are permanently discarded. You should therefore only save an image as JPEG once, when you are finished making any other necessary adjustments. Repeatedly saving an image in JPEG format can make it blurry.

- For computer-generated images, use GIF format (with LZW compression). We'll discuss this more on page 67.

add photos to page p. 25

- You can create a folder within your web folder to organize your images, say sarahs_images. Then, the src attribute will need to reflect that new location: /sarahs_images/park_guell.jpg.

- While you can use the height and width attributes to change the size of the image in your web page, it's not the best method for doing so. To make an image smaller, crop (page 20) or resize it (page 22). To make an image bigger, reshoot it!

label a photo p. 26

- Insert non-breaking spaces ( ) between words in a label to avoid nasty line breaks like the one shown on page 26.

- The only limit I've found to the quantity of text you can put in a title is the amount of time your visitors have to read it before it automatically disappears.

- If your label contains double quotes, you can use single quotes to enclose the whole label. For example, title='These are the "Sagrada Familia" ceramics'.

use special characters p. 28

- You only need to use a character reference for a special symbol if that symbol is not part of your web page's encoding, which reflects the page's principal language. For web pages written in English on English operating systems, that means any symbols beyond the first 128 in ASCII. You'll find a list of these symbols with their corresponding character references in Appendix D.

- For full details about writing pages with large portions in other languages, see Chapter 20, "Symbols and Non-English Characters", in my HTML VQS (described on page xvi).

change font size p. 30

- You can set a specific font size in pixels (px), points (pt), centimeters (cm), millimeters (mm), or picas (pc). Only pixels should be used for setting a specific size on screen; the others are good for controlling printed output.

- You can also use keywords to specify a specific size—xx-small, x-small, small, medium, large, x-large, or xx-large—however, browsers interpret these keywords in different ways.

- You can set the font size relative to the parent element (that is, the element that contains the one you're defining) by using ems (em) or a percentage (%). You can also use the relative keywords larger or smaller.

- The line height can be specified as an absolute value in pixels (px), or relative to the element's font-size, either as a number (say, 1.2), as a percentage (120%), or in ems (em). The difference lies in how the values are inherited by elements contained in the one you're defining. We'll discuss this in more detail in Chapter 2.

pad the images p. 32

- The padding is the space between an element's content and its border (which is discussed on page 34).

- The padding is applied with the same system as the margin. See adjust spacing on page 49.

- Padding is the same color as the element's background.

- If two adjacent elements both have padding, both values are added together and may result in too much space. (In contrast, adjacent vertical margins are combined, resulting in a value equal to the larger of the two.)

draw a border p. 34

- The border is the outer edge of the padding and the inner edge of the margin.

- The border-style can be none, dotted, dashed, solid, double, groove, ridge, inset, or outset.

- The default border-style is none, which means if you don't specify a style, you won't get a border.

- You can apply only one aspect of a border (to one or more sides of an element) by using border-color, border-width, or border-style. Use one to four values in the same way as described for margins on page 49.

- You can apply one or more border aspects to one particular side of a border by using border-right, border-top, etc., along with up to three desired values.

extra bits

draw a border (cont.)

- You can even apply a single border aspect to a single side of an element with something like border-top-color.

- If you specify only some aspects of a border, the other aspects are set to their defaults.

add line breaks p. 37

- Note that the br element is empty. The text, 10 notecards for $12.99 , is in the p element, not the br element.

add local formatting p. 38

- You can also use the logical HTML elements, strong and em (for emphasis) to add local formatting. Text marked with strong is usually displayed bold, em text is usually displayed in italics.

- You can make text bigger and smaller with big and small.

- You can format text as a subscript (sub) or superscript (sup).

- You can underline text with ins (for insert), and you can strike out text with del (for delete).

- Local formatting should only be used for small amounts of text. Use styles for whole paragraphs or divisions.

add structure p. 39

- The div element has no default formatting. However, it is a block-level element, which means it will always start on its own line.

clear floats p. 41

- The clear property can be set to both, left, right, or none.

2. creating the home page

A home page is not only the front door to your web site but also the directory of its contents. The idea is to capture your visitors' interest as you explain who you are and why this site exists.

We'll create a set of images that function as links to the rest of the site, and then duplicate the links in the left-hand navigation bar in case for some reason the images should fail to load.

what we'll do

1 On pages 55–60, to get set up, we'll create and begin writing a new HTML file (index.html), apply to it the existing styles (sarahs_styles.css), create a new style sheet (home.css), and apply that too.

2 Next, from pages 61–64, we'll create a low-contrast background image and add it to the HTML code.

3 On pages 65–68 we'll create a GIF image for the header logo and add it to the HTML.

7 Last but not least, on pages 82–89, we'll create a left navigation bar with an image and four text links (to the same pages as the image links, just in case the images don't load).

4 Next, on pages 69–72, we'll add the main paragraph and create a link to the ceramics.html page we created in Chapter 1. Then we'll make the link beautiful.

6 On pages 79–81, we'll add a copyright notice on the bottom of the page, complete with copyright symbol, and add some local styles.

5 On pages 73–78, we'll then create the four images that we'll use to link to the inner pages of our web site, add them to the HTML, and make them into links.

create a new html file

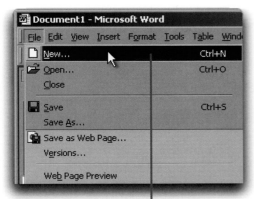

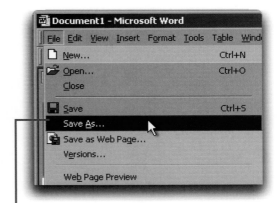

1 Choose File > New from your preferred text editor.

2 Before you start writing your web file, save it in the proper format by choosing File > Save As from your text editor or word processor (not Save as Web Page).

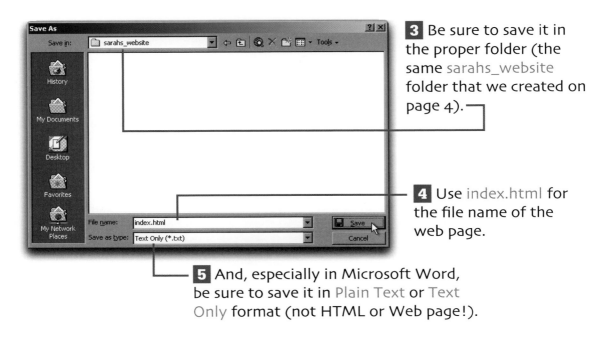

3 Be sure to save it in the proper folder (the same sarahs_website folder that we created on page 4).

4 Use index.html for the file name of the web page.

5 And, especially in Microsoft Word, be sure to save it in Plain Text or Text Only format (not HTML or Web page!).

start the home page

Always start your web page with `<html>` (or `!DOCTYPE`, see page 48).

Next, comes the head section.

```
<html>
<head>
<title>Sarah's Notecards</title>


</head>

</html>
```

The title of the home page goes in the head section between opening and closing title tags.

The title is displayed in the browser's window bar, often next to the browser's name.

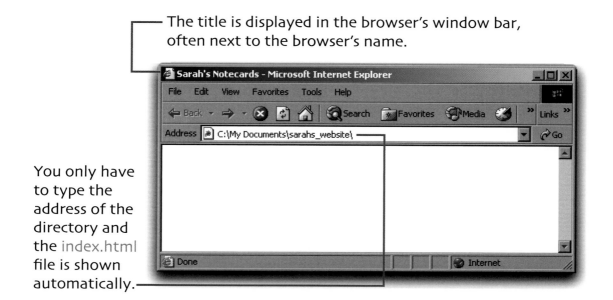

You only have to type the address of the directory and the index.html file is shown automatically.

structure the page

A web page's content is always enclosed in its body. The body on this page is further organized into two main divisions: a central content area (main) and a navigation bar (nav_bar).

```
. . .
</head>
<body>
<div class="main">



</div>

<div class="nav_bar">



</div>
</body>
</html>
```

It's generally a good idea to name your divisions according to their purpose, not their appearance. Don't use spaces or punctuation, except the underscore (_).

link existing style sheet

```
. . .
<title>Sarah's Notecards</title>
<link rel="stylesheet" type="text/css"
href="sarahs_styles.css" />
. . .
```

Here we link our new index.html file to the style sheet that we created throughout Chapter 1, sarahs_styles.css. This makes it easy to use the same styles throughout your entire web site.

The only thing that we have so far in the new index.html page whose style is already defined in the sarahs_styles.css file is the body—which is a nice shade of blue (#EDF2FF).

creating the home page

create new style sheet

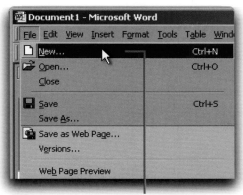

1 Choose File > New from your preferred text editor.

2 Before you start writing your style sheet, save it in the proper format by choosing File > Save As from your text editor or word processor.

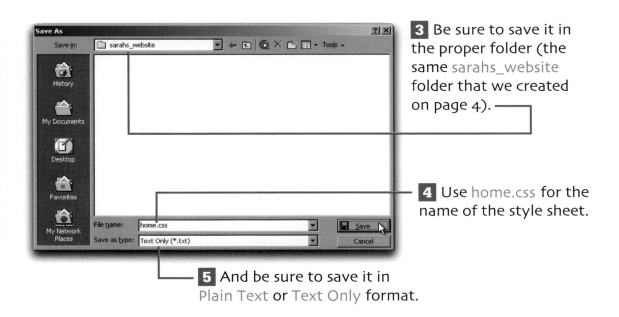

3 Be sure to save it in the proper folder (the same sarahs_website folder that we created on page 4). ─────

4 Use home.css for the name of the style sheet.

5 And be sure to save it in Plain Text or Text Only format.

link to new styles

The order in which style sheets are linked is very important. Style sheets that are linked later—like home.css here—take precedence over earlier style sheets—like sarahs_styles.css here. (We'll see this better as the chapter progresses.)

```
<head>
<title>Sarah's Notecards</title>
<link rel="stylesheet" type="text/css"
href="sarahs_styles.css" />
<link rel="stylesheet" type="text/css"
href="home.css" />
</head>
. . .
```

Type the new style sheet's file name exactly as you saved it on the previous page.

create a background

Here is the original image that I used to create the background. It has too much contrast to be a suitable background. In order for your visitors to read the content on your page, we'll have to reduce the contrast.

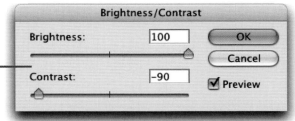

The image still has too much contrast.

Increase the brightness and reduce the contrast until the image detail all but disappears. (In Photoshop Elements, choose Enhance > Adjust Brightness/Contrast > Brightness/Contrast.)

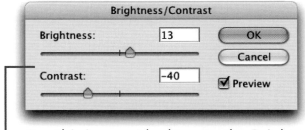

For this image, I had to use the Brightness/Contrast controls twice before the image was sufficiently "bland".

colorize background

You can then colorize the grayish, low-contrast image by changing the Hue/Saturation (Command-U in Photoshop Elements).

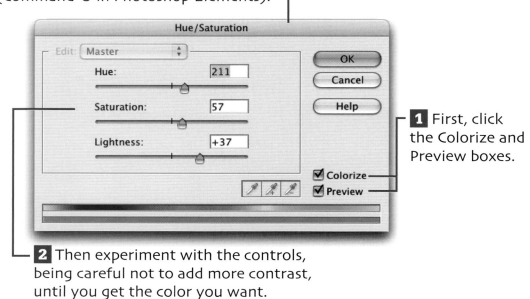

1 First, click the Colorize and Preview boxes.

2 Then experiment with the controls, being careful not to add more contrast, until you get the color you want.

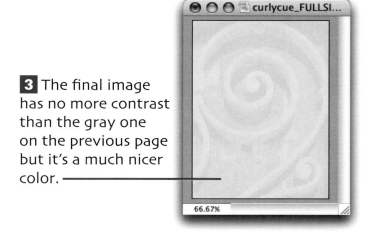

3 The final image has no more contrast than the gray one on the previous page but it's a much nicer color.

save the background

We'll increase the size of the background image to 700 pixels wide so that it won't repeat unnecessarily. Since it's going to be in the background, the minor resulting blurriness won't be a problem.

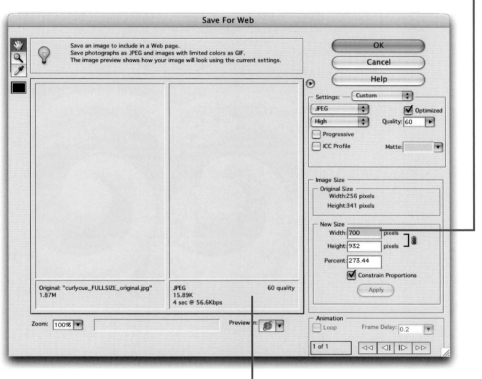

In fact, the blurring that results from increasing the image's size makes it a prime candidate for JPEG compression. Even at the relatively high quality level of 60, the image is squeezed down to little more than 15K. Call the image curly.jpg and place it in the sarahs_website folder.

add background image

This will be the first line of the home.css document that we created on page 59.

```
body {background: url(curly.jpg)}
```

Type the name of your background image exactly as you saved it on the previous page. As long as it's contained in the same folder as your style sheet, you don't need any additional path information.

The new background property conflicts with the background property that we set for body in the sarahs_styles.css file (where we said it should be EDF2FF blue). Since we linked this home.css file later (see page 60), it wins the fight and we get the curly.jpg image shown. However, if the image cannot be loaded for some reason, we'll get the EDF2FF blue background instead.

begin the header logo

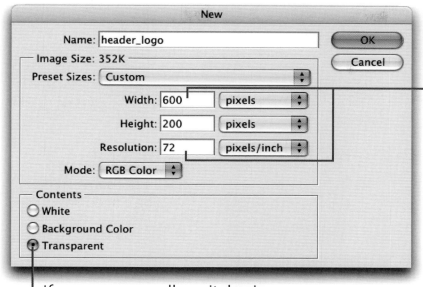

In your image editor, start with a file around 600 pixels wide (at 72dpi)—about the same width as the average browser window—so you can judge visually how big your header should be.

If your program allows it, begin with a transparent background.

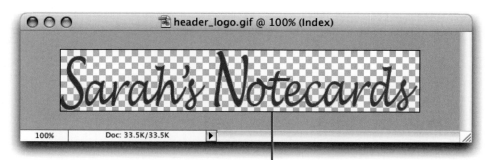

Because we will save the file as an image, you can take advantage of your font library to make a pleasing logo. This font is Lucida Handwriting.

make logo transparent

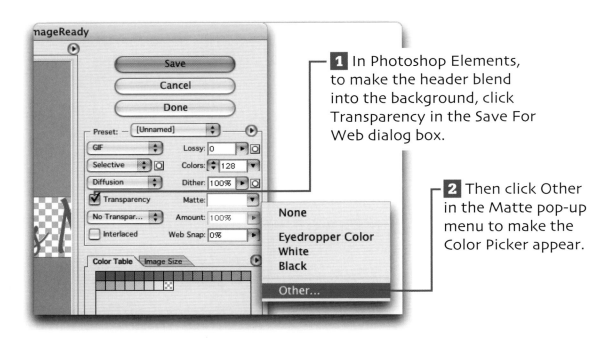

1 In Photoshop Elements, to make the header blend into the background, click Transparency in the Save For Web dialog box.

2 Then click Other in the Matte pop-up menu to make the Color Picker appear.

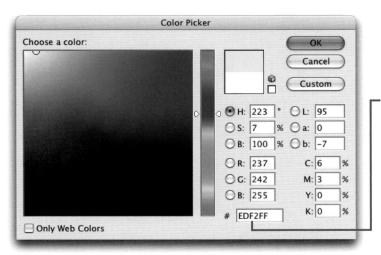

3 In the Color Picker, type EDF2FF to specify the color that the header will blend into. (Here we have it blend into the main color of our page's background.)

save logo as gif

1 Choose GIF format for computer-generated images like text and logos. (This is Photoshop Elements' Save For Web dialog box.)

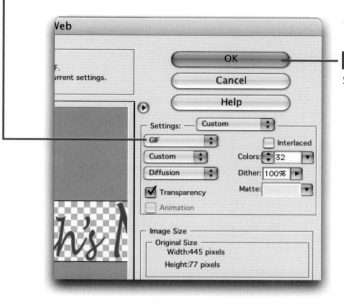

2 Then click OK to save the image.

3 Call the file header_logo.gif and place it in the sarahs_website folder.

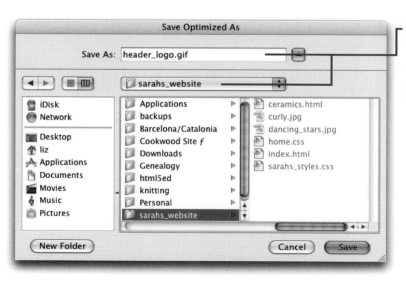

add header logo

```
. . .
<body>
<div class="main">
<p><img src="header_logo.gif" alt="Sarah's
Notecards" width="445" height="77" /></p>
. . .
```

The width of the header logo is just about perfect—slightly more narrow than the average web page.

Whenever you replace text with an image, you should reproduce the text in the alt attribute. This "translates" your GIF image for search engines like Google that can then use the information to set their rankings, or for software that makes web pages accessible, say to the blind.

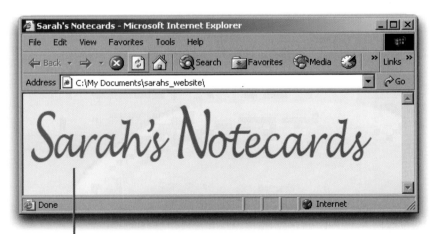

One well-placed GIF image can make your page look really sharp. You should not, however, make all your text into GIF images; GIFs are too hard to update, search, and rank, too inflexible, and not universal enough for the web.

creating the home page

add text

```
. . .
<p><img src="header_logo.gif" alt="Sarah's
Notecards" width="445" height="77" /></p>
<p>I've been wanting to combine a love of
both art and architecture. On our last trip
to Barcelona, I took a bunch of pictures that
I used as the foundation for a new series of
postcards and notecards. There are closeups
of beautiful mosaics and pottery, full shots
of architectural treasures, and candid photos
of traditional cultural events. I hope you'll
enjoy them. </p>
. . .
```

Our new paragraph gets its formatting from the styles
in the sarahs_styles.css file that we created in Chapter 1.
I think the text is too small for a home page introduction.

increase font size

```
p {font-size: 16px}
```

We'll increase the font size of the p elements on the home page. Note that the p elements on the inner pages will not be affected.

Note that the font size and the line height are both increased. The p elements inherited a factor of 1.2 for the line height from sarahs_styles.css, which gives a pleasing value of 19.2 here (the new font size of 16 pixels times 1.2).

create a link

The anchor element (abbreviated as a) lets you create links to other pages, either on your site or on someone else's.

```
. . .
I hope you'll enjoy them.</p>

<p>You can begin browsing the catalog with
the <a href="ceramics.html">ceramics</a>
postcards.</p>
. . .
```

If the linked page is in the same directory as the page you're linking from, you don't need any additional path information besides the file name itself.

The text between the opening and closing a tags will be highlighted on your page and will "invite" your visitor's clicks.

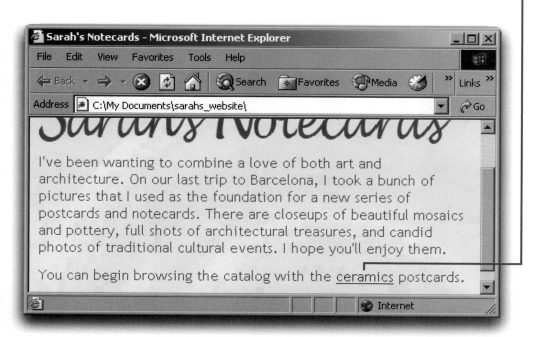

style the links

Instead of that familiar bright blue, we want both new (a:link) and already visited (a:visited) links to be the same color blue as our text (# 4D65A0).

Remember that we can apply the same style rule to one or more kinds of elements by separating them with a comma (see page 33).

```
. . .
a:link, a:visited {color:#4D65A0}
a:focus, a:hover, a:active {color:#7A4DA0;
     text-decoration:none; font-weight:bold}
```

For links that are selected, say, by the Tab key (a:focus), are being pointed at (a:hover), or are being clicked (a:active), we want to apply a purple color (#7A4DA0), remove the underlining (text-decoration:none), and make them bold (font-weight:bold).

postcards and notecards. There are
nd pottery, full shots of architectural
traditional cultural events. I hope you'll

alog with the ceramics postcards.

Browsers underline links by default. Changing the color makes them a bit more subtle, without hiding them completely.

postcards and notecards. There are
nd pottery, full shots of architectural
traditional cultural events. I hope you'll

alog with the **ceramics** postcards.

ecards/ceramics.html"

When the visitor selects or points at the link (and, indeed, as they click it), the link calls attention to itself by losing its underline, and becoming bold and purple.

create little images

Part of our web page consists of four images that will serve as links to the inner pages of the site. They have to be little. One way to do this in Photoshop is to use the crop tool, and specify the desired final size in pixels (with a resolution of 72 dpi).

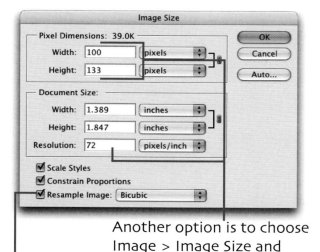

Another option is to choose Image > Image Size and specify the new size there in pixels (at 72 dpi).

The Resample Image box will have to be checked.

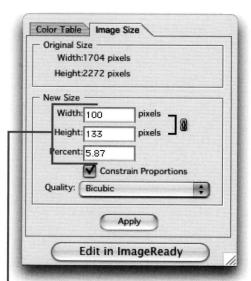

Or you can use the Image Size tab in the Save For Web dialog box.

create an images folder

Now that we've added the four little images to the sarahs_website folder, its contents are becoming a bit unorganized. (You can download the images from the web site—see page xiii.)

Choose File > New > Folder to create a new folder for the little images. Call it little.

Drag the four little images to the little folder.

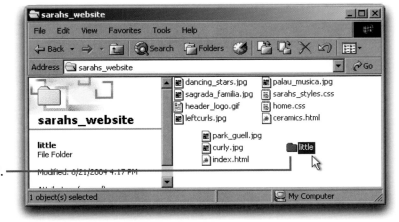

make image links

There are two new paragraphs. The first introduces the image links, the other contains them.

The anchor (a) elements are virtually identical to the one on page 71. The difference is that instead of enclosing text, they enclose an image.

```
. . .
the <a href="ceramics.html">ceramics</a>
postcards.</p>
<p>Or you can click on one of the images below
to go directly to that set of postcards.</p>

<p><a href="ceramics.html">
<img src="little/sagrada_lit.jpg" width="100"
height="133" alt="Ceramics" /></a>
<a href="architecture.html">
<img src="little/spiral_lit.jpg" width="100"
height="133" alt="Architecture" /></a>
<a href="market.html">
<img src="little/market_lit.jpg" width="100"
height="133" alt="Market" /></a>
<a href="festivals.html">
<img src="little/festival_lit.jpg" width="100"
height="133" alt="Festivals" /></a>
</p>
. . .
```

Each img element begins after its respective opening <a> tag and ends before the corresponding closing </a> tag.

Since the images are in the little folder, you must precede the file name with the folder name (little) and a slash (/).

make image links (continued)

In some browsers, an image link appears with a bright blue border by default.

Notice that when a visitor hovers the mouse over the image, the pointer turns into a hand, the alt text appears, and the link address appears in the status bar at the bottom of the window.

adjust link borders

```
...
<p><a href="ceramics.html">
<img src="little/sagrada_lit.jpg" width="100"
height="133" alt="Ceramics" class="little"/>
</a>
...
```

Add a class attribute, set to little, to each of the four image links.

```
...
img.little {border: 1px solid #4D65A0}
```

Then we'll create a style rule that will add a 1 pixel rule just around those images in links—but with our blue (#4D65A0), not the default bright blue that browsers use for links.

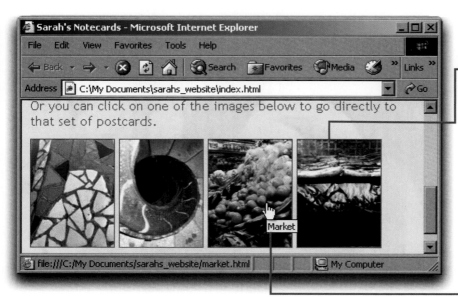

The image links are much more attractive with our more subtle blue border. The pointer still changes to a hand and displays the alt text so that visitors know they are links.

keep images together

Add a class attribute set to image_links to the p element that contains the image links.

```
. . .
<p class="image_links"><a href="ceramics.html">
. . .
```

```
. . .
p.image_links {white-space:nowrap}
```

When you set the white-space property to nowrap, the paragraph is displayed with no line breaks.

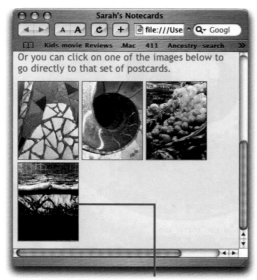

Before: If your visitor makes the window too narrow, the images wrap to the next line. The effect is not pretty.

After: No matter how narrow the window, the image links will stay together on the same line.

add the copyright

Add a new paragraph to contain the copyright information. We'll add the copyright class so that we can format it later.

Use © to add the copyright symbol (©). You can find a whole list of references for symbols in Appendix D.

```
. . .
<img src="little/festival_lit.jpg"
alt="Festivals" width="100" height="133"
class="little" /></a></p>

<p class="copyright">&copy; Copyright 2004.
All Rights Reserved. Sarah's Notecards, Inc.
</p>

</div>
. . .
```

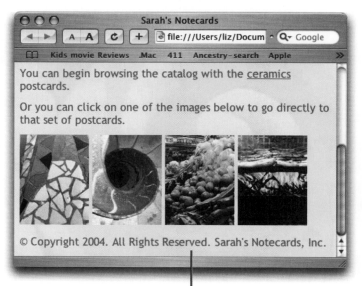

The copyright information begins with the basic styles that are already applied to all p elements (some of which are inherited from the body element).

make copyright smaller

```
. . .
p.image_links {white-space:nowrap}

p.copyright {font-size: smaller;
             padding-top: 40px}
```

The smaller value for the font-size property is calculated with respect to the element that contains this element (called the parent element), which in this case is the main div.

We'll also add padding to the top of the copyright paragraph to keep it a respectable distance from the rest of the content.

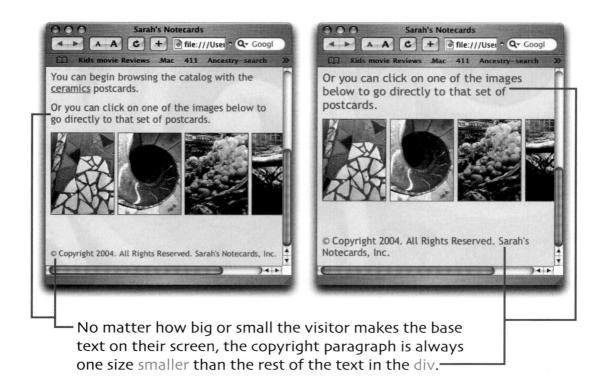

No matter how big or small the visitor makes the base text on their screen, the copyright paragraph is always one size smaller than the rest of the text in the div.

add styles in html

The span element has no default formatting and so works well for adding styles to a chunk of text that is otherwise hard to identify.

The style attribute is followed by an equals sign (=) and then a double quotation mark ("). Then add the CSS properties in the same property:value format as you've been doing all through this book.

```
. . .
<p class="copyright">&copy; Copyright 2004.
All Rights Reserved.<span style="font-family:
'Lucida Handwriting'">Sarah's Notecards,
Inc.</span>
</p>

</div>
. . .
```

Values that need to be enclosed in quotes should use single quotes (') instead of double ones ("), so they are not confused with the double quotes that delimit the value of the style attribute.

© Copyright 2004. All Rights Reserved. *Sarah's Notecards, Inc.*

The font will only display correctly if it is available on the visitor's system (as shown here). Otherwise, it will be ignored.

create a navigation bar

A navigation bar is a common device for helping your visitors find all the pages on your site. Ours runs along the left side of the page and consists of a long image followed by four text links.

You can download the image from the web site. It's called leftcurls.jpg and is the same image that the background came from originally.

The links go to the same pages as the image links we just created. If the images should not load properly for some reason, these links will give our visitors another way to get to the inner pages of our site.

begin navigation bar

```
. . .
Handwriting'"> Sarah's Notecards, Inc.</a></p>
</div>

<div class="nav_bar">
<p><img src="leftcurls.jpg" alt="" width="75"
height="314" /></p>
. . .
```

It's a good idea to start a navigation bar division *after* the main content. That way, if the styles don't work for some reason, the content will still be the first thing your visitors see.

Our navigation bar starts with the long image. Since it's just used for decoration, no *alt* text is necessary.

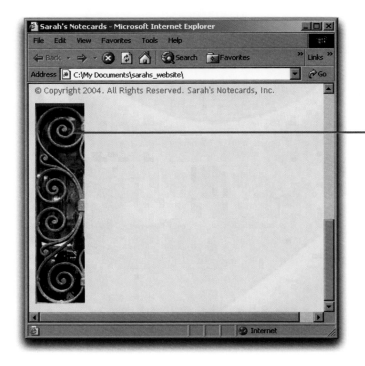

By default, the image appears after the element that precedes it (the *copyright* paragraph).

position navigation bar

```
. . .
div.nav_bar {position: absolute;
             left: 10px;
             top: 10px}
```

The position property determines if a given element should be part of the flow (that is, naturally appear after the element that precedes it), or be positioned absolutely as here, and thus be removed from the flow and begin 10 pixels from the left (left: 10px) and 10 pixels to the top (top: 10px) of the parent element, which is the body, in this case.

The nav_bar div has been removed from the flow and, instead of appearing after the copyright paragraph, it appears 10 pixels from the left and 10 pixels from the top of the body element, its parent. We'll fix that overlap on the next page.

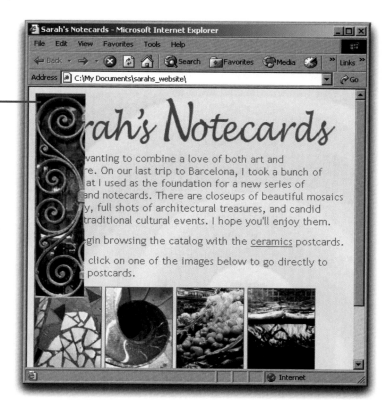

creating the home page

move main div over

```
. . .
div.nav_bar {position: absolute;
             left: 10px;
             top: 10px}
div.main {margin-left:90px}
```

We'll add a left margin of 90 pixels to the entire main div to leave room for the 75 pixel-wide navigation bar image.

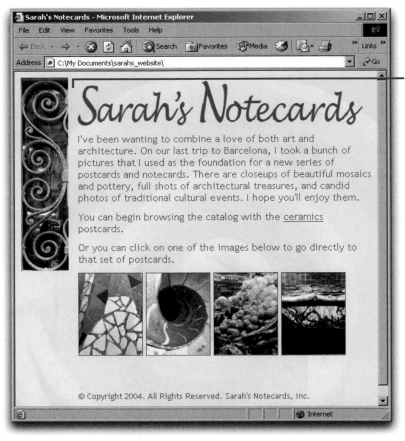

The contents of the two div elements now sit side by side. The extra 15 pixels (90 from the margin minus 75 from the image width) leave a pleasing gap between the two div elements.

add links to nav-bar

```
. . .
<div class="nav_bar">
<img src="leftcurls.jpg" alt="" width="75"
height="314" />
<p><a href="ceramics.html">Ceramics</a>
<br /><a href="architecture.html">
Architecture</a>
<br /><a href="market.html">Market</a>
<br /><a href="festivals.html">Festivals</a>
<br /></p>
. . .
```

Here we recreate the four image links—both to reinforce the navigation system in general, as well as to offer an alternative should the images not load for some reason.

The links get their formatting from the styles we defined earlier (on page 72). They're too big; we'll fix them on the next few pages.

creating the home page

align links to right

```
...
div.nav_bar {position: absolute; left: 10px;
top: 10px; text-align: right}
div.main {margin-left:90px}
```

The links will look better in the navigation bar if they're all aligned to the right (text-align:right).

The links (and indeed, the leftcurls.jpg file) are aligned to the right edge of the nav_bar div. The width of that div is determined by the largest element it contains, which in this case is the set of links. They're so big that they're pushing the whole nav_bar div over onto the contents of the main div. We'll fix that on the next page.

reduce size of links

```
...
div.nav_bar {position: absolute; left: 10px;
top: 10px; text-align: right}
div.nav_bar a {font-size: 11px}
div.main {margin-left:90px}
```

The space says "only apply this style to the a elements that are in the nav_bar div".

When the links are reduced in size, the nav_bar div itself is reduced in size and no longer overlaps the text in the main div. The width of the navigation bar is still determined by the widest element it contains, but that is now the leftcurls.jpg image.

creating the home page

italicize main content

```
. . .
div.main {margin-left:90px}

div.main p {font-style:italic}
```

The space says "this style applies only to the p elements that are in the main div".

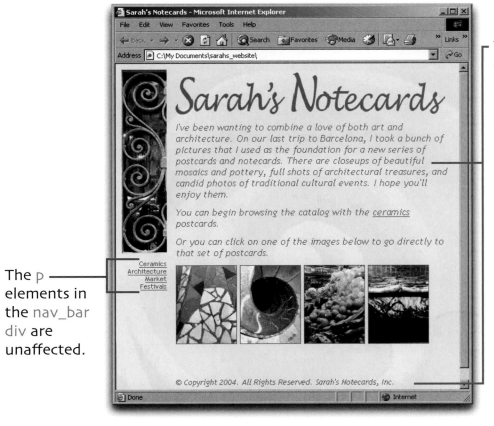

The p elements in the main div are italicized.

The p elements in the nav_bar div are unaffected.

extra bits

create a new html file p. 55

- When you name a file index.html, it is designated as the default file that should open when someone types the address of the directory that contains it. For example, at my site, when someone types http://www.cookwood.com/ the file that they actually see is http://www.cookwood.com/index.html.

link existing style sheet p. 58

- The genius of style sheets is that you can use the same style sheet for as many pages as you want. Not only does this save you time in defining the styles for each page, but it makes global changes very easy to implement.

link to new styles p. 60

- You can link to as many style sheets from a single HTML page as you like. Style sheets that are linked later generally take precedence over conflicting rules from earlier style sheets—as long as the rules share the same level of specificity. So, if an earlier style sheet says p elements should be blue and a later one says they should be red, they will be red. If the earlier style sheet says p elements of class special should be purple, the later, but more general red rule will not affect those special p elements.

begin the header logo p. 65

- For this logo, I scaled the letters horizontally, used oversized capitals, and then reduced the space between the caps and the lowercase letters that follow them. You needn't go to such lengths, however. Simply choosing an attractive font is half of the battle.

add header logo p. 68

- The alt text can contain single straight quotes as long as it is enclosed in double quotes. If you want the alt text to contain double quotes, you must enclose it in single quotes (or use the character reference).

- Since the paragraphs in our main sarahs_styles.css style sheet have a bottom margin but no top margin (page 18), we'll enclose the GIF image in a paragraph. That way there will be a bit of space between the image and the paragraph below it (that we'll add next).

creating the home page

increase font size p. 70

- If we had used a percentage instead of a factor to set the line-height property for p elements in the sarahs_styles.css file, the line height would be inherited a different way. Instead of multiplying the percentage by a new font size, it would be the computed value (say, 120% of the original 12 pixels, or 14.4 pixels) that would be inherited, regardless of the new font size.

create a link p. 71

- You can create links to pages on other web sites by adding the full URL (including the http protocol part) in the href attribute. For example, to link to my site, use `<a href="http://www.cookwood.com">go to Liz's site</a>` .

style the links p. 72

- Because a link can be in more than one state at a time, say, both unvisited and being pointed at, it's a good idea to style your links in order: link, visited, focus, hover, and then active.

- The text-decoration property can also accept values of underline, overline, line-through, blink, none, or inherit.

- The font-weight property can accept the following values: normal, bold, bolder, lighter, 100, 200, 300, 400, 500, 600, 700, 800, 900, or inherit.

create little images p. 73

- You can create these images yourself or get them from the web site: http://www.cookwood.com/htmlvqj/

make image links p. 75

- You can link to nested folders by using additional folder names and slashes (/). So, if there were an image called mosaic.jpg in a folder called ceramics in the little folder you would link to it from a file that was in the sarahs_website folder by using little/ceramics/mosaic.jpg.

- You can control the appearance of the cursor itself with the cursor property. You can consult my HTML VQS (see page xvi in the introduction) for more details.

extra bits

adjust link borders p. 77

- While some browsers show an empty image box when images don't load properly, others don't (below left). If the images have a CSS border, the border shows up even if the image doesn't and the visitor will more easily realize that there is a link there (below right).

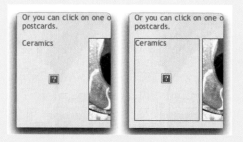

keep images together p. 78

- Use a value of pre for the white-space property to have the browser display all the returns and spaces in the original text. Use a value of normal to treat white space as usual.

make copyright smaller p. 80

- The font-size property also can be set to larger.

- You can also set the font-size property to a factor or to a percentage of the parent element's font size.

add styles in html p. 81

- The styles that you add with the style attribute within an HTML element take precedence over styles in a local or linked style sheet.

position navigation bar p. 84

- An element can also be positioned relative to its normal position in the flow (offset with the values of top and left), or it can be fixed to a static position on the window. However the latter property is only recently becoming more widely supported by browsers.

move main div over p. 85

- You may find it interesting to note that the div elements themselves are not side by side. Rather, the nav_bar div is on top of the main div. However, since the content of the main div has a left margin of 90 pixels, the illusion is that they're next to each other.

align links to right p. 87

- You can set the width manually in pixels or as a percentage of the parent element with the width property (e.g., width:100px). The relationship between the width, margin, border, and the padding properties is somewhat complex. See my HTML VQS for details.

3. publishing your web site

Once you've created your web site, the only step left is to make it available to the Internet by publishing it on a server and then letting people know it's there.

get a web host

Most ISPs (from whom you get your Internet connection) offer a small amount of free space—perhaps 25Mb—for a web site. Your address typically looks like the ISP's name, followed by a tilde (~) followed by your user name.

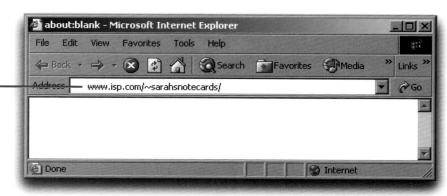

If you need more space or power, you can contract the services of a dedicated web host. Their job is to make your web files available to the Internet. They often offer not only additional space but the ability to run scripts, use databases, employ shopping carts, and more. You can research web hosts at webhostingratings.com.

get a web domain

Whether you have your site hosted by your ISP
or by a dedicated web host, you also have the
option of registering your own domain name
(search for domain registration on Google).
Having your own domain name makes your
site look much more professional—and it
makes it easier to get to, since the address is
presumably easier to remember. And if you
become dissatisfied with your current web
host, you can leave it behind and take your
domain name (and current visitors) with you
to a new host.

set up the ftp program

1 You use an FTP program to transfer files from your computer to the server. This one is Cute FTP for Windows, but any FTP program is fine (see extra bits). Open the Site Manager (or New Connection dialog box, as it's known in Fetch for Mac).

2 Give this group of settings a name—typically, that of your web site, but it doesn't really matter.

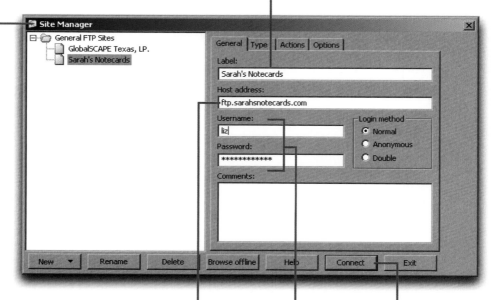

3 The first essential bit of setup information is the Host or FTP address, typically something like ftp.yourdomain.com. If you're not sure what to put here, contact your web host.

5 Finally click Connect to close the Site Manager window and connect to the specified FTP site.

4 Next, enter your user name and password. (Your web host should have provided you with these as well.)

publishing your web site

transfer files to server

1 Navigate through your computer's file system until you find the sarahs_website folder that you created throughout this book.

Cute FTP gives you the connection status in the window bar.

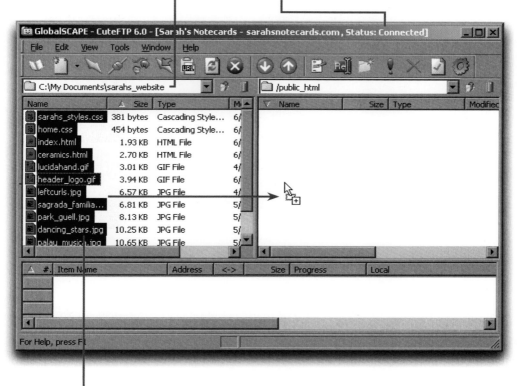

2 Select the files from the sarahs_website folder on your computer and drag them over to the FTP site.

test pages online

Once you've uploaded all your files, be sure to go online and test that your page is working properly. This page, for example, is missing a few images.

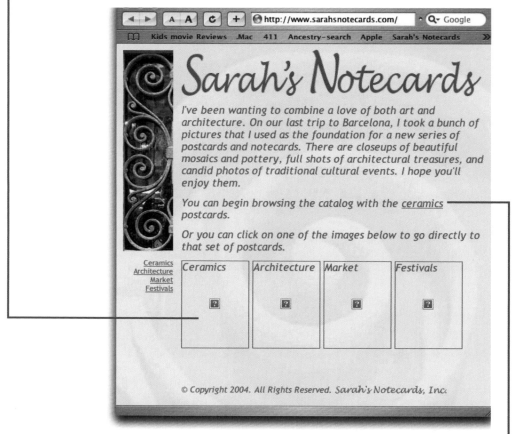

It's also a good idea to test all your links to make sure they lead where they should.

fix and retest

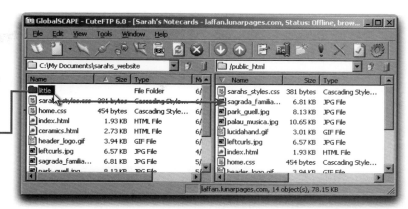

The error in this case was rather common, at least for me: I forgot to upload the little folder, together with the images it contains.

Once the problem has been fixed, choose View > Refresh from your browser. Or click the Refresh icon on the browser's toolbar.

The images now appear as they should.

get indexed

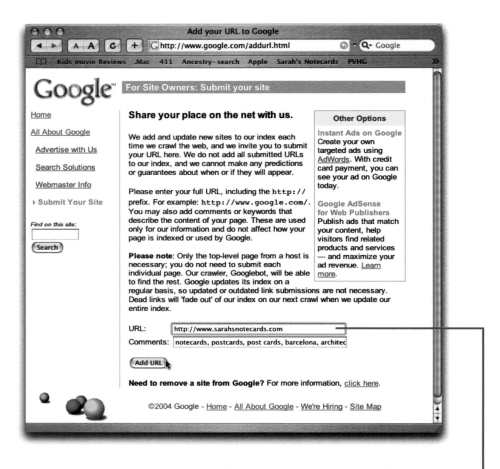

Once your site is published, you can invite Google to visit and add your site to its index by sending your URL (web address) through the Submit your site page at http://www.google.com/addurl.html.

extra bits

get a web host p. 94

- Questions that you should ask a prospective web host include how much they charge each month, how much they charge for "setup", if they have a money-back guarantee, if they have toll-free or email tech support, what their guaranteed uptime is (the percentage they are actually connected to the Internet serving your files), how much space you have on the server, and how many gigabytes you're allowed to serve each month (then divide this by the total size of all your web site files to determine how many users you'll be allowed to have).

get a web domain p. 95

- For a non-professional site, the most important reason to get your own domain name is so that you don't have to change your site's address (or your email) should you decide to change your web host (or ISP). I highly recommend it.

- There used to be only one company that could register domains: Network Solutions. That's no longer the case, and you can often get a better deal by going to the competition.

set up the ftp program p. 96

- Only your web host can tell you what the FTP address is for your site. If you get web space from your ISP, they often have this information on their web site.

- Your web host is also the only one who will know what your user name and password are (though it's often the same as what you use to get your email).

- Fetch for Macintosh is an excellent FTP program. Cute FTP also has a Macintosh version. And there's also WS_FTP for Windows, from Ipswitch.com, among many other possibilities.

transfer files to server p. 97

- As long as the files on the server have the same relative location with respect to the other files, all the links and images will continue to work. So, if index.html and ceramics.html were in the same sarahs_website folder on your computer, they should be in the same folder on your server. In the same way, since the link images were in the little folder on your computer, they should also be in a little folder on the server.

- Transferring files with other FTP programs is virtually the same as with Cute FTP. The basic process is setup, connect, and transfer.

transfer files to server (cont.)

- Some FTP programs require you to set the upload format. In that case use ASCII for text (HTML and CSS files) and Binary for images.

test pages online p. 98

- Missing images is one of the most common problems with a web page. (Remember that we duplicated the links to prepare for this eventuality.) The images may not have been uploaded, may not have been uploaded to the proper folder, or may not have been uploaded properly (images must be uploaded in binary format, and not all FTP programs do that automatically). Another common problem with images is that the file name in the src attribute of the img element does not exactly match the file name of the actual image, including upper and lowercase letters.

- It's also not a bad idea to test your web pages on a variety of browsers and platforms (Windows, Macintosh, Unix). While browsers have begun to embrace the standards that will make such testing unnecessary, there are still important differences, especially with older browsers in wide use (particularly Internet Explorer 5.5 for Windows).

- My number one tip for troubleshooting is to check the easy things first. I can't tell you how many times I've spent hours going over some new tricky technique just to find that the problem was that I misspelled the file name, or a too familiar attribute. Once you've ruled out the obvious culprits, then you can look for more complicated answers.

get indexed p. 100

- There are people who make a living by getting web sites indexed. There are three important techniques: 1. Use the words that peo - ple will search for in order to find you (called keywords) throughout your site and in a meaningful way, especially in the title, headers, and first paragraph. 2. Get linked from other sites. 3. Submit your site to Google.

appendix a:
html reference

In this appendix, you'll find a listing of the HTML elements and attributes that we've covered in this book. If you'd like to see what other HTML elements there are, you can consult my complete listing online: http://www.cookwood.com/html/ (in the extras section).

html reference

element/ attribute	description
— most tags —	The following attributes may be used with most HTML elements
class	For identifying a set of tags in order to apply styles (p. 35)
style	For adding local style sheet information (p. 81)
title	For labeling elements with tool tips (p. 26)
!DOCTYPE	Theoretically required. For indicating the version of HTML used (p. 48)
a	For creating links (p. 71)
href	For specifying the web address (URL) of the page that the link goes to
b	For displaying text in boldface (p. 38)
body	For enclosing the main content of a page (p. 10)
br	For creating a line break (p. 37)
div	For dividing a page into logical sections (p. 39, 57)
class	For giving a name to each class of divisions
h1, h2, ... h6	For creating headers (p. 14, 27)
head	For creating head section of a page (p. 8)
html	For identifying a text file as a web page (p. 7)
i	For displaying text in italics (p. 38)
img	For inserting images on a page (p. 25)
alt	For offering alternate text that is displayed if the image is not
src	For specifying the web address (URL) of the image
width, height	For specifying the size of the image so that the page is loaded more quickly
link	For linking to an external style sheet (p. 12, 58, 60)
href	For specifying the web address (URL) of the style sheet
type	For noting a style sheet's MIME type
rel	For indicating that the link is to a style sheet
p	For creating new paragraphs (p. 17)
span	For creating custom character styles (p. 81)
class	For naming individual custom character styles
title	Required. For creating the title of the page in the title bar area (p. 9)

appendix b:
css reference

In this appendix, you'll find an alphabetical listing of the CSS properties that we've covered in this book. You can find a complete listing of CSS properties on my web site: http://www.cookwood.com/html in the extras section.

css reference

property/values	description/notes
background any combination of the values for background-attachment, background-color, background-image, background-repeat, and/or background-position, or inherit	for changing the background color and image of elements (p. 13, 64) initial value depends on individual properties; not inherited; percentages allowed for background-position
background-color either a color, transparent, or inherit	for setting just the background color of an element (p. 13) initial value: transparent; not inherited
background-image either a URL, none, or inherit	for setting just the background image of an element (p. 64) initial value: none; not inherited
border any combination of the values of border-width, border-style, and/or a color, or inherit	for defining all aspects of a border on all sides of an element (p. 34) initial value depends on individual properties; not inherited
border-color from one to four colors, transparent, or inherit	for setting only the color of the border on one or more sides of an element (p. 34, 51) initial value: the element's color property; not inherited
border-style one to four of the following values: none, dotted, dashed, solid, double, groove, ridge, inset, outset, inherit	for setting only the style of a border on one or more sides of an element (p. 34, 51) initial value: none; not inherited
border-top, border-right, border-bottom, border-left any combination of a single value each for border-width, border-style, and/or a color, or use inherit.	for defining all three border properties at once on only one side of an element (p. 34, 51) initial value depends on individual values; not inherited
border-top-color, border-right-color, border-bottom-color, border-left-color one color or inherit	for defining just the border's color on only one side of an element (p. 34, 51) initial value: the value of the color property; not inherited
border-top-style, border-right-style, border-bottom-style, border-left-style one of none, dotted, dashed, solid, double, groove, ridge, inset, outset, or inherit	for defining just the border's style on only one side of an element (p. 34, 51–52) initial value: none; not inherited
border-top-width, border-right-width, border-bottom-width, border-left-width one of thin, medium, thick, or a length	for defining just the border's width on only one side of an element (p. 34, 51) initial value: medium; not inherited

property/values	description/notes
border-width one to four of the following values: thin, medium, thick, or a length	for defining the border's width on one or more sides of an element (p. 34, 51) initial value: medium; not inherited
clear one of none, left, right, both, or inherit	for keeping elements from floating on one or both sides of an element (p. 41) initial value: none; may only be applied to block-level elements; not inherited
color a color or inherit	for setting the foreground color of an element (p. 16) initial value: parent's color, some colors are set by browser; inherited
float one of left, right, none, inherit	for determining on which side of an element other elements are permitted to float (p. 31, 44) initial value: none; may not be applied to positioned elements or generated content; not inherited
font if desired, any combination of the values for font-style, font-variant, and font-weight followed by the required font-size, an optional value for line-height, and the also required font-family, or use inherit	for setting at least the font family and size, and optionally the style, variant, weight, and line-height of text initial value depends on individual properties; inherited; percentages allowed for values of font-size and line-height
font-family one or more quotation mark-enclosed font names followed by an optional generic font name, or use inherit	for choosing the font family for text (p. 15) initial value: depends on browser; inherited
font-size an absolute size, a relative size, a length, a percentage, or inherit	for setting the size of text (p. 30) initial value: medium; the computed value is inherited; percentages refer to parent element's font size
font-style either normal, italic, oblique, or inherit	for making text italic (p. 36, 89) initial value: normal; inherited
font-weight either normal, bold, bolder, lighter, 100, 200, 300, 400, 500, 600, 700, 800, 900, or inherit	for applying, removing, and adjusting bold formatting (p. 72) initial value: normal; the numeric values are considered keywords and not integers (you can't choose 150, for example); inherited

appendix b: css reference

css reference

property/values	description/notes
left either a length, percentage, auto, or inherit	for setting the distance that an element should be offset from its parent element's left edge (p. 84) initial value: auto; may only be applied to positioned elements; not inherited; percentages refer to width of containing block
line-height either normal, a number, a length, a percentage, or inherit	for setting the amount of space between lines of text (p. 30) initial value: normal; inherited; percentages refer to the font size of the element itself
margin one to four of the following: length, percentage, auto, or inherit	for setting the amount of space between one or more sides of an element's border and its parent element (p. 18) initial value depends on browser and on value of width; not inherited; percentages refer to width of containing block
margin-top, margin-right, margin-bottom, margin-left either a length, percentage, auto, or inherit	for setting the amount of space between only one side of an element's border and its parent element initial value: 0; not inherited; percentages refer to width of containing block; the values for margin-right and margin-left may be overridden if sum of width, margin-right, and margin-left are larger than parent element's containing block
padding one to four lengths or percentages, or inherit	for specifying the distance between one or more sides of an element's content area and its border (p. 40) initial value depends on browser: not inherited; percentages refer to width of containing block
padding-top, padding-right, padding-bottom, padding-left either a length, percentage, or inherit	for specifying the distance between one side of an element's content area and its border (p. 32, 44) initial value: 0; not inherited; percentages refer to width of containing block
position either static, relative, absolute, fixed, or inherit	for determining how an element should be positioned with respect to the document's flow (p. 84) initial value: static; may not be applied to generated content; not inherited
text-align one of left, right, center, justify, a string, or inherit	for aligning text (p. 87) initial value depends on browser and writing direction; may only be applied to block-level elements; inherited

property/values	description/notes
text-decoration	for decorating text (mostly with lines) (p. 72)
any combination of underline, overline, line-through, and blink, or none or inherit	initial value: none; not inherited
top	for setting the distance that an element should be offset from its parent element's top edge (p. 84)
either a length, percentage, auto, or inherit	initial value: auto; may only be applied to positioned elements; not inherited; percentages refer to height of containing block
white-space	for specifying how white space should be treated (p. 78)
either normal, pre, nowrap, or inherit	initial value: normal; may only be applied to block-level elements; inherited
width	for setting the width of an element (p. 92)
either a length, percentage, auto, or inherit	initial value: auto; may not be applied to non-replaced inline elements, table rows, or row groups; not inherited; percentages refer to width of containing block

appendix b: css reference

appendix c: colors

Colors add life to your web site. In this appendix, you'll see how to create the color codes that you'll use in your style sheets. You'll also find a table of the sixteen named colors, as well as a selection of 234 colors, along with their corresponding codes, that you can use as is or as a foundation for choosing your own.

color codes

Here is a bit of one of the style sheets created with this book.

Begin the color code with the hash symbol (#).

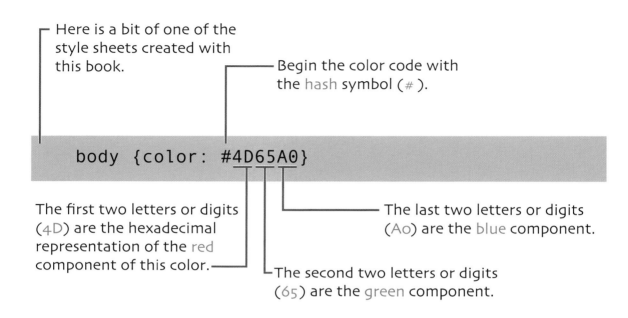

```
body {color: #4D65A0}
```

The first two letters or digits (4D) are the hexadecimal representation of the red component of this color.

The last two letters or digits (A0) are the blue component.

The second two letters or digits (65) are the green component.

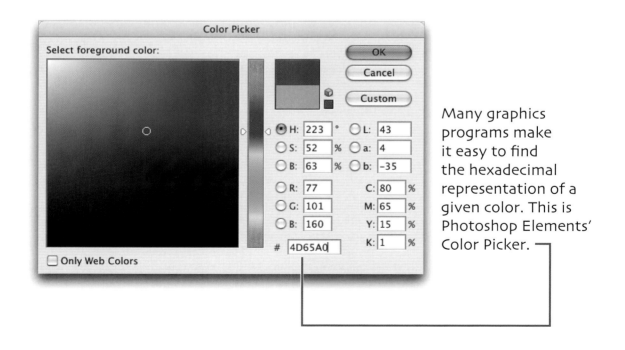

Many graphics programs make it easy to find the hexadecimal representation of a given color. This is Photoshop Elements' Color Picker.

sixteen named colors

There are sixteen
predefined colors.

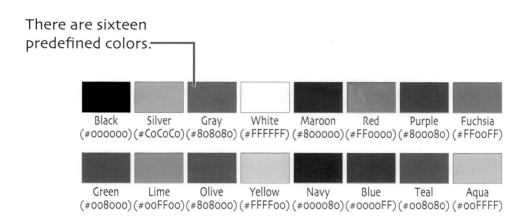

Black	Silver	Gray	White	Maroon	Red	Purple	Fuchsia
(#000000)	(#C0C0C0)	(#808080)	(#FFFFFF)	(#800000)	(#FF0000)	(#800080)	(#FF00FF)
Green	Lime	Olive	Yellow	Navy	Blue	Teal	Aqua
(#008000)	(#00FF00)	(#808000)	(#FFFF00)	(#000080)	(#0000FF)	(#008080)	(#00FFFF)

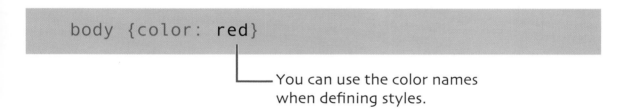

```
body {color: red}
```

You can use the color names
when defining styles.

a selection of colors

#3D001C	#58002B	#6F0039	#840045	#990050	#AD005B	#BE0066	#D20071	#E3007B
#24001D	#35002C	#440039	#530046	#600051	#6D005C	#7A0067	#860071	#92007B
#0A011D	#12022C	#190438	#200645	#260751	#2C0A5C	#330B67	#380D71	#3D107B
#01172E	#002443	#022F55	#023A67	#044476	#004E87	#005796	#0561A5	#0469B3
#002B40	#003F5B	#005073	#006189	#00709E	#0080B4	#008DC6	#009CDA	#00A8EC
#002927	#003D39	#004E4A	#005E5A	#006D68	#007B76	#008983	#009790	#00A49D
#002809	#003B12	#004B18	#005B1E	#006A25	#00782B	#008531	#009337	#009F3C
#1D3403	#2D4B08	#395F0B	#47720F	#528412	#5E9619	#69A61D	#72B720	#7DC623
#444200	#605F00	#7A7700	#918E00	#A7A400	#BDBA00	#D2CE00	#E6E100	#F8F400
#412700	#5C3900	#744A00	#8C5900	#A06800	#B57600	#C98300	#DC9000	#EF9C00
#3C0005	#560007	#6C000A	#820010	#960014	#A90017	#BC001D	#CF0021	#DF0024
#3D0011	#57001A	#6E0023	#83002C	#980034	#AB003C	#BD0043	#D1004B	#E10052
#000000	#121212	#252525	#363636	#464646	#555555	#636363	#707070	#7D7D7D

#E62B86	#EA5493	#EE71A2	#F289AE	#F5A0BD	#F7B5CB	#F9C8D8	#FCDBE4	#FDEDF2
#9C2C86	#A74992	#B1629F	#BC7AAC	#C790B9	#D2A6C7	#DEBDD6	#E9D2E4	#F4E8F0
#4A2885	#5C3E90	#6F559D	#826BA9	#9781B7	#AA99C5	#BFB2D3	#D4CAE2	#EAE4EF
#2D73B9	#497FBF	#648DC7	#7C9BCF	#93A9D5	#AABADD	#C0CBE7	#D5DCEF	#EBECF6
#00AEED	#00B5EF	#49BDEF	#6EC6F1	#8DCFF4	#A5D8F6	#BFE2F9	#D4ECFB	#EBF5FC
#00A9A4	#00B1AE	#49BAB6	#6FC3C1	#8CCCCA	#A7D6D5	#BEE0DF	#D5EAE9	#EBF4F3
#00A54E	#00AD63	#3EB677	#69C08A	#89CA9D	#A4D4B0	#BEDFC4	#D5E9D7	#EBF4EA
#8DCB41	#9DD05B	#AED673	#BBDB88	#C7E19E	#D4E7B2	#E0EDC5	#EAF3DA	#F5F8EC
#FAF519	#FCF64C	#FEF76E	#FEF886	#FFF99D	#FFFAB2	#FFFBC6	#FFFDDA	#FFFDED
#F1A629	#F3B044	#F5BA5C	#F8C473	#FACD8A	#FBD7A1	#FDE2B8	#FDEBCF	#FFF5E8
#E3372E	#E7573B	#EB714D	#EF8861	#F39E77	#F6B28F	#FAC6AA	#FCD9C5	#FEEDE3
#E5325E	#E9556A	#ED717A	#F0888A	#F49F9C	#F6B3AD	#F9C7C2	#FCDAD5	#FEEDEA
#898989	#959595	#A0A0A0	#ACACAC	#B7B7B7	#C2C2C2	#CCCCCC	#D7D7D7	#ECECEC

appendix c: colors   **115**

extra bits

color codes p. 112

- You can also represent colors by specifying their red, green, and blue components either as a percentage or as a numerical value from 0–255. For example, to create our blue 4D65A0, you would use 30% red, 40% green and 63% blue. That could be written as rgb(30%, 40%, 63%) or as rgb(77, 101, 160) (since 77 is 30% of 255, etc). Nevertheless, the hexadecimal system is the most common.

- Hexadecimal means base 16. It is used commonly in computer programming. You can find a table of hexadecimal values on my web site: http://www.cookwood.com/html/ in the extras section.

sixteen named colors p. 113

- There are other color names that some browsers will understand. The color names listed here are the names that all browsers will understand.

- Because the sixteen predefined colors are RGB colors—designed to be viewed on screen, rather than paper—they may look slightly different printed than they do on your monitor.

a selection of colors p. 114

- You can find this collection of colors (as well as the 16 predefined colors and a group of "web-safe" colors that are good for old monitors) on my web site: http://www.cookwood.com/html/ in the extras section.

appendix d: symbols

In this appendix, you'll find a listing of the most common accented characters and special symbols, along with their code names (entities), as well as number references. The entities are perhaps easier to remember, but both systems are equally valid.

Note that the tables were generated with a browser, for authenticity's sake, and thus appear slightly more pixelated than regular text in this book.

symbols and characters

Characters with special meaning in html

Entity	Entity Displayed	Number	Number Displayed	Description
&	&	&	&	ampersand
>	>	>	>	greater-than sign
<	<	<	<	less-than sign
"	"	"	"	quotation mark = APL quote

Accented characters, accents, and other diacritics from Western European languages

Entity	Entity Displayed	Number	Number Displayed	Description
´	´	´	´	acute accent = spacing acute
¸	¸	¸	¸	cedilla = spacing cedilla
ˆ	^	ˆ	^	modifier letter circumflex accent
¯	¯	¯	¯	macron = spacing macron = overline = APL overbar
·	·	·	·	middle dot = Georgian comma = Greek middle dot
˜	˜	˜	˜	small tilde
¨	¨	¨	¨	diaeresis = spacing diaeresis
Á	Á	Á	Á	latin capital letter A with acute
á	á	á	á	latin small letter a with acute
Â	Â	Â	Â	latin capital letter A with circumflex
â	â	â	â	latin small letter a with circumflex
Æ	Æ	Æ	Æ	latin capital letter AE = latin capital ligature AE
æ	æ	æ	æ	latin small letter ae = latin small ligature ae
À	À	À	À	latin capital letter A with grave = latin capital letter A grave
à	à	à	à	latin small letter a with grave = latin small letter a grave
Å	Å	Å	Å	latin capital letter A with ring above = latin capital letter A ring
å	å	å	å	latin small letter a with ring above = latin small letter a ring
Ã	Ã	Ã	Ã	latin capital letter A with tilde
ã	ã	ã	ã	latin small letter a with tilde
Ä	Ä	Ä	Ä	latin capital letter A with diaeresis
ä	ä	ä	ä	latin small letter a with diaeresis
Ç	Ç	Ç	Ç	latin capital letter C with cedilla

Accented characters, accents, and other diacritics from Western European languages (continued)

Entity	Entity Displayed	Number	Number Displayed	Description
&ccedil;	ç	&#231;	ç	latin small letter c with cedilla
&Eacute;	É	&#201;	É	latin capital letter E with acute
&eacute;	é	&#233;	é	latin small letter e with acute
&Ecirc;	Ê	&#202;	Ê	latin capital letter E with circumflex
&ecirc;	ê	&#234;	ê	latin small letter e with circumflex
&Egrave;	È	&#200;	È	latin capital letter E with grave
&egrave;	è	&#232;	è	latin small letter e with grave
&ETH;	Ð	&#208;	Ð	latin capital letter ETH
&eth;	ð	&#240;	ð	latin small letter eth
&Euml;	Ë	&#203;	Ë	latin capital letter E with diaeresis
&euml;	ë	&#235;	ë	latin small letter e with diaeresis
&Iacute;	Í	&#205;	Í	latin capital letter I with acute
&iacute;	í	&#237;	í	latin small letter i with acute
&Icirc;	Î	&#206;	Î	latin capital letter I with circumflex
&icirc;	î	&#238;	î	latin small letter i with circumflex
&Igrave;	Ì	&#204;	Ì	latin capital letter I with grave
&igrave;	ì	&#236;	ì	latin small letter i with grave
&Iuml;	Ï	&#207;	Ï	latin capital letter I with diaeresis
&iuml;	ï	&#239;	ï	latin small letter i with diaeresis
&Ntilde;	Ñ	&#209;	Ñ	latin capital letter N with tilde
&ntilde;	ñ	&#241;	ñ	latin small letter n with tilde
&Oacute;	Ó	&#211;	Ó	latin capital letter O with acute
&oacute;	ó	&#243;	ó	latin small letter o with acute
&Ocirc;	Ô	&#212;	Ô	latin capital letter O with circumflex
&ocirc;	ô	&#244;	ô	latin small letter o with circumflex
&OElig;	Œ	&#338;	Œ	latin capital ligature OE
&oelig;	œ	&#339;	œ	latin small ligature oe (note)
&Ograve;	Ò	&#210;	Ò	latin capital letter O with grave
&ograve;	ò	&#242;	ò	latin small letter o with grave
&Oslash;	Ø	&#216;	Ø	latin capital letter O with stroke = latin capital letter O slash
&oslash;	ø	&#248;	ø	latin small letter o with stroke, = latin small letter o slash

symbols and characters

Accented characters, accents, and other diacritics from Western European languages (continued)

Entity	Entity Displayed	Number	Number Displayed	Description
&Otilde;	Õ	&#213;	Õ	latin capital letter O with tilde
&otilde;	õ	&#245;	õ	latin small letter o with tilde
&Ouml;	Ö	&#214;	Ö	latin capital letter O with diaeresis
&ouml;	ö	&#246;	ö	latin small letter o with diaeresis
&Scaron;	Š	&#352;	Š	latin capital letter S with caron
&scaron;	š	&#353;	š	latin small letter s with caron
&szlig;	ß	&#223;	ß	latin small letter sharp s = ess-zed
&THORN;	Þ	&#222;	Þ	latin capital letter THORN
&thorn;	þ	&#254;	þ	latin small letter thorn
&Uacute;	Ú	&#218;	Ú	latin capital letter U with acute
&uacute;	ú	&#250;	ú	latin small letter u with acute
&Ucirc;	Û	&#219;	Û	latin capital letter U with circumflex
&ucirc;	û	&#251;	û	latin small letter u with circumflex
&Ugrave;	Ù	&#217;	Ù	latin capital letter U with grave
&ugrave;	ù	&#249;	ù	latin small letter u with grave
&Uuml;	Ü	&#220;	Ü	latin capital letter U with diaeresis
&uuml;	ü	&#252;	ü	latin small letter u with diaeresis
&Yacute;	Ý	&#221;	Ý	latin capital letter Y with acute
&yacute;	ý	&#253;	ý	latin small letter y with acute
&yuml;	ÿ	&#255;	ÿ	latin small letter y with diaeresis
&Yuml;	Ÿ	&#376;	Ÿ	latin capital letter Y with diaeresis

Currency characters

Entity	Entity Displayed	Number	Number Displayed	Description
&cent;	¢	&#162;	¢	cent sign
&curren;	¤	&#164;	¤	currency sign
&euro;	€	&#8364;	€	euro sign
&pound;	£	&#163;	£	pound sign
&yen;	¥	&#165;	¥	yen sign = yuan sign

Punctuation

Entity	Entity Displayed	Number	Number Displayed	Description
¦	¦	¦	¦	broken bar = broken vertical bar
•	•	•	•	bullet = black small circle (note)
©	©	©	©	copyright sign
†	†	†	†	dagger
‡	‡	‡	‡	double dagger
⁄	/	⁄	/	fraction slash
…	...	…	...	horizontal ellipsis = three dot leader
¡	¡	¡	¡	inverted exclamation mark
ℑ	ℑ	ℑ	ℑ	blackletter capital I = imaginary part
¿	¿	¿	¿	inverted question mark = turned question mark
‎		‎		left-to-right mark (for formatting only)
—	—	—	—	em dash
–	–	–	–	en dash
¬	¬	¬	¬	not sign
‾	‾	‾	‾	overline = spacing overscore
ª	ª	ª	ª	feminine ordinal indicator
º	º	º	º	masculine ordinal indicator
¶	¶	¶	¶	pilcrow sign = paragraph sign
‰	‰	‰	‰	per mille sign
′	′	′	′	prime = minutes = feet
″	″	″	″	double prime = seconds = inches
ℜ	ℜ	ℜ	ℜ	blackletter capital R = real part symbol
®	®	®	®	registered sign = registered trade mark sign
‏		‏		right-to-left mark (for formatting only)
§	§	§	§	section sign
­		­		soft hyphen = discretionary hyphen (displays incorrectly on Mac)
¹	¹	¹	¹	superscript one = superscript digit one
™	™	™	™	trade mark sign
℘	℘	℘	℘	script capital P = power set = Weierstrass p

symbols and characters

Punctuation (continued)

Entity	Entity Displayed	Number	Number Displayed	Description
&bdquo;	„	&#8222;	„	double low-9 quotation mark
&laquo;	«	&#171;	«	left-pointing double angle quotation mark = left pointing guillemet
&ldquo;	"	&#8220;	"	left double quotation mark
&lsaquo;	‹	&#8249;	‹	single left-pointing angle quotation mark (note)
&lsquo;	'	&#8216;	'	left single quotation mark
&raquo;	»	&#187;	»	right-pointing double angle quotation mark = right pointing guillemet
&rdquo;	"	&#8221;	"	right double quotation mark
&rsaquo;	›	&#8250;	›	single right-pointing angle quotation mark (note)
&rsquo;	'	&#8217;	'	right single quotation mark
&sbquo;	‚	&#8218;	‚	single low-9 quotation mark
				em space
				en space
				no-break space = non-breaking space
				thin space
&zwj;		&#8205;		zero width joiner
&zwnj;		&#8204;		zero width non-joiner

Mathematical symbols

Entity	Entity Displayed	Number	Number Displayed	Description
&deg;	°	&#176;	°	degree sign
&divide;	÷	&#247;	÷	division sign
&frac12;	$\frac{1}{2}$	&#189;	$\frac{1}{2}$	vulgar fraction one half = fraction one half
&frac14;	$\frac{1}{4}$	&#188;	$\frac{1}{4}$	vulgar fraction one quarter = fraction one quarter
&frac34;	$\frac{3}{4}$	&#190;	$\frac{3}{4}$	vulgar fraction three quarters = fraction three quarters
&ge;	≥	&#8805;	≥	greater-than or equal to
&le;	≤	&#8804;	≤	less-than or equal to
&minus;	−	&#8722;	−	minus sign
&sup2;	²	&#178;	²	superscript two = superscript digit two = squared
&sup3;	³	&#179;	³	superscript three = superscript digit three = cubed
&times;	×	&#215;	×	multiplication sign

index

index

C

ceramics.html, file name
  linking to 71
  saving 6
characters, special 28
  references for 51
character references 51
  and encodings 50
child element 49. See
  also inheritance
class, attribute 104
  adding italics 36
  adjusting link borders 77
  floating images 44
  in div element 39
  in img element 77
  in p element 35, 78, 79
  style rules for 40, 44
classifying
  divisions 39
  images 44, 77
  paragraphs 35, 78, 79
clear, property 41, 52, 107. See
  also float, property
clearing floats 41, 52
color
  background 13
  background image 62
  text 16
color, property 16, 107
colors 111–116
  codes for 112
  selection of 114
  sixteen named 113
  tips 116
commas, in style rules 15, 33
compression 50, 63
contrast 16
  adjusting 21, 61
copyright, adding 79
copyright symbol 79
Corel WordPerfect 5
creating
  borders 34
  folders 4
  headers 14
  HTML file 5–6, 55
  images 19–23
  style sheets 11
  subheaders 27

cropping images 20, 73
CSS, Cascading Style Sheets 12
  reference 105–110
  See also style sheets
.css extension 11
curly.jpg, background image 63
  adding 64
  getting xiii
curly brackets 13
curly quotes 28
currency characters 120
cursor, property 91
Cute FTP for Macintosh 101
Cute FTP for Windows xv,
  96, 101

D

del, element 52. See also text-
  decoration, property
div, element 92, 104
  adding new 42
  clearing floats 41
  creating 39, 57
  default formatting 52
  location of 83
  padding 40
  positioning 84–85
  width of 87
divisions. See div, element
DOCTYPE declarations 48,
  56, 104
domains 95
  advantages of 101
download time 22
  JPEG quality 23, 63

E

EDF2FF (background color
  value) 13
ellipsis, meaning of xi, 9
em, element 52. See also font-
  style, property
encodings, for non-English
  languages 50
entities 117–122
example files, for this book xiii
extensions, file. See file
  extensions

extra bits
  description xii
  for colors 116
  for home page 90–92
  for inner pages 48–52
  for publishing 101–102

F

favorites, and title of web page 9
Fetch for Macintosh 101
file extensions
  for style sheets 11
  for web pages 6
file names
  conventions for 6, 11, 24
  See also file extensions
float, property 31, 107. See
  also clear, property
floating
  clearing 41
  images 31
  to the right 44
folders
  creating 4
  for images 50, 74
  importance of 6
font, property 49, 107
font-family, property 15,
  81, 107
font-size, property 30, 51, 70,
  88, 107
  relative values 80, 92
font-style, property 36, 89, 107.
  See also italics
font-weight, property 72, 108.
  values for 91
  See also bold
fonts
  choosing 15, 49, 81
  saving as GIF image 65–67
  size 51
  standard 49
  See also individual font
   properties
format
  of style sheets 11, 59
  of web page 6, 55
formatting, local 38, 52. See
  also bold, italics, and style
  sheets

index

index

Full-color projects
from the folks
who bring you
Visual QuickStart
Guides…

Visual QuickProject

Creating a Web Page
in Dreamweaver

NOLAN HESTER

creating
a web page
in dreamweaver

Visual QuickProject Guide

by Nolan Hester

Peachpit
Press

Visual QuickProject Guide
Creating a Web Page in Dreamweaver
Nolan Hester

Peachpit Press

1249 Eighth Street
Berkeley, CA 94710
510/524-2178
800/283-9444
510/524-2221 (fax)

Find us on the World Wide Web at: www.peachpit.com
To report errors, please send a note to errata@peachpit.com
Peachpit Press is a division of Pearson Education

Copyright © 2005 by Nolan Hester

Editor: Nancy Davis
Production Editor: Lisa Brazieal
Compositor: David Van Ness
Proofreader: Ted Waitt
Indexer: FireCrystal Communications
Cover design: The Visual Group with Aren Howell
Interior design: Elizabeth Castro
Interior photos: Ali Pearson and Shannon Smith
Cover photo credit: Getty One

Notice of Rights
All rights reserved. No part of this book may be reproduced or transmitted in any form by any means, electronic, mechanical, photocopying, recording, or otherwise, without the prior written permission of the publisher. For information on getting permission for reprints and excerpts, contact permissions@peachpit.com.

Notice of Liability
The information in this book is distributed on an "As Is" basis, without warranty. While every precaution has been taken in the preparation of the book, neither the author nor Peachpit Press shall have any liability to any person or entity with respect to any loss or damage caused or alleged to be caused directly or indirectly by the instructions contained in this book or by the computer software and hardware products described in it.

Trademarks
Visual QuickProject Guide is a registered trademark of Peachpit Press, a division of Pearson Education.
All other trademarks are the property of their respective owners.

Throughout this book, trademarks are used. Rather than put a trademark symbol with every occurrence of a trademarked name, we state that we are using the names in an editorial fashion only and to the benefit of the trademark owner with no intention of infringement of the trademark. No such use, or the use of any trade name, is intended to convey endorsement or other affiliation with this book.

ISBN 0-321-27843-7

Printed and bound in the United States of America

To Mary, for helping create this life of startling delight.

Special Thanks to...

Terry Wardwell for sharing the fun of making Tuffits and the Web site,

Marjorie Baer and Cary Norsworthy for helping me get this book off the ground,

Nancy Davis, my editor and nerves-of-steel ground controller, for helping me land safely when the book was up in the air,

Nancy Aldrich-Ruenzel, Peachpit's publisher, for letting me fly in the first place,

David Van Ness and Lisa Brazieal for keeping the layouts and wing bolts tight,

Emily Glossbrenner for turning around the index faster than LAX does planes,

Laika for not eating all the free peanuts,

and my readers for fastening their safety belts during such extended metaphors.

contents

contents

introduction

The Visual QuickProject Guide that you hold in your hands offers a unique way to learn about new technologies. Instead of drowning you in theoretical possibilities and lengthy explanations, this Visual QuickProject Guide uses big, color illustrations coupled with clear, concise step-by-step instructions to show you how to complete one specific project in a matter of hours.

Our project in this book is to create a beautiful Web site using Macromedia Dreamweaver MX 2004, one of the best programs for building Web sites. Our Web site displays the products for a real company that makes cast concrete stepping stones that look like couch pillows. Because the project covers all the techniques needed to build a basic Web site, you'll be able to use what you learn to create your own Web site. Thanks to Dreamweaver, you'll do all this without having to enter a single line of HTML, the code that drives the Web.

what you'll create

These two pages represent just some of the things you'll learn how to create.

Format text and headings in the font, size, and colors you want. (See page 12.)

Add images and wrap text around them. (See page 23.)

Create a site-wide navigation bar to guide visitors as they explore your site. (See page 93.)

Reduce and resample images to make them quicker to download. (See page 30.)

Create internal, external, and email links, then give them a consistent appearance using external style sheets. (See page 55.)

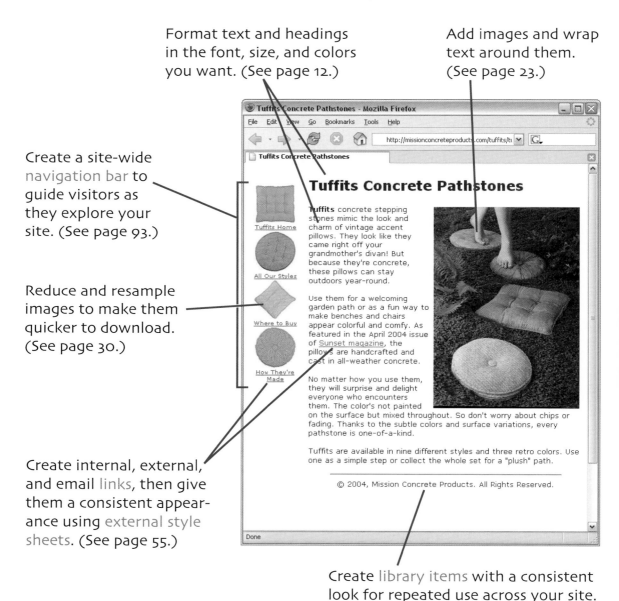

Create library items with a consistent look for repeated use across your site. (See page 76.)

Build tables for displaying everything from images to tabular data. (See page 37.)

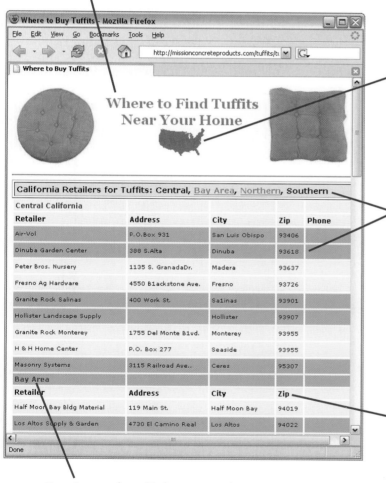

Create image maps that link specific parts of images to different files. (See page 68.)

Apply colors and formatting to tables to make them easier to read. (See page 50.)

Sort data alphabetically or numerically within a table's columns or rows. (See page 51.)

Create anchor links so readers can jump to the right spot in a long document. (See page 65.)

introduction

how this book works

The title explains what is covered in that section.

Names of Dreamweaver elements, file names, and other important concepts are shown in orange.

Numbered steps lead you through the sequence of actions, showing only the details you really need.

Screenshots focus on what part of Dreamweaver you'll be using for that particular project step.

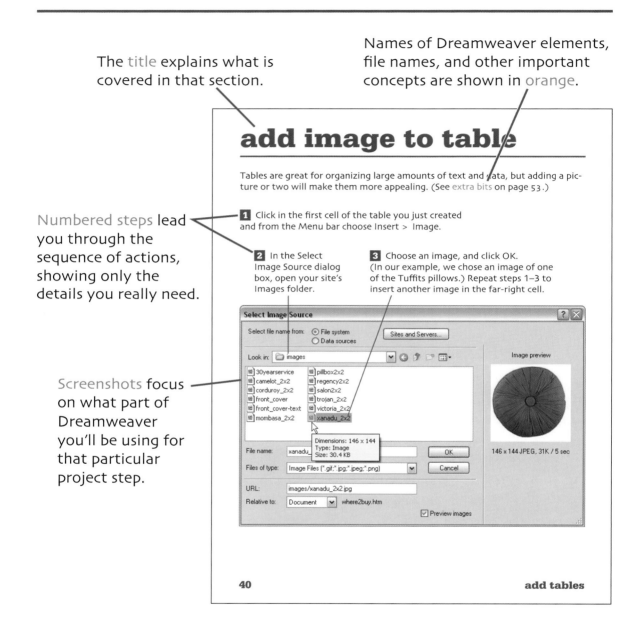

add image to table

Tables are great for organizing large amounts of text and data, but adding a picture or two will make them more appealing. (See extra bits on page 53.)

1 Click in the first cell of the table you just created and from the Menu bar choose Insert > Image.

2 In the Select Image Source dialog box, open your site's Images folder.

3 Choose an image, and click OK. (In our example, we chose an image of one of the Tuffits pillows.) Repeat steps 1–3 to insert another image in the far-right cell.

40   add tables

The extra bits section at the end of each chapter contains additional tips and tricks that you might like to know—but that aren't absolutely necessary for creating the Web page.

import tabular data

extra bits

add a table p. 38
- Use the Table dialog box's Accessibility section to create an explanatory Caption that will be read aloud by special audio Web browsers for visually impaired visitors. If needed, add details in the Summary field.

add image to table p. 40
- If you're having trouble selecting a table, just click near the table and then press Ctrl A in Windows or Cmd A on the Mac.

add labels p. 42
- The Table dialog box Header options—None, Left, Top, and Both—let you skip adding labels, label only the rows, label only the columns, or label both rows and columns.

save and apply style p. 44
- To insert a new column, select a column and press Ctrl Shift A in Windows or Cmd Shift A on the Mac. The new column will appear left of the selected column.
- For more information on formatting text, see Chapter 2.

import tabular data p. 46
- Before importing, use your spreadsheet or word-processing program to save the data in comma- or tab-delimited form.
- Sometimes the Set drop-down menu in the Table Width section of the Import Tabular Data dialog box will switch to Percent—even if you previously set it to Pixels. So double-check before clicking OK.
- Our copy-and-paste example works because each table had the same number of columns. You cannot, for example, copy 6 columns and paste them into 4 columns.

format table colors p. 50
- By using Ctrl-click in Windows or Cmd-click on the Mac, you also can select non-adjacent columns or cells. Then you can format all the selections at once.

sort tables p. 51
- By default, the Options in the Sort Table dialog box are not checked, since you seldom want the header or footer rows sorted.

add tables   53

The heading for each group of tips matches the section title. (The colors are just for decoration and have no hidden meaning.)

Next to the heading there's a page number that also shows which section the tips belong to.

the web site

You can find this book's companion site at http://www.waywest.net/dwvqj/.

You'll find all the example files used in the book, including the images.

You'll also find extra tips on working with Dreamweaver, plus corrections if any mistakes are found.

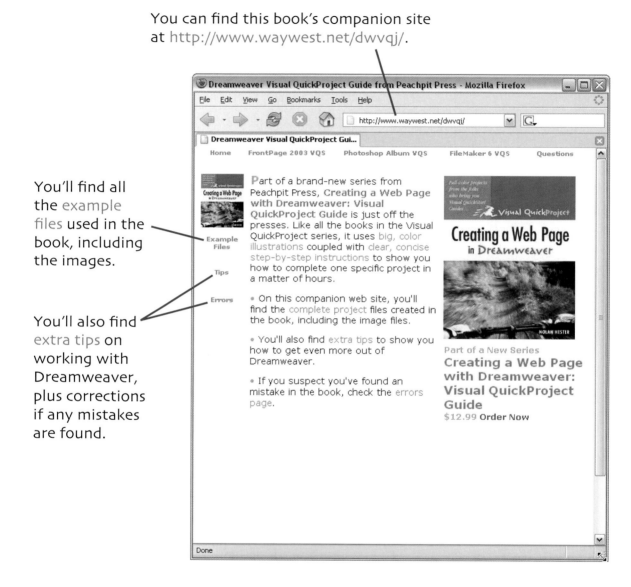

useful tools

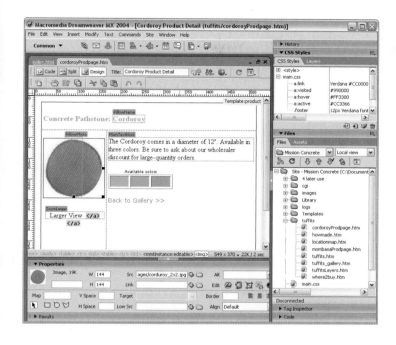

Naturally, you'll need a computer, and you'll need Dreamweaver MX 2004, which is packed with most of the tools you'll need, including a way to publish to the Web.

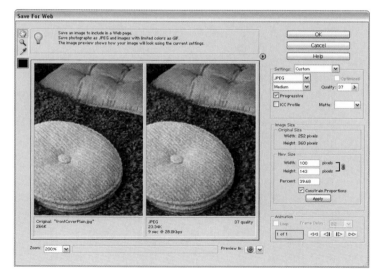

You'll also need an image editor. If you bought Dreamweaver as part of Macromedia Studio MX 2004, then you'll be able to use Fireworks, which is a full-fledged image editor designed to work hand-in-hand with Dreamweaver. Your digital camera may have included an image-editing program. Otherwise, consider Adobe Photoshop Elements, which also contains specific tools for working with Web images.

the next step

While this Visual QuickProject Guide gives you a good start on creating a Web site using Dreamweaver, there is a lot more to learn. If you want to dive into all the details, try Macromedia Dreamweaver MX 2004 for Windows and Macintosh: Visual QuickStart Guide, by J. Tarin Towers.

The Macromedia Dreamweaver MX 2004 Visual QuickStart Guide features clear examples, concise step-by-step instructions, and tons of helpful tips. With more than 700 pages, it covers darn near every aspect of Dreamweaver.

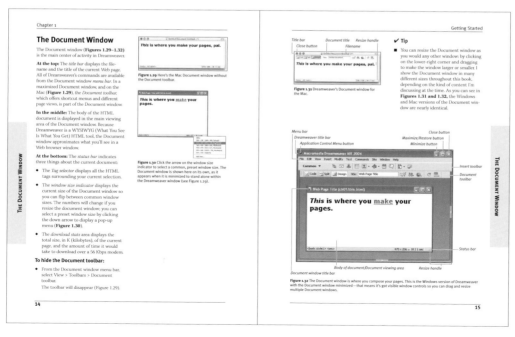

1. welcome to dreamweaver

Dreamweaver is a powerful program, packed with cool features to create Web sites. So packed, in fact, that it can be a bit overwhelming.

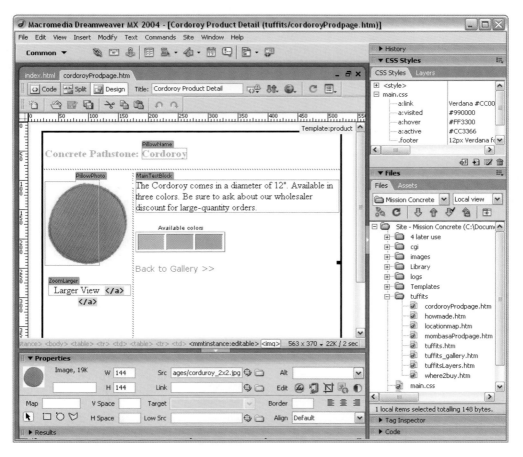

Not to worry. We aren't going to explain every possible option—just the crucial ones to keep you going, no matter how daunting Dreamweaver may seem initially. We'll have some fun along the way, too, so let's get started.

explore dreamweaver

A series of key toolbars, windows, and panels surround your main Dreamweaver document. Take a moment to understand how they work and you'll save yourself frustration later. (See extra bits on page 8.)

When you open more than one file, a series of tabs will appear across the top of the main window to indicate which ones are open.

The current file's title appears at the center of the toolbar, followed by some buttons related to posting your site on the Web. Use the last button if you want to see a ruler or grid while building pages.

Just below the tabs run two toolbars. The Document toolbar is set by default to the Design view. You can change it to show only the Code view or use the Split view to show the Code and Design views.

Use the buttons in the Standard toolbar to create new files, open folders, cut and paste, save files, and undo actions.

Depending on what you're doing, switch the Insert toolbar to display the relevant buttons using the drop-down menu.

Many of the toolbar's buttons have their own drop-down menus.

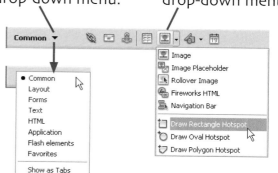

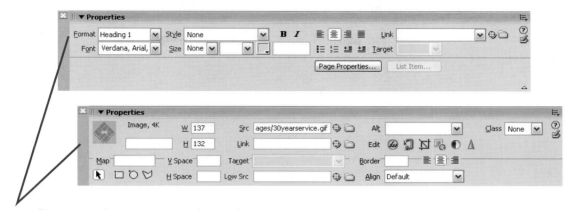

Depending on what you've selected, the Property inspector changes to display the relevant information and tools, such as those for text or images. To see or hide the inspector, press [Ctrl][F11] (Windows) or [Cmd][F11] (Mac).

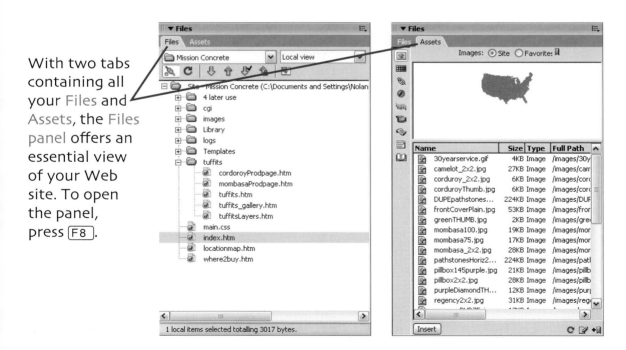

With two tabs containing all your Files and Assets, the Files panel offers an essential view of your Web site. To open the panel, press [F8].

welcome to dreamweaver

set up local site

Once you've installed Dreamweaver, your first step is to set up a local version of your Web site on your computer. (See extra bits on page 8.)

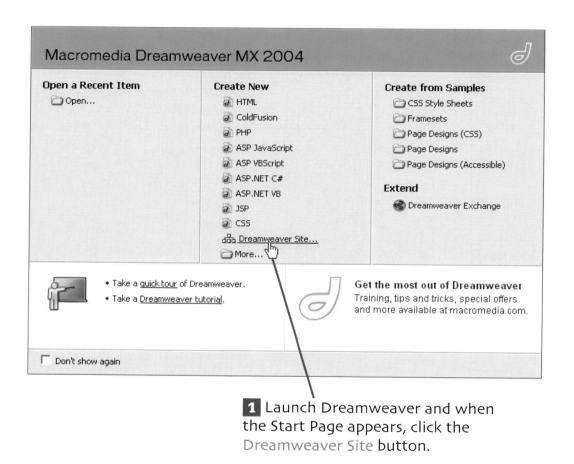

1 Launch Dreamweaver and when the Start Page appears, click the Dreamweaver Site button.

2 Dreamweaver will automatically assign a generic name to your new site and highlight it.

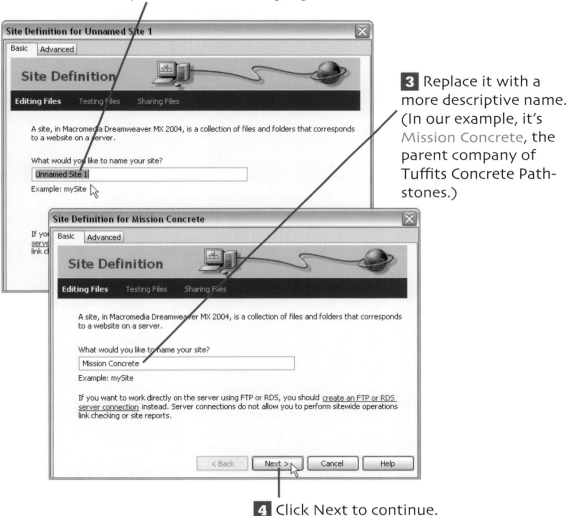

3 Replace it with a more descriptive name. (In our example, it's Mission Concrete, the parent company of Tuffits Concrete Path-stones.)

4 Click Next to continue.

set up local site (cont.)

5 When the next Site Definition window appears, choose No and click Next.

6 In the next window, choose Edit local copies on my machine....

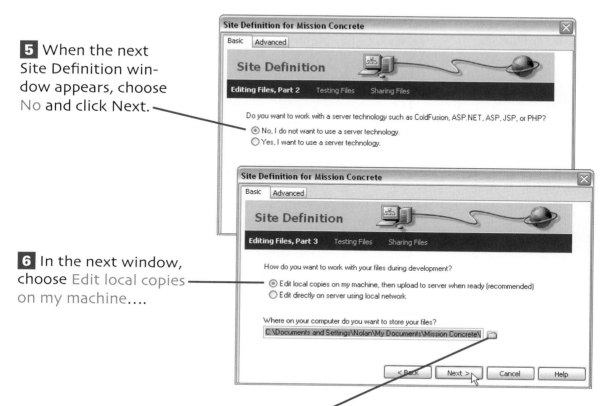

7 In general, you don't need to change where Dreamweaver creates the site folder, but if you want to change it, click the Folder icon and navigate to your preferred location. Click Next to continue.

8 In the next window, choose FTP from the drop-down menu.

Fill in the FTP address for your new site, based on information provided by the firm that will be hosting your site.

Fill in your login and password, again based on the information from your Web host.

Assuming you're already online, click Test Connection and it will take only a moment for Dreamweaver to determine if the connection's working. Click Next to continue.

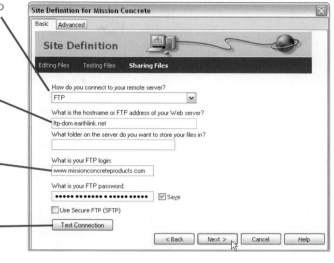

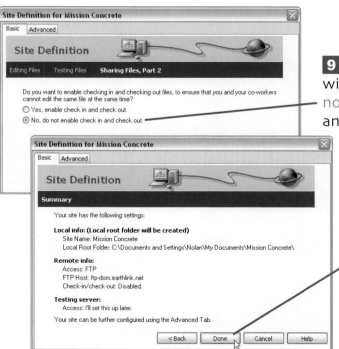

9 When the next Site Definition window appears, choose No, do not enable check in and check out and click Next.

10 Double-check the Summary information before clicking Done. You're ready to build your site. See create a basic home page on page 9.

welcome to dreamweaver

extra bits

explore dreamweaver p. 2

- Unless you're familiar with HTML or CSS coding, leave the toolbar set to Design.

- Rather than explain every tool and button here, we'll cover them in the coming chapters as we need them.

- You also can see or hide the contents of any panel by clicking the triangle-shaped arrow at the upper left of the panel.

- Using Dreamweaver's keyboard shortcuts greatly speeds your work.

  To download the Windows short-cuts, go to: http://download. macromedia.com/pub/dream weaver/documentation/dwmx_ kb_shortcuts.zip.

  To download the Mac shortcuts, go to: http://download.macro media.com/pub/dreamweaver/ documentation/dwmx_kb_ shortcuts.sit.

set up local site p. 4

- The name you enter in the Site Definition window only appears within Dreamweaver, not on your actual Web site. Pick one to distinguish this site from the many others you'll no doubt be creating soon.

- Web-hosting firms usually email you a login name and password for posting your files. Keep the original email where you won't delete it and can find it later. If you ever buy a new computer, you'll need that password because Dreamweaver never reveals the password, just those black dots.

- If the test connection fails, double-check your entries in the Site Definition window. Note that entries are case sensitive. Almost inevitably, you'll find a mistyped entry.

- Use the check-in system only if there are several people building the Web site; it keeps you from overwriting each other's work.

2. create a basic home page

As the front door to your Web site, the home page invites visitors to step in and take a look around. In this chapter, you'll build a simple home page to quickly orient visitors to what your site offers. In later chapters, you'll learn how to dress it up a bit with images and some special features. Here, however, we'll focus on the basics: creating, naming, titling, and saving this all-important page.

Working within Dreamweaver's Property inspector, you'll add text to the page, and set the font, size, color, and alignment. You'll also use the Property inspector to add headings and a bulleted list of items. Such lists help group multiple items into an easy-to-scan format. The graphics you add later will add snap to your Web pages, but such simple steps as formatting text and setting heading sizes establish an essential sense of order and visual rank on your pages.

create your home page

The mechanics of making your home page are pretty simple. The first step is to create a new page, then name the file, give it a title, and save it. While you can give the home page any title you wish, try to use something that helps visitors immediately understand your site's purpose. If you have not already done so, launch Dreamweaver, and the site you created in Chapter 1 will open by default. (See extra bits on page 22.)

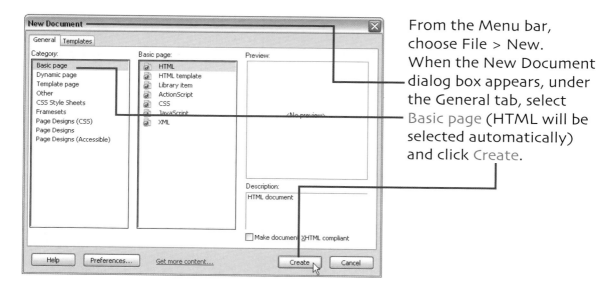

From the Menu bar, choose File > New. When the New Document dialog box appears, under the General tab, select Basic page (HTML will be selected automatically) and click Create.

create a basic home page

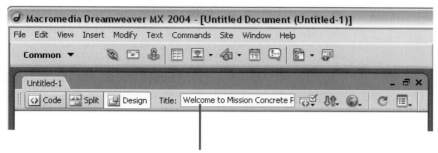

When a new untitled page appears in Dreamweaver's main window, click inside the Title text window, and type in your own title for the page. (Our sample site uses Welcome to Mission Concrete Products.) Visitors to your site will see the title at the top of their browser window, where it acts as a label for your site. It's not the same as the page's file name.

From the Menu bar, choose File > Save and in the Save As dialog box that opens, navigate to the site folder you created in Chapter 1. This will be your home page, so name it index and click Save. (Dreamweaver will automatically add the appropriate .htm or .html suffix.) The page will be saved and appear as part of your site in Dreamweaver's Files tab.

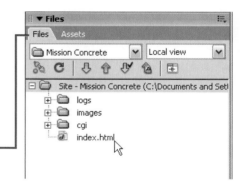

add text

Adding text to your Web page in Dreamweaver is not that different from using a word processing program. However, Macintosh computers will display Web page text at about three-fourths the size of the text that appears on a Windows machine. (See extra bits on page 22.)

Click anywhere in your still-blank home page and type the first line of text. In our example, the company name, Mission Concrete Products, is the first thing we want the viewer to see.

Select the text you just typed, and open the Property inspector (from the Menu bar, choose Window > Properties) if it's not already visible.

Click the inspector's Format drop-down menu and choose Paragraph. Click the Font drop-down menu and choose Vendana, Arial, Helvetica, san-serif. The six font groups listed are found on nearly every computer, ensuring that your Web visitors will see a font similar to what you are using.

Click the Align Center icon within the group of four alignment icons to center the line on the page.

create a basic home page

Press [Enter] (Windows) or [Return] (Mac) to start a new paragraph, and just as you would with a word processing program, type your text where we've entered Concrete Landscape Products.

Select the text you just typed and in the Property inspector, click the Align Center icon again. Then click the Text Color box and in the drop-down Color Picker choose a basic red, labeled #CC0000 in the hexadecimal system used on the Web.

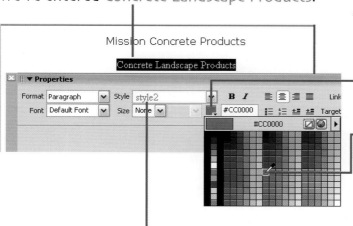

As soon as you apply the color change, the label in the Style box changes from style1 in black to style2 in red.

Press [Enter] (Windows) or [Return] (Mac) to start a new paragraph and enter your next bit of text. Our example lists the first category of products: Stepping stones / Pavers / Edgers. Dreamweaver automatically applies style2 to the text since that's what you last used. But you want this line formatted like the page's first line, so click the style drop-down menu and choose style1. You don't need to select the text; the entire line will switch to style1.

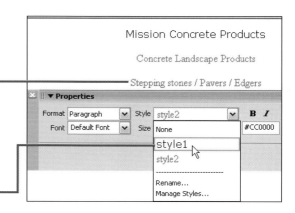

create a basic home page

add text (cont.)

Continue to add lines and style text until you have all your
information in place. Here we've added five more paragraphs
of text, all using the centered black text of style1.

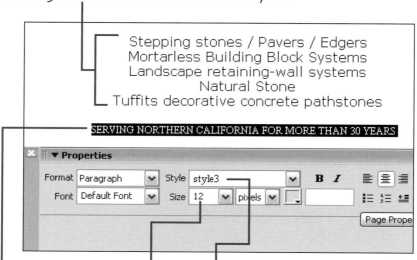

Press [Enter] (Windows) or
[Return] (Mac) to create one
last paragraph for a slogan,
catchphrase, motto, or
marketing message—some-
thing that quickly tells
visitors what your site's all
about and entices them to
linger. We've used SERVING
NORTHERN CALIFORNIA
FOR MORE THAN 30 YEARS
in all capital letters, selected
the entire line, and chosen
12 in the Size drop-down
menu.

That will make the text about 12 pixels
high—just slightly smaller than the
default 14 pixels that's applied when
you set the Size drop-down menu to
None. Notice that Dreamweaver saves
this change as a new style, in this case
style3 in the Style box.

Press [Enter] (Windows) or [Return] (Mac) to start a new paragraph for your site's contact information. Type Contact Us and then, because we want to present the rest of this information as a single item, press [Shift] [←Enter] (Windows) or [Shift] [Return] (Mac) to create a simple line break. (Paragraph returns would leave too much space between each line.)

Type the site's e-mail address, and add more line breaks to place the street address and phone number on separate lines of their own.

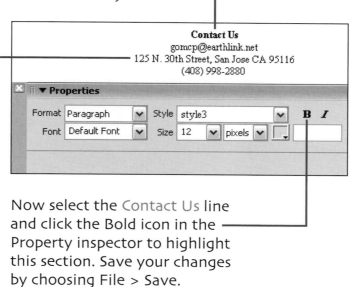

Contact Us
gomcp@earthlink.net
125 N. 30th Street, San Jose CA 95116
(408) 998-2880

Now select the Contact Us line and click the Bold icon in the Property inspector to highlight this section. Save your changes by choosing File > Save.

create a basic home page

create headings

Just like newspaper and magazine headlines, headings on a Web page are larger and more noticeable than regular text. They range from size 1 (the largest) to size 6 (the smallest). Use larger sizes for more important items and smaller sizes for less important items. (See extra bits on page 22.)

Select the first line of text in your home page (Mission Concrete Product in our sample project). In the Property inspector, select Heading 1 in the Format drop-down menu. The top line on the page will change from regular text to the larger, bolder Heading 1 style.

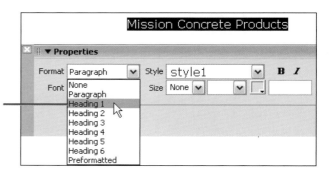

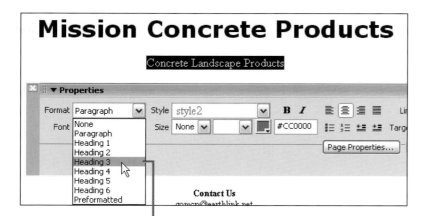

Select the second line (Concrete Landscape Products) and in the Property inspector, select Heading 3 in the Format drop-down menu. While the text will retain the red color last used for style2, its size and boldness change to reflect addition of the Heading 3 styling.

Click and drag your cursor to select the next five lines, which in our example lists various Mission Concrete products. In the Property inspector, select Heading 5 in the Format drop-down menu. All the lines change size, making it clearer that they are the items being referred to by the previous Concrete Landscape Products heading. To make that distinction even clearer, the next section shows how to format the products as a list. First, however, save your changes by choosing File > Save.

create lists

Organizing information into lists, whether numbered or simply marked with bullets, makes it easy to group lots of items in a way that anyone can instantly recognize. Ordered lists are great when you need to highlight a specific sequence of steps or materials, but here we want to highlight the items without numbering them.

Return to your home page and select lines 3–7 on the home page. If it's not already vis - ible, open the Property inspector (Window > Properties) and click the Ordered List icon, just above the Page Properties button.

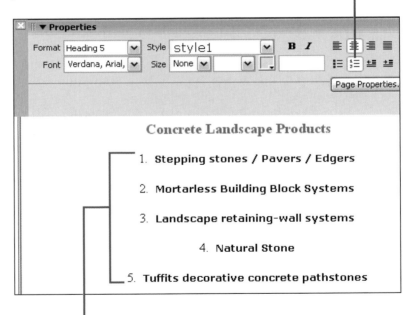

The selected lines will be numbered in sequence from 1 to 5 below the larger Concrete Landscape Products heading.

Reselect the five lines
if they are no longer
selected and click the
Unordered List icon.

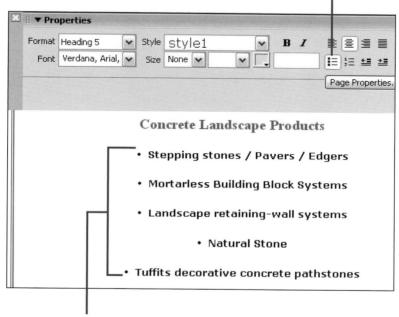

The selected lines now will have small bullets instead, which in our example more
clearly indicates that these are examples
of Concrete Landscape Products. Save your
changes by choosing File > Save.

change the background

You often see Web pages that use background images behind the text. Many of these pages use what's called a tiled image, where a small image is repeated across the page. Others use a single large image. In either case, unless the image is a very simple one, it can make it hard to read the page's text. Instead of adding an image, you can simply change the page's background from the default white to a color that makes your home page pop—without giving your visitors a headache.

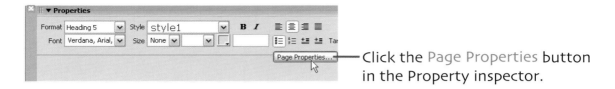

Click the Page Properties button in the Property inspector.

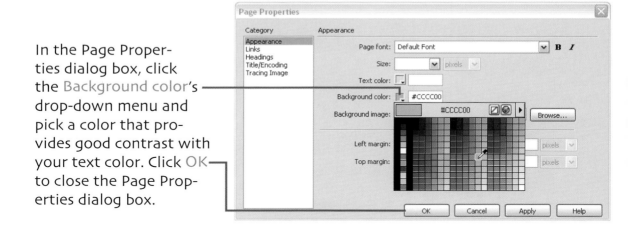

In the Page Properties dialog box, click the Background color's drop-down menu and pick a color that provides good contrast with your text color. Click OK to close the Page Properties dialog box.

Mission Concrete Products

Concrete Landscape Products

- Stepping stones / Pavers / Edgers

- Mortarless Building Block Systems

- Landscape retaining-wall systems

- Natural Stone

- Tuffits decorative concrete pathstones

SERVING NORTHERN CALIFORNIA FOR MORE THAN 30 YEARS

Dreamweaver applies your changes to your home page. Save your changes by choosing from the Menu bar File > Save. In the next chapter, you'll learn how to add graphics to your pages to catch a visitor's attention—without interfering with the text's readability.

extra bits

create your home page p. 10

- The page's file name and title serve different purposes. The file name is used behind the scenes to help you and Dreamweaver keep track of how your files are organized. For example, home pages should always be named index, which helps Web servers know that this page is the "front door" to your site. The page title is what the viewer's Web browser displays when your page is onscreen.

- The Basic Page column offers lots of choices, including templates and library items. Both are explained in later chapters (see pages 76 and 82). Working with non-HTML pages, such as those using CSS and XML, is covered in the Dreamweaver MX 2004: Visual QuickStart Guide.

- If your options are set so the Start Page appears when Dreamweaver launches, you can create a new page by clicking HTML in the Create New column.

add text p. 12

- If you are building your Web site on a Windows PC, be kind to Mac-based visitors by not using the smallest text sizes. If you're creating pages with a Mac, remember that text columns should have enough space at the bottom to handle the text running about 25 percent longer when viewed on a Windows machine.

- While you can choose Edit Font List to pick a particular font installed on your own computer, there's no guarantee visitors will have the font, so stick to the six most common font groups.

- Dreamweaver automatically defines and saves your different type settings as separate styles, based on a system called Cascading Style Sheets (CSS). The information includes such things as the text's format, font, size, alignment, and color. Dreamweaver arbitrarily names your first text setting style 1. When you create or change that type setting—as you did by adding red to the second line of text—Dreamweaver saves the new style as style 2. While entire books are devoted to CSS, you don't need to know much more than such style sheets make it easy to reuse text styles without starting from scratch.

create headings p. 16

- To keep your pages uncluttered, limit yourself to no more than two or three heading sizes on the same page.

create a basic home page

3. add images

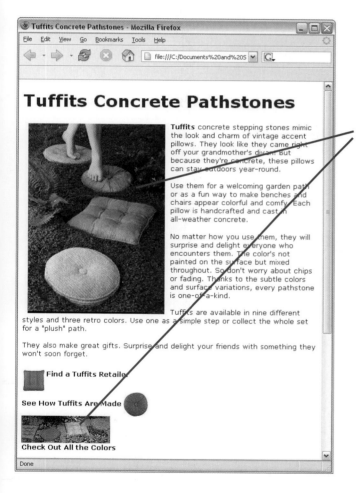

While text and headlines lend structure and meaning to Web pages, it's images that give them real impact.

Dreamweaver can handle basic image editing; for more demanding tasks use a dedicated graphics program. If you don't already have a graphics program, take a look in the graphics section of www.versiontracker.com where you can compare prices, features, and user comments.

image tools

As with text-related tasks, the Property inspector acts as your main tool for most image work.

Displayed near the image thumbnail is the file size (53K in our example) and its W (width) and H (height) in pixels.

Src tells you where the image is stored, while Link tells you what file (if any) the image is linked to if clicked.

Alt lets you create a label to be read aloud by browsers created for visually handicapped visitors. Use Alt to describe an image for visitors who have turned off image downloading for speedier surfing.

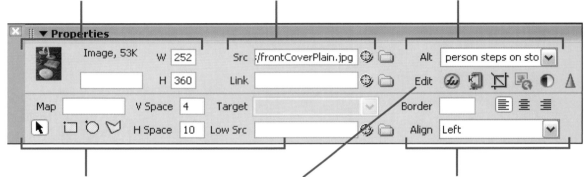

The items from Map to Target are used to create image maps, as explained on pages 68–70.

Three of the Edit buttons only work if you have installed Macromedia Fireworks. Without Fireworks, you're limited to using the Crop, Contrast/Brightness, and Sharpen buttons (see pages 27, 29, and 30).

Use Border to set the border width around the image. The three buttons to the right control whether your image is set at the left, center, or right of the page. Use the Align drop-down menu to control how text wraps around the image (see pages 32–34).

add image

After preparing images in an external program, you're ready to add them to your Web pages. (See extra bits on page 35.)

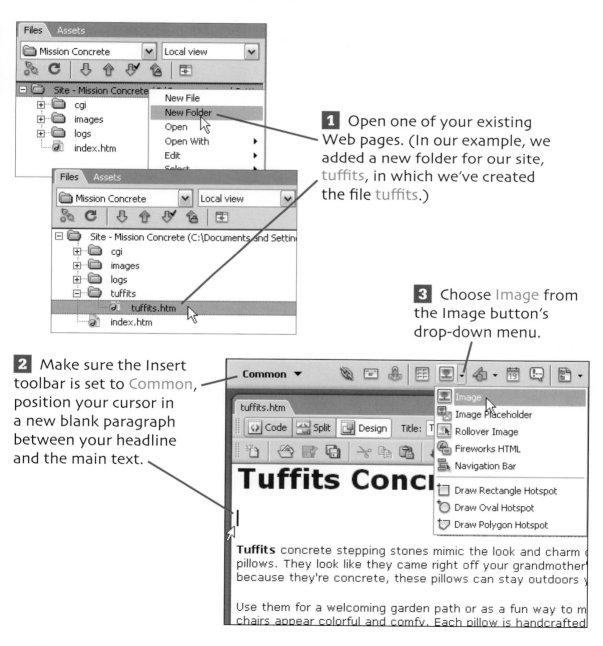

1 Open one of your existing Web pages. (In our example, we added a new folder for our site, tuffits, in which we've created the file tuffits.)

3 Choose Image from the Image button's drop-down menu.

2 Make sure the Insert toolbar is set to Common, position your cursor in a new blank paragraph between your headline and the main text.

add image (cont.)

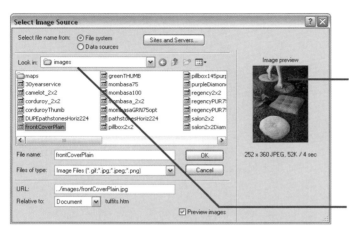

4 When the Select Image Source dialog box appears, navigate to the image you want to use (using the preview area to help you choose), and click OK.

5 If the image isn't already a part of your Web site, Dreamweaver will ask if you want to save it in the site's root folder. Choose Yes, navigate to your site's images, and save the image there. The selected image will appear between the headline and the main text.

6 Once inserted on the page, the image remains selected, so click the align center button in the Property inspector to center the image on the page.

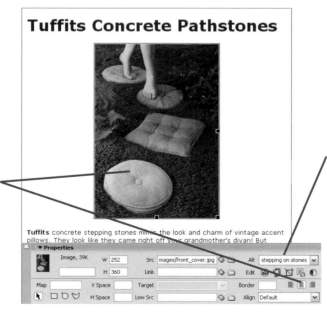

7 Type a brief description of the image in the Alt text box. Save the page before continuing.

crop image

You don't need a separate graphics program for cropping images—just don't use your original image. Cropping permanently alters your image, so if you make a mistake, immediately choose Undo Crop in the Edit menu. (See extra bits on page 35.)

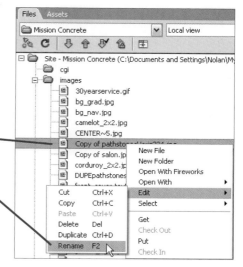

Select the original image in your site's Files panel and duplicate it ([Ctrl] in Windows, [Cmd] on the Mac). Dreamweaver automatically adds Copy of to beginning of the duplicate's file name.

If you want to name it something else, right-click (Windows) or [Ctrl]-click (Mac) it and choose Rename from the Edit drop-down menu. Once the name is highlighted, type in a new name and press [Enter] (Windows) or [Return] (Mac).

Insert the image on the page and select it by clicking on it. Make sure the Property inspector is visible and click the Crop button in the Property inspector. A selection area, marked by a dashed line and darker surrounding area, will appear in the middle of the image.

crop image (cont.)

Click and drag any of the black handles along the selection's edge to set your crop lines or click-and-drag in the middle to reposition the entire crop.

Double-click inside the selection and the image will be trimmed.

add images

adjust brightness

A single button in the Property inspector lets you adjust an image's brightness or contrast. Sometimes minor adjustments of either can really help a so-so image. You do not need to make a duplicate of the image. (See extra bits on page 35.)

Click to select the image on your page that you want to adjust.

Now click the Brightness and Contrast button in the Property inspector.

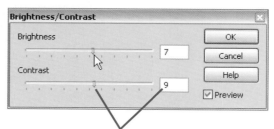

To change the brightness or contrast drag the sliders or enter new values in the adjacent text windows. (Increase the effects by sliding to the right or entering a larger number.) Click OK to apply your adjustments.

reduce image

If you have an image without lots of details, which would disappear if shrunk, you can use it to create a tiny thumbnail to add some graphic variety to a page. Detail lost from reducing and resampling cannot be recovered, so use a duplicate of your original image. (See extra bits on page 35.)

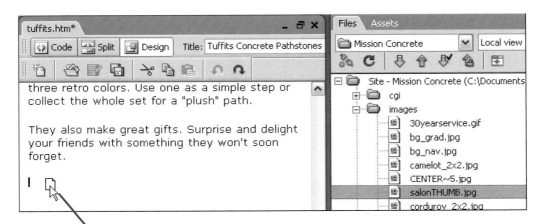

1 Make a duplicate of your original image, and drag the renamed image—salonTHUMB.jpg in our example—onto the page. The image will appear on the page with small black handles at its corners.

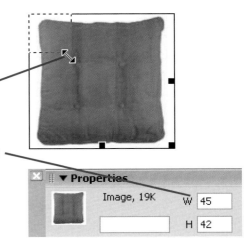

2 Press (Shift) while dragging a corner handle to reduce the image yet maintain its proportions.

Watch the pixel dimensions change in the W and H text windows in the Property inspector to gauge how much to reduce the image.

3 Release the cursor and the image will appear with the new dimensions in bold—even though the actual size of the file remains the same.

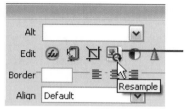

4 Click the Property inspector's Resample button to reduce the actual file size, indicated afterward by a smaller K size in the Property inspector.

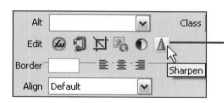

5 Greatly reduced images often lose some crispness, so click the Sharpen button.

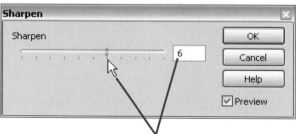

6 Use the slider or text window in the Sharpen dialog box to adjust the amount. (Drag slider to the right or enter a higher number in the text window to increase the sharpening.) Click OK when you're satisfied. Save the page before continuing.

wrap text with images

Wrapping blocks of text around your images, instead of putting each image in its own paragraph, creates a tighter, more professional page layout. (See extra bits on page 35.)

1 Click at the beginning of the text paragraph and press (←Backspace) (Windows) or (Delete) (Mac) once to remove the paragraph break separating the image from the text below it.

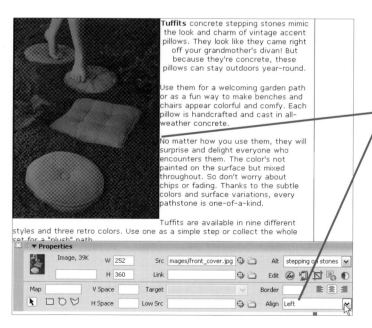

2 Select the image and use the Align drop-down menu to choose Left. The image will be aligned on the left side of the page with the text wrapping along its right side.

add images

3 To add a little more space between the image and the surrounding text, make sure the image is selected. Now use the H Space text box to specify how many pixels of space you want between the image and text. In our example, we set the H at 10 , which adds a moderate amount of space.

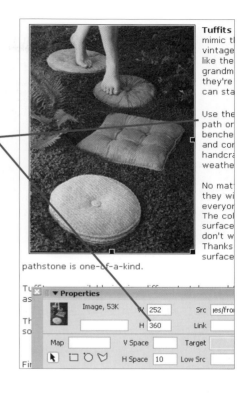

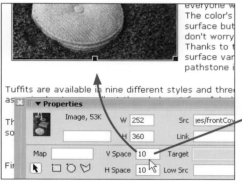

4 Use the V Space text box to set how many pixels are added above and below the image, which affects how closely the text wraps under the image. Save the page before continuing.

align text with image

The same Align drop-down menu used to wrap blocks of text around images also can be used to precisely position an image next to a single line of text. It's especially useful for pairing button-sized images with text labels.

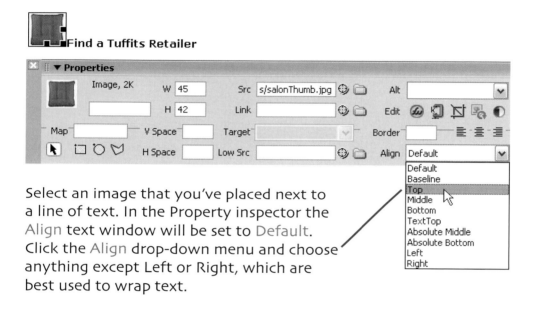

Select an image that you've placed next to a line of text. In the Property inspector the Align text window will be set to Default. Click the Align drop-down menu and choose anything except Left or Right, which are best used to wrap text.

Release your cursor and the image will realign itself with the adjacent text.

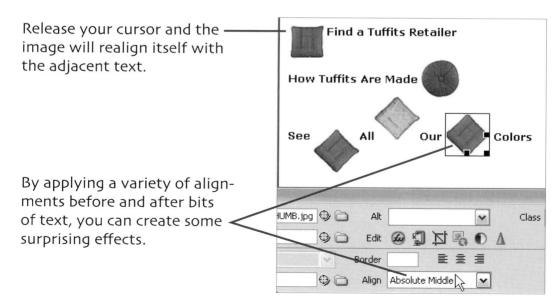

By applying a variety of alignments before and after bits of text, you can create some surprising effects.

add images

extra bits

image tools p. 24

- The blank text window right of the thumbnail is for scripts.

add image p. 25

- Keep your site's top-level folder uncluttered by creating new sub-folders when you have more than three or four related pages. Open the Files panel and right-click (Windows) or Ctrl-click (Mac) to reveal the New Folder choice.

- The root folder contains all your Web site's files. (In our example, it's Mission Concrete.) Save photos/graphics to the auto-generated subfolder, images, to easily find them.

- Listed below the image preview are its dimensions, file size, and estimated download time.

- Always add Alt text for your images. For dialup Web visitors, the alt text appears quickly, enabling them to skip the page if they don't want to wait for the full image. Alt text also is used by special audio Web browsers for visually impaired visitors. If the image is something like a horizontal rule, choose <empty> from the drop-down menu.

crop image p. 27

- Dreamweaver's built-in image editing only works for JPEG and GIF images, the two formats used for most photos and graphics.

adjust brightness p. 29

- The sliders can be hard to control, so type numbers in the text windows for fine adjustments.

reduce image p. 30

- You could use resampling to enlarge an image, but don't. The quality will suffer noticeably. Instead, use your regular image-editing program with the (presumably) larger original.

- When you click the Resample button, a dialog box warns you that the change is permanent. Since we're using a duplicate, click OK.

wrap text with images p. 32

- To put the image on the right side with the text down the left, choose Right in the Property inspector's Align drop-down menu.

- The Property inspector's H Space and V Space values are added to both sides of the image (right and left, top and bottom).

4. add tables

You are not limited to the simple approach used to build your home page in Chapter 2. By using tables to lay out a page, you can create pages more quickly and consistently. Tables also allow you to mix text, data, images, and headers, yet present it all in an easy to organize manner.

California Retailers for Tuffits			
Retailer	**Address**	**City**	**Zip**
Big B Lumber	6600 Brentwood Blvd..	Brentwood	94513
Norman's Brentwood Nursery	Route 3 Box 526	Brentwood	94513
Masonry Systems	3115 Railroad Ave..	Ceres	95307
L.H.Voss	2445 Vista Del Monte.	Concord	94520
Yamagami's Nursery	1361 South DeAnza Blvd.	Cupertino	95014
Dinuba Garden Center	388 S.Alta	Dinuba	93618
Agorra Bldg Supply	5965 Dougherty Road	Dublin	94568
Christy Vault Co.	44100 Christy St.	Fremont	94538
Regan Nursery.Inc.	4268 Decoto Rd.	Fremont	94555
Fresno Ag Hardware	4550 Blackstone Ave.	Fresno	93726

add a table

Tables can be a big help in creating simple layouts for your pages. (See extra bits on page 53.)

1 As you did in the previous chapter, create a new basic Web page (⎣Ctrl⎦⎣N⎦ in Windows, ⎣Cmd⎦⎣N⎦ on the Mac) and give it a title by typing inside the Title text window.———

2 Save it before continuing (⎣Ctrl⎦⎣S⎦ in Windows, ⎣Cmd⎦⎣S⎦ on the Mac). (In our example, we titled the new page Where to Buy Tuffits and saved the file as where2buy.)

Take a moment to set several Dreamweaver options that will make using tables easier.

3 Set the Insert toolbar to Layout.

4 And click the Standard button near the center of the toolbar...

...which will display buttons for inserting tables and columns.

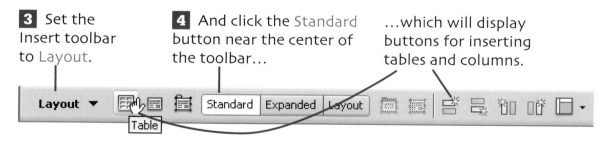

5 To make it easier to align your tables and cells, turn on the ruler (View > Rulers > Show), the grid (View > Grid > Show Grid), and set the grid so your drawn objects snap to it (View > Grid > Snap To Grid).

6 Click inside your page, then click the Insert Table button in the Layout toolbar. When the Table dialog box appears, use the text boxes to set the Table size and whether you want a Header, which lets you create labels for your rows or columns. In our example, we've set Rows to 1, Columns to 3, Table width to 500 pixels, Border thickness to 1 pixel, and the Header to None. Click OK to insert the new table.

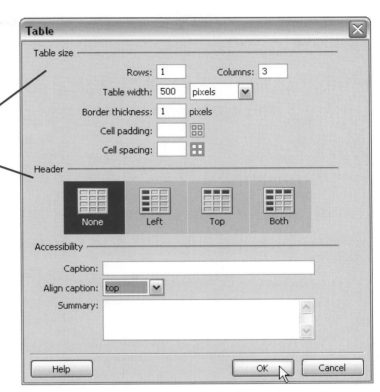

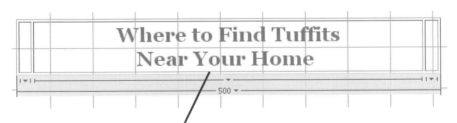

7 When the new table appears, click inside the middle cell to type a headline for the page. (Our example includes a line break right after Tuffits.) Based on what you learned in Chapter 2, use the Property inspector to format the cell's text.

add tables

add image to table

Tables are great for organizing large amounts of text and data, but adding a picture or two will make them more appealing. (See extra bits on page 53.)

1 Click in the first cell of the table you just created and from the Menu bar choose Insert > Image.

2 In the Select Image Source dialog box, open your site's Images folder.

3 Choose an image, and click OK. (In our example, we chose an image of one of the Tuffits pillows.) Repeat steps 1–3 to insert another image in the far-right cell.

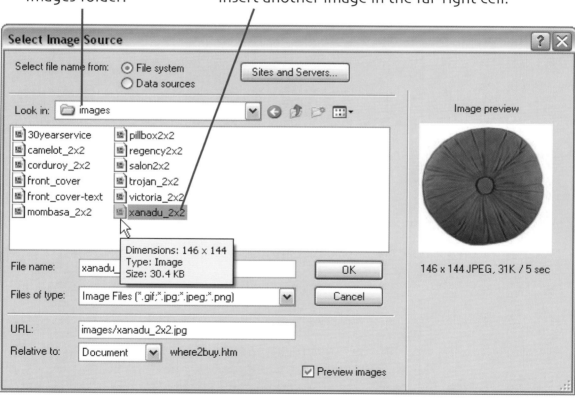

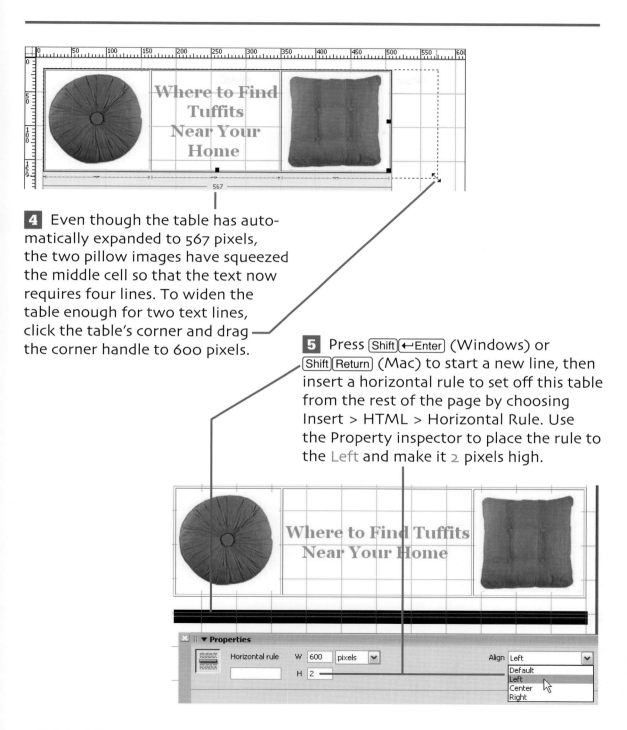

4 Even though the table has automatically expanded to 567 pixels, the two pillow images have squeezed the middle cell so that the text now requires four lines. To widen the table enough for two text lines, click the table's corner and drag the corner handle to 600 pixels.

5 Press Shift ←Enter (Windows) or Shift Return (Mac) to start a new line, then insert a horizontal rule to set off this table from the rest of the page by choosing Insert > HTML > Horizontal Rule. Use the Property inspector to place the rule to the Left and make it 2 pixels high.

add tables

add labels

Dreamweaver automatically formats row and column labels as centered and bold. That makes the labels, also known as table headers, easy to scan for anyone viewing the table. (See extra bits on page 53.)

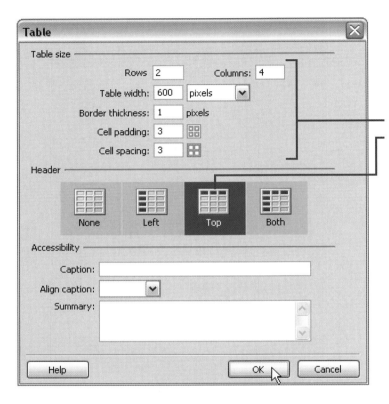

Press Enter (Windows) or Return (Mac) to start a new line below the first table, then insert a new table and use the Table dialog box to set the Table size, and create a Header with labels across the Top.

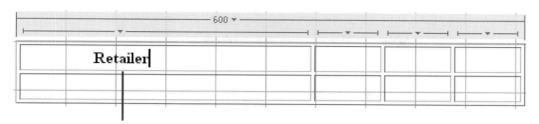

When the new table appears on the page, click in the header's far-left cell and type in a label for the first column. Add labels for the rest of the headers, pressing ⬚Tab⬚ to move from cell to cell. (In our example, we use Retailer, Address, City, and Zip, which match the tabular data we'll soon import.)

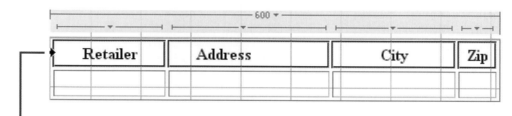

Select the header row by moving your cursor to the row's left edge until it becomes a bold arrow and the selected row is outlined in red. With the row selected, use the Property inspector to change the font and size and press ⬚Tab⬚ to apply the changes to all the text in the row.

save and apply style

By saving and renaming the CSS-based styles that Dreamweaver automatically generates as you change text settings, you can reapply those same settings later to other text selections. (See extra bits on page 53.)

In our table header example, the Font is set to Verdana, Arial, Helvetica, san-serif, the Size at 12 in Bold, with a light-gray Bg (background color) of #CCCCCC. By default, Dreamweaver automatically generated a temporary name of style12 for all these changes.

Since we want to apply this same style for other table headers, we'll give it an easy to recognize permanent name. Click the Style drop-down menu and choose Rename.

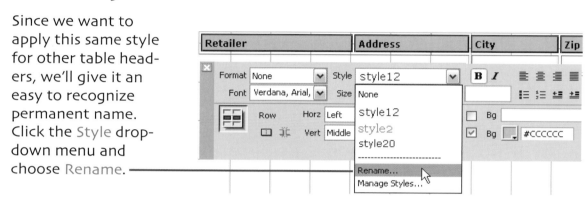

When the Rename Style dialog box appears, type a quick descriptive name in the New name text box (no spaces allowed) and click OK to save the new name. The new name will appear in the Property inspector's Style text box.

add tables

Now, let's apply the style to a new row inserted just above the header row. Select the header, and press Ctrl M in Windows or Cmd M on the Mac to insert the row.

In our example, the new row has four cells, just like the row below it. To merge them into a single cell, select the new row and press Ctrl Alt M in Windows or Cmd Option M on the Mac.

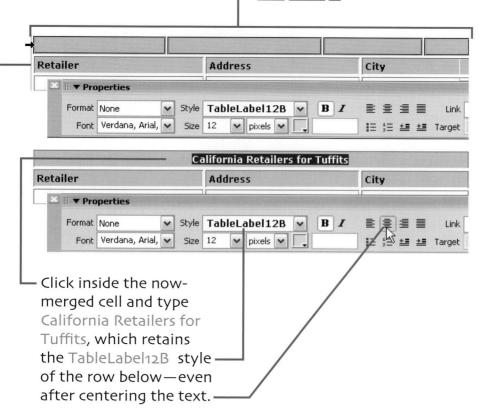

Click inside the now-merged cell and type California Retailers for Tuffits, which retains the TableLabel12B style of the row below—even after centering the text.

import tabular data

Nothing beats a table for clearly presenting spreadsheet data or tab-separated text imported from a word-processing document. (See extra bits on page 53.)

1 Press (Enter) (Windows) or (Return) (Mac) to start a new paragraph just below the table you've already created.

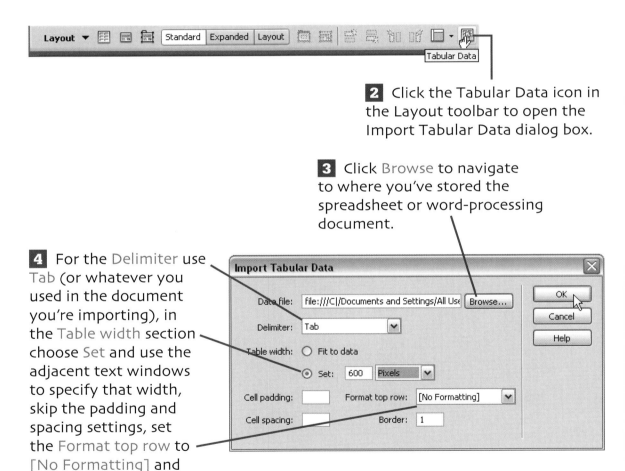

2 Click the Tabular Data icon in the Layout toolbar to open the Import Tabular Data dialog box.

3 Click Browse to navigate to where you've stored the spreadsheet or word-processing document.

4 For the Delimiter use Tab (or whatever you used in the document you're importing), in the Table width section choose Set and use the adjacent text windows to specify that width, skip the padding and spacing settings, set the Format top row to [No Formatting] and click OK.

add tables

California Retailers for Tuffits

Retailer	Address	City	Zip
Agorra Bldg Supply	5965 Dougherty Road	Dublin	94568
Clark's Home and Garden	23040 Clawiter Rd.	Hayward	94545
Christy Vault Co.	44100 Christy St.	Fremont	94538
Diamond K Supply	3671 Mt.Diablo Blvd.	Lafayette	94549
L.H.Voss	2445 Vista Del Monte.Concord	94520	
Morgan's Masonry	P.O. Box 127	San Ramon	94583

5 The data will appear on the Web page arranged in its own table. Save the page (Ctrl S in Windows, Cmd S on the Mac).

6 Click and drag your cursor until you select all the cells in the second table, then copy them (press Ctrl C in Windows, Cmd C on the Mac).

Agorra Bldg Supply	5965 Dougherty Road	Dublin
Clark's Home and Garden	23040 Clawiter Rd.	Hayward
Christy Vault Co.	44100 Christy St.	Fremont
Diamond K Supply	3671 Mt.Diablo Blvd.	Lafayette
L.H.Voss	2445 Vista Del Monte.Concord	94520
Morgan's Masonry	P.O. Box 127	San Ramo
Morgan Bros. Patio	14305 Washington Ave.	San Lean

mino Real	Los Altos	94022
Blvd.	Redwood City	94062
lyn Ave.	Mountain View	94041
t.	Mountain View	94041
re Blvd.	San Francisco	94124
Ave.	Sunnyvale	94086
lway	Vallejo	94591

7 Click in the first cell in the blank row of the top table and paste your selection there (press Ctrl V in Windows, Cmd V on the Mac). The copied cells will appear in the first table with their cell formatting intact. Having moved the second table's contents to the first table, select the second table and delete it.

California Retailers for Tuffits

Retailer	Address	City	Zip
Agorra Bldg Supply	5965 Dougherty Road	Dublin	94568
Clark's Home and Garden	23040 Clawiter Rd.	Hayward	94545
Christy Vault Co.	44100 Christy St.	Fremont	94538
Diamond K Supply	3671 Mt.Diablo Blvd.	Lafayette	94549
L.H.Voss	2445 Vista Del Monte.Concord	94520	
Morgan's Masonry	P.O. Box 127	San Ramon	94583
Morgan Bros. Patio	14305 Washington Ave.	San Leandro	94578
Orco Const. Supply	P.O. Box5058	Livermore	94550

add tables

edit table

Inevitably, our example table has a few errors. Several blank cells appear because the imported data mistakenly had an extra tab character between several retailers' names and addresses. Dreamweaver makes it easy to fix the problem, but let's first change the new table text formatting.

1 Click and drag your cursor to select all the text cells in the table and use the Property inspector to set the Font, Size, and cell alignment.

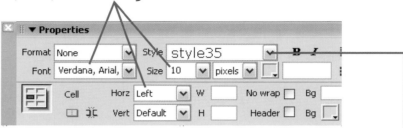

2 Press ⟨Tab⟩ to apply the formatting and to trigger Dreamweaver to generate a generic name for your new style. (In our example, Dreamweaver named it style35 .) Use the Style drop-down menu to rename it something easy to remember for reuse. (In our example, we will name it TableText10 since we want to reuse the 10-pixel style in future tables.)

3 You cannot directly delete a blank cell in a table because of the table's interlocking grid of rows and columns. But you can move data from several cells and delete the blank row created by the shift. (In our example, we select the cell with the street address for the first retailer.)

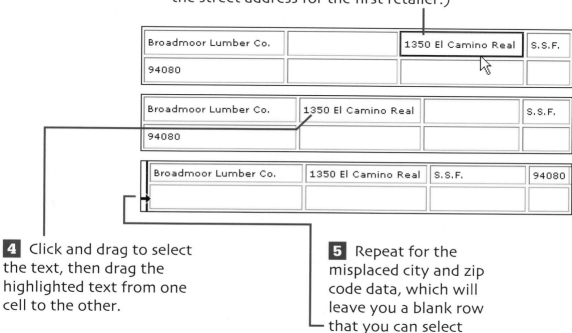

4 Click and drag to select the text, then drag the highlighted text from one cell to the other.

5 Repeat for the misplaced city and zip code data, which will leave you a blank row that you can select and delete.

format table colors

To make it easier for your Web visitors to read the information in long tables, we'll apply some color formatting. (See extra bits on page 53.)

Select the entire table and choose Commands > Format Table to open the Format Table dialog box, which includes more than a dozen preset table color combinations.

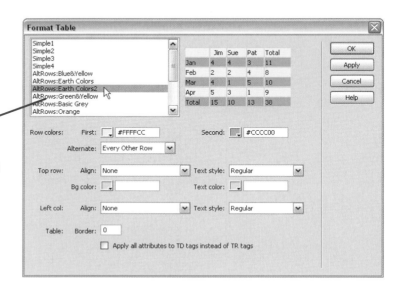

Use the various drop-down menus to pick your colors and how often the colors of the rows alternate.

In our example, we've changed the First and Second row colors to echo the page's pillow colors and set Alternate to Every Two Rows for a less busy look.

Click Apply to preview your choices and click OK to close the dialog box. Be sure to save the page when you're done.

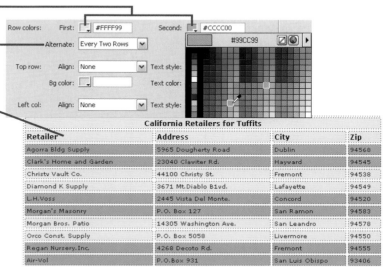

sort tables

Dreamweaver can automatically sort tabular data by column—a neat trick that lets you tinker with how the data is organized long after you've imported it into your table. There's just one catch: tables cannot be sorted if they include a cell that spans multiple columns. We've got just such a cell in our example, but we can do a quick cut and paste to work around this restriction. (See extra bits on page 53.)

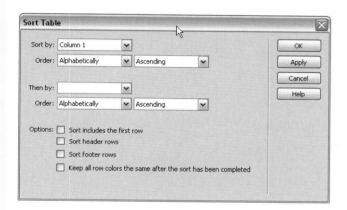

Select the column-spanning cell (in our example, it's California Retailers for Tuffits) and cut it from the page (Ctrl X in Windows, Cmd X on the Mac). Now select the table and choose Commands > Sort Table to open the Sort Table dialog box.

Use the Sort by drop-down menu to choose which column will control the sort, then use the Order drop-down menu to set whether the sort is done Alphabetically (or numerically) and whether it's Ascending (or descending) order. (In our example, we sort by Column 3 (City) because that will be the easiest way for site visitors to find a nearby store. We also set Then by to sort using Column 4 (Zip), which will help big-city residents. Click Apply to preview the sort and click OK to close the dialog box.

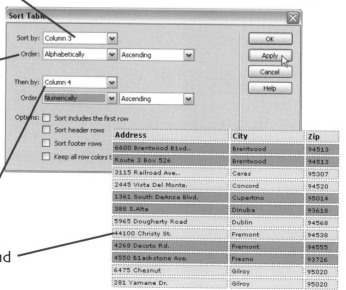

add tables

sort tables (cont.)

Once the sort's done, insert a row above the header row, merge those new cells into one and paste back in your original header. (In our example, it's California Retailers for Tuffits.) Be sure to save the page and you're done.

California Retailers for Tuffits			
Retailer	**Address**	**City**	**Zip**
Big B Lumber	6600 Brentwood Blvd..	Brentwood	94513
Norman's Brentwood Nursery	Route 3 Box 526	Brentwood	94513
Masonry Systems	3115 Railroad Ave..	Ceres	95307

add tables

extra bits

add a table p. 38

- Use the Table dialog box's Accessibility section to create an explanatory Caption that will be read aloud by special audio Web browsers for visually impaired visitors. If needed, add details in the Summary field.

add image to table p. 40

- If you're having trouble selecting a table, just click near the table and then press [Ctrl][A] in Windows or [Cmd][A] on the Mac.

add labels p. 42

- The Table dialog box Header options—None, Left, Top, and Both—let you skip adding labels, label only the rows, label only the columns, or label both rows and columns.

save and apply style p. 44

- To insert a new column, select a column and press [Ctrl][Shift][A] in Windows or [Cmd][Shift][A] on the Mac. The new column will appear left of the selected column.
- For more information on formatting text, see Chapter 2.

import tabular data p. 46

- Before importing, use your spreadsheet or word-processing program to save the data in comma- or tab-delimited form.
- Sometimes the Set drop-down menu in the Table Width section of the Import Tabular Data dialog box will switch to Percent—even if you previously set it to Pixels. So double-check before clicking OK.
- Our copy-and-paste example works because each table had the same number of columns. You cannot, for example, copy 6 columns and paste them into 4 columns.

format table colors p. 50

- By using [Ctrl]-click in Windows or [Cmd]-click on the Mac, you also can select non-adjacent columns or cells. Then you can format all the selections at once.

sort tables p. 51

- By default, the Options in the Sort Table dialog box are not checked, since you seldom want the header or footer rows sorted.

5. create links

The Web's magic comes largely from the hyperlink, which lets Web users jump from page to image to email to almost anywhere on the Internet. Links fall into two categories: internal links, which connect different items within your own Web site, and external links, which connect to items out on the larger Web. Before we begin linking some of the pages created in previous chapters, switch the Insert toolbar to Common, which includes link-related buttons.

Add link   Add anchor link

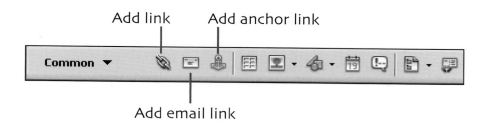

Add email link

link text internally

Dreamweaver makes creating links between pages on your Web site a point-and-click affair. (See extra bits on page 71.)

1 Open your home page and select text you want to link to another page on your Web site. (In our example, we are linking text on the Mission Concrete home page to the Tuffits products page.)

2 Make sure the Files panel and the Property inspector are both visible.

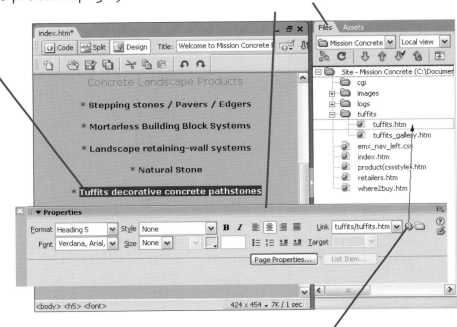

3 Click the compass-like Point to File icon and drag the line that appears to your to-be-linked file in the Files panel. Release your cursor and the file path for the other file will appear in the Link text window.

create links

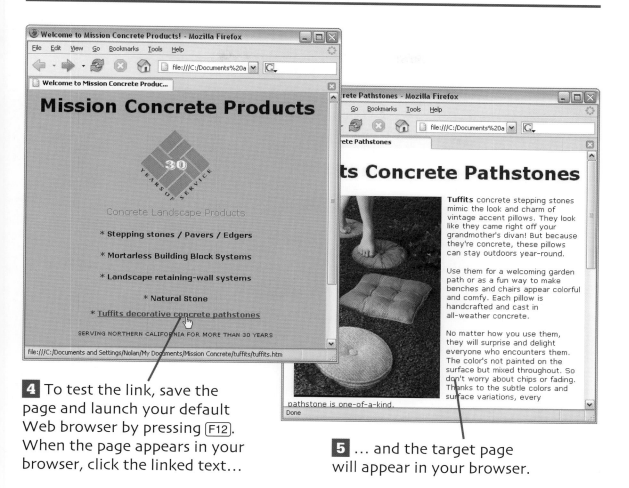

4 To test the link, save the page and launch your default Web browser by pressing F12. When the page appears in your browser, click the linked text...

5 ... and the target page will appear in your browser.

link text externally

Links to items not part of your own Web site are called external links. While we use text in this example, you can create external links using images as well. (See extra bits on page 71.)

1 Make sure the Files panel and Property inspector are visible, then select the text you want to link to a page out on the Web.

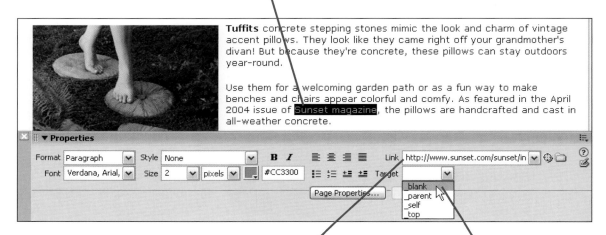

2 Type the full Web address for the outside page, including the http://, directly into the Link text window...

3 ...then select _blank from the Target drop-down menu. Save the page and test the link in your browser, where the outside link will open in a new window.

color page links

By default, unvisited Web links are blue and underlined while visited links are purple and underlined. Dreamweaver, however, makes it easy to change the color and style of all your links to match your Web site's overall look. (See extra bits on page 71.)

1 Open your home page, which already contains a link, and click the Page Properties button in the Property inspector.

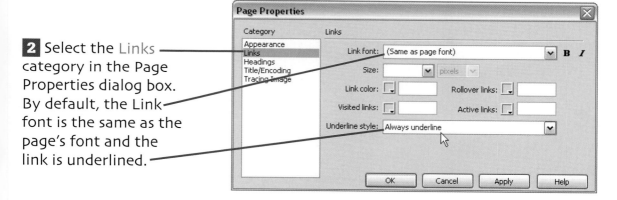

2 Select the Links category in the Page Properties dialog box. By default, the Link font is the same as the page's font and the link is underlined.

3 While you can change the font and size of the link text, in our example, we have changed only the colors used to indicate different link states: the Link color of the page's linked text; Visited links for after the link's been clicked; Rollover links for when the visitor's cursor hovers over the link without clicking it; and Active links for the moment when the link is clicked. Once you set the link colors and styles, click OK to apply the change and close the dialog box. Save the page before continuing.

color site links

Once you set the link colors and style of a single page, you can quickly apply them to other pages on your site—without affecting any other styles you've created for those pages.

1 Leave the home page open and select the CSS Styles tab in the Design panel.

2 Click to expand the <style> listing and you'll see the link colors you set. This internal style sheet applies only to this page.

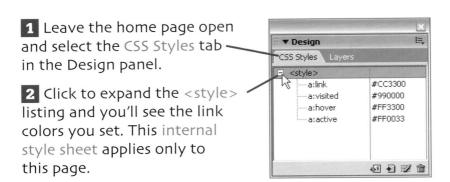

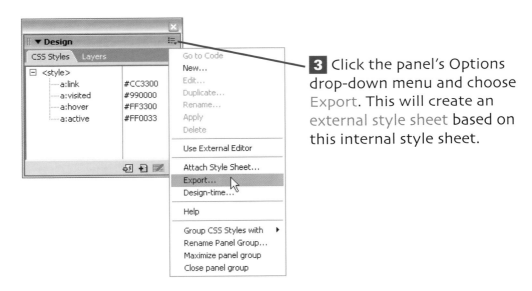

3 Click the panel's Options drop-down menu and choose Export. This will create an external style sheet based on this internal style sheet.

4 Navigate within the Export Styles As CSS File dialog box to your Web site's folder (in our example, Mission Concrete).

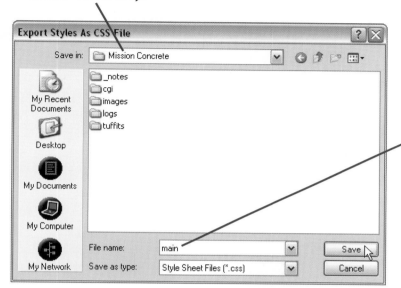

5 Name the file main and click Save. Dreamweaver will automatically append .css to the file and generate the external style sheet.

6 You need to replace the home page's internal style sheet with the new external one, so select any link-related styles listed in the Design panel's CSS Styles tab.

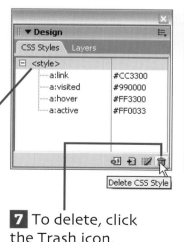

7 To delete, click the Trash icon.

8 The styles will be cleared from the CSS Styles tab.

create links

color site links (cont.)

9 Click the CSS Styles tab's Attach Style Sheet button.

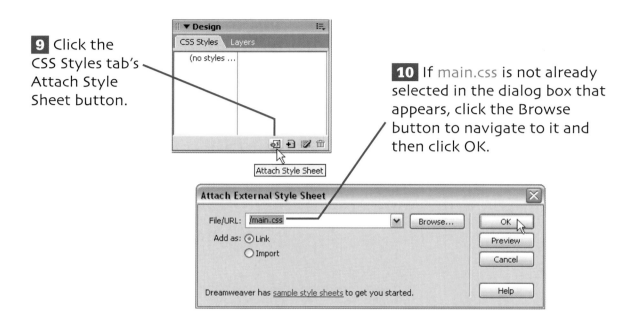

Attach Style Sheet

10 If main.css is not already selected in the dialog box that appears, click the Browse button to navigate to it and then click OK.

11 The main.css style sheet will immediately appear in the page's CSS Styles tab, indictating that it has been attached.

12 You then can attach the main.css style sheet to any other page on your site.

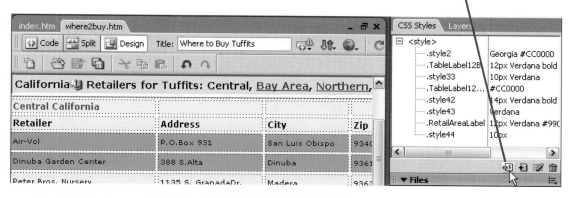

13 The main.css styles will be added to the page's existing styles and immediately change the color of the page's links.

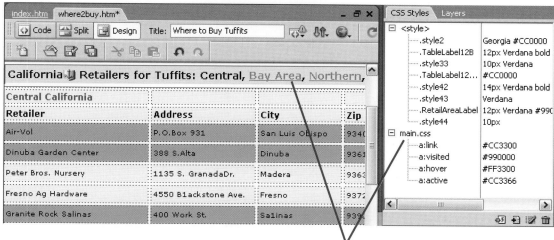

add email link

By embedding addresses in your email links, you make it easy for readers to send email to you and others listed on your Web site. (See extra bits on page 71.)

1 Select the text on your page that you want to link to email. (In our example, we've selected Contact us! on the Mission Concrete home page.)

2 Click the Email button on the Insert toolbar.

3 The selected text will be highlighted in the Email Link dialog box. Type the email address into the bottom text window and click OK.

4 The text selected on your page will become a link. Test it by saving the page, opening it in your Web browser and clicking the link. Your default email program will automatically create a new message addressed to the email address on the Web page.

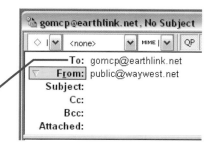

add anchor link

Anchor links enable Web visitors to jump to a specific spot within a long Web page, sparing readers from scrolling through it. You must first create an anchor to mark the particular spot in the target document. Then you create a link to that spot. (See extra bits on page 71.)

1 Open a Web page and click at the particular spot where you want to add an anchor link. (In our example, we're marking the start of our Northern California retailers in a list of suppliers.)

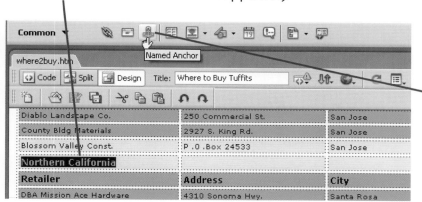

2 Click the Named Anchor button in the Insert toolbar.

3 Type a distinctive name in the Named Anchor dialog box and click OK.

An anchor icon will be added next to the selected text. Save the page, which will also save the anchor name.

add anchor link (cont.)

4 Now select the text you want linked to the anchor.

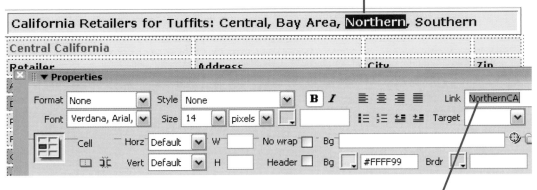

5 Type the anchor name exactly as you created it into the Property inspector's Link text window. (In our example, we're linking to the anchor we just created, NorthernCA.) Press [Enter] (Windows) or [Return] (Mac) to activate the link.

link image

Images are easy to spot on a page and easy to click, so don't limit yourself to creating just text links. Creating internal vs. external links with images works exactly as it does for text links. (See extra bits on page 71.)

With the Files panel and Property inspector both visible, open the page containing the image you want to link to something, and select it.

Use the Point to File icon to draw a line to the file you want to link the image to. (In our example, we are linking a button-sized image to our list of Tuffits retailers.)

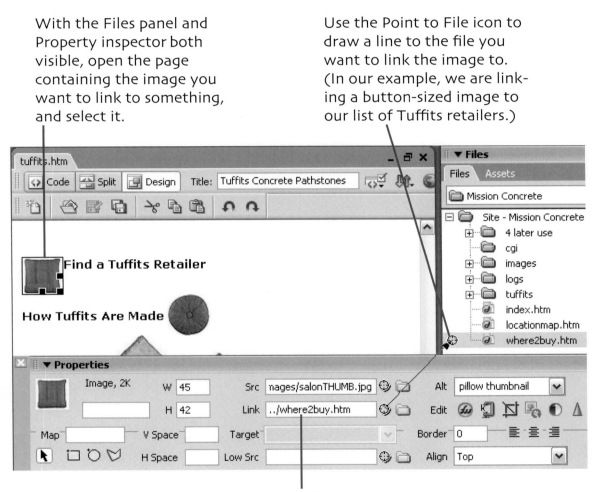

The file path for the other file will appear in the Link text window. Release your cursor to create the link.

create image map

Image maps take the basic idea behind an image link and give it extra power by making it possible to link separate "hot spots" within the image to multiple files. It saves space on the page and provides an elegant, easy-to-understand interface for your site. (See extra bits on page 72.)

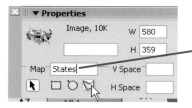

1 With the Property inspector visible, open the image for which you want to create an image map. Type a name for the image map in the Map text window.

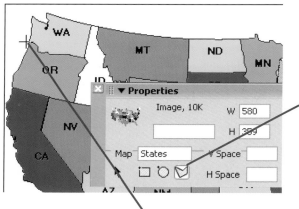

2 Based on the shape of the hot spot you'll be creating, click one of the three shape buttons. (In our example, we've chosen the freeform polygon to create an Oregon-shaped hot spot.)

3 Click in your image where you want to begin creating the hot spot, which will be marked by a cross-hair.

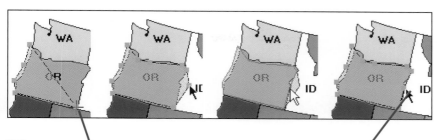

4 Build your hot spot one click at a time along the boundary of the underlying image.

5 If you need to adjust the hot spot's boundary, click any square-shaped handle and drag it to a new spot.

6 After building your hot spots, select one and use the Property inspector's Point to File icon to link it to a document. (In our example, we've linked to an anchor within the file.)

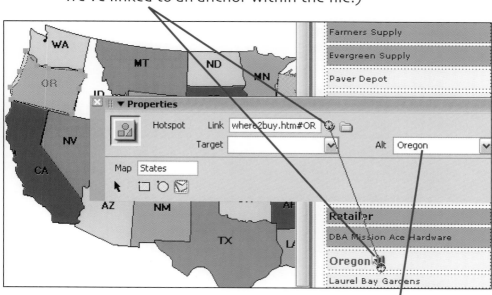

7 Be sure to add an Alt name for the hot spot to help you keep them straight. Repeat these steps for each hot spot you've created, giving each its own Alt name.

create links

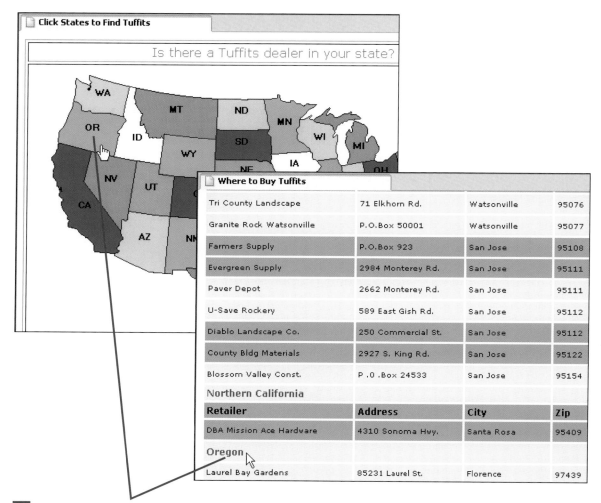

8 To test the link, save the page and launch your default Web browser by pressing F12. Click any of the image's hot spots and the linked page will appear in your browser.

extra bits

link text internally p. 56

- If the file to which you're linking is not already part of your Web site, click the Folder icon next to the Link drop-down menu and navigate to it. When Dreamweaver asks to import the file into the site, click Yes.

link text externally p. 58

- Reduce the chance of typing in the wrong Web address by copying the outside page's URL from your browser and pasting it directly into the Link text window.

- Selecting _blank from the Target drop-down menu will open a new window in the visitor's browser—ensuring that your site will remain visible as the visitor looks at the external Web page.

color page links p. 59

- Used since the birth of the Web, underlined blue and purple links are recognized by virtually all Web surfers. It's fine to change the color scheme but be prudent. Making unvisited links purple, for example, would be akin to making stop lights green.

- Our example uses shades of red for all four link states. The colors are different enough from each other to signal link-state changes

without creating a kaleidoscope of colors that might distract from the page's overall color scheme.

color site links p. 60

- In our example, we use the home page but you can replace the internal style sheet on any page on your site.

add email link p. 64

- With robot programs scouring the Web for email addresses, it's a sad fact that putting an email link on your Web site almost guarantees that your inbox will be flooded with spam. One workaround: enter your email as "myname AT earthlink DOT net" instead of as "myname@earthlink.net." For now, address-harvesting robots can't cope with this trick, while your human visitors will realize they need to replace the AT with @ and the DOT with a period.

extra bits

add anchor link p. 65

- The anchor can be placed any-where and doesn't need to be tied to a text selection.

- Dreamweaver inserts the anchor-shaped icon next to your anchor-link text just to help you spot it. It will not be visible on your Web site. To turn these icons off or on, choose View > Visual Aids > Invisible Elements.

create image map p. 68

- Image map names should not include any blank spaces or special characters.

- The hot spot need not exactly match the underlying shape. Just cover the portion your visitors will most likely click.

- If you can't arrange your document windows to point directly to an anchor, use Browse to reach the file. Then type #nameofanchor at the end of the file name selected in the Link text window.

- As with text and images, a hot spot can link to an internal or external file.

6. reuse items to save time

Think of the Assets tab as Dreamweaver's grand central timesaver. It automatically lists which images, color swatches, and external links you use on your site. If you want to use those items again, the Assets tab makes it easy to quickly find what you need. The Assets tab also includes two other major timesavers—library items and templates, both of which we'll use in our project.

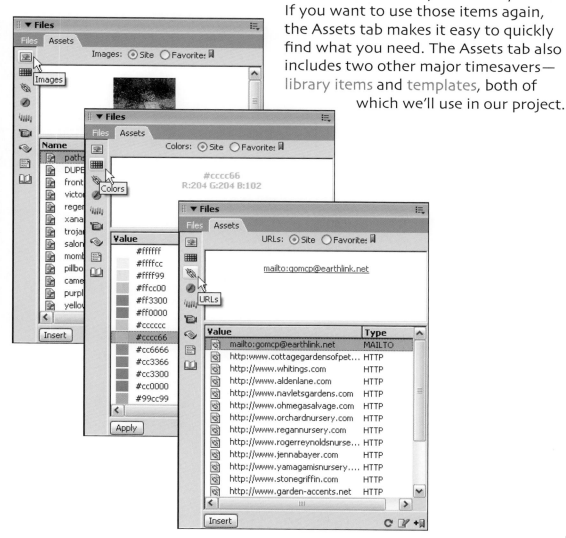

create a favorite

By creating favorites from the lists generated by the Assets tab, you always have your most-used items handy.

1 Press F11 to open the Assets tab and make sure the Site radio button is selected.

2 Select the category button you need in the left-hand column. (In our example, we've chosen the Images button because with so many images used, creating a shorter favorites list is essential.)

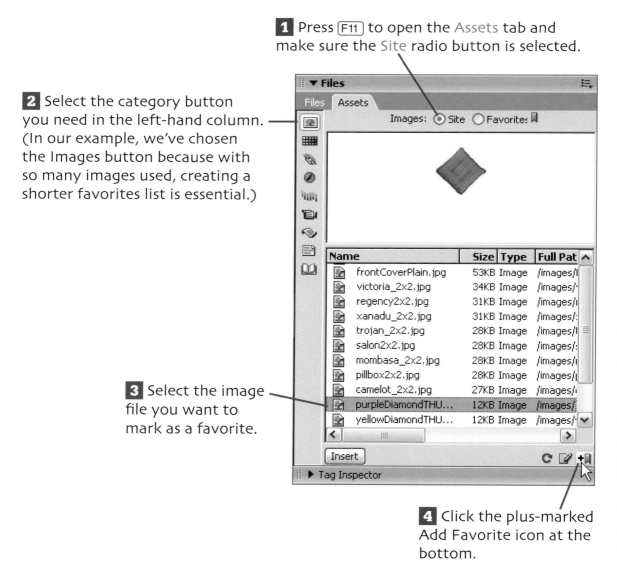

3 Select the image file you want to mark as a favorite.

4 Click the plus-marked Add Favorite icon at the bottom.

reuse items to save time

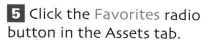

5 Click the Favorites radio button in the Assets tab.

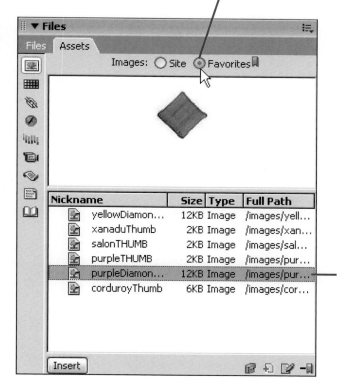

6 The image you marked as a favorite will appear in the list of favorite images.

create a library item

Make library items of anything you use repeatedly. It can be something simple like a 2 x 400-pixel rule. Or it can be as elaborate as an entire table containing images and links. Short or long, the real benefit of a library item comes when you need to make a change—change it once and all pages using it automatically update. (See extra bits on page 91.)

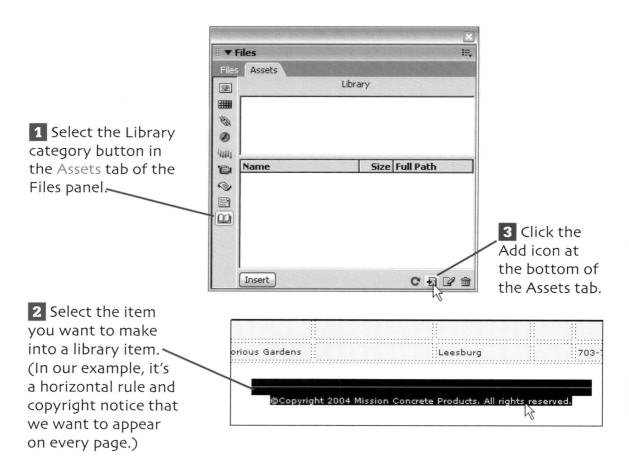

1 Select the Library category button in the Assets tab of the Files panel.

3 Click the Add icon at the bottom of the Assets tab.

2 Select the item you want to make into a library item. (In our example, it's a horizontal rule and copyright notice that we want to appear on every page.)

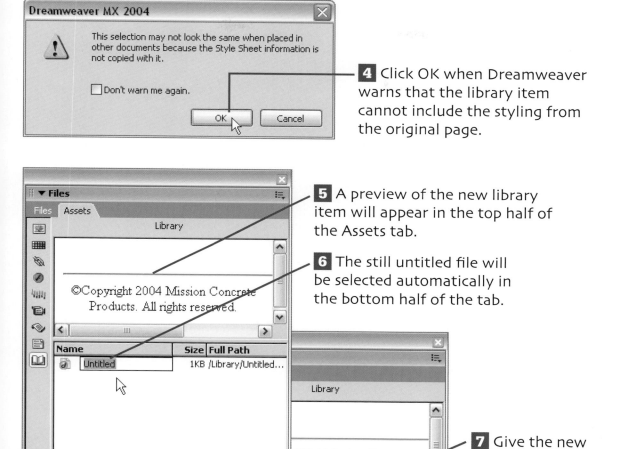

4 Click OK when Dreamweaver warns that the library item cannot include the styling from the original page.

5 A preview of the new library item will appear in the top half of the Assets tab.

6 The still untitled file will be selected automatically in the bottom half of the tab.

7 Give the new library item a distinctive name and press [Tab] to apply it.

edit library item

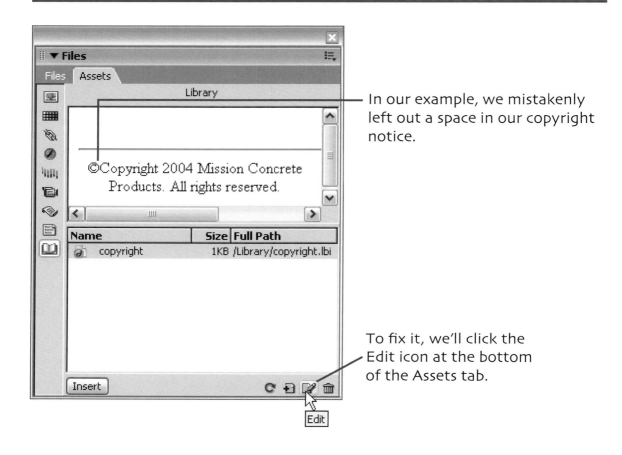

In our example, we mistakenly left out a space in our copyright notice.

To fix it, we'll click the Edit icon at the bottom of the Assets tab.

reuse items to save time

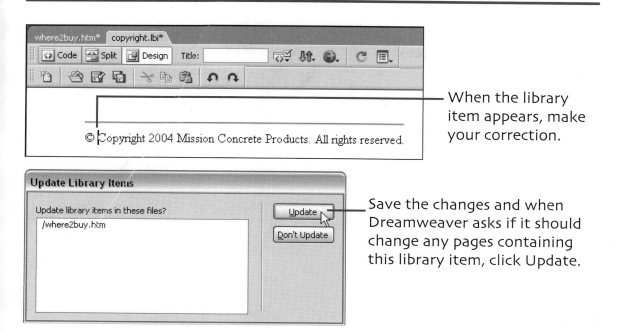

When the library item appears, make your correction.

Save the changes and when Dreamweaver asks if it should change any pages containing this library item, click Update.

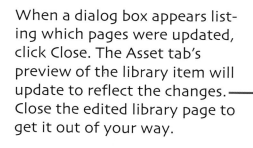

When a dialog box appears listing which pages were updated, click Close. The Asset tab's preview of the library item will update to reflect the changes. Close the edited library page to get it out of your way.

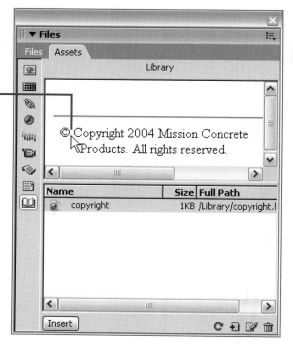

reuse items to save time

insert library item

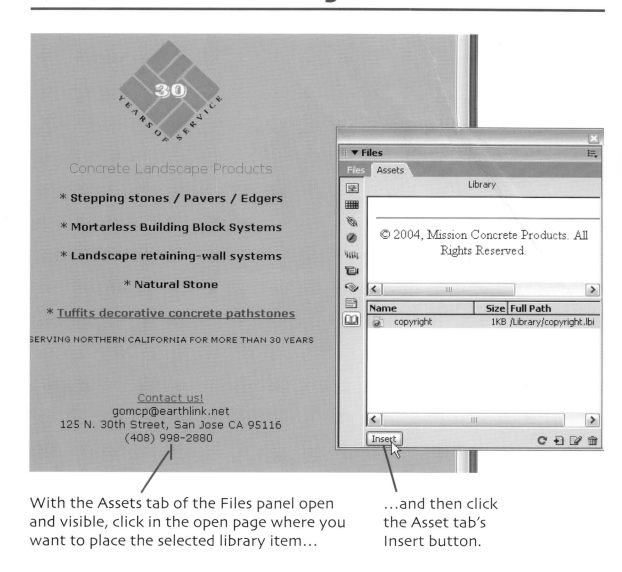

With the Assets tab of the Files panel open and visible, click in the open page where you want to place the selected library item...

...and then click the Asset tab's Insert button.

reuse items to save time

The item will appear in the page with a light yellow background indicating that it's a library item.

When you save the page and view it within a Web browser, however, this yellow marker will not be visible.

reuse items to save time

create a template

Templates are great timesavers for building pages with an identical layout but with variable content. In our example, we've created a Tuffits product template, which can then be used to generate pages for each product. Templates require that you mark which parts can be changed in the individual pages created from it. (See extra bits on page 91.)

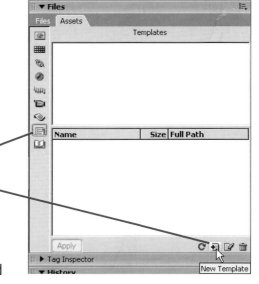

1 Select the Templates category button in the Assets tab and click the New Template button.

2 The still untitled file will be selected automatically in the bottom half of the tab. Give the new template item a distinctive name and press Tab to apply it. (In our example, we've named it product since we'll be using it as the template for all Tuffits products.)

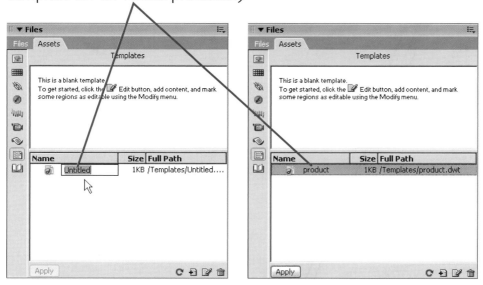

reuse items to save time

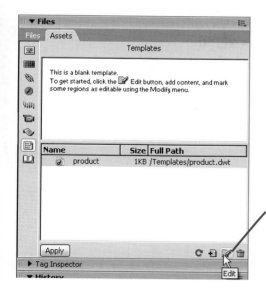

3 With the template still selected, click the Edit button at the bottom of the Assets tab.

4 The new—and entirely blank—template page will open.

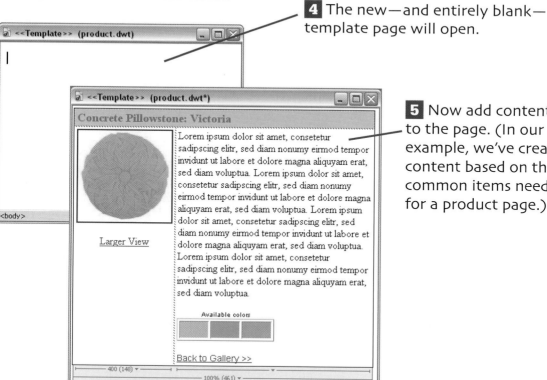

5 Now add content to the page. (In our example, we've created content based on the common items needed for a product page.)

reuse items to save time

create a template (cont.)

6 Once you finish adding your content, you need to mark which items in the template can be changed, or edited. Make sure the Insert toolbar is set to Common, then select a page item (in our example, the main text block).

7 Click the Templates button in the toolbar and choose Editable Region in the drop-down menu.

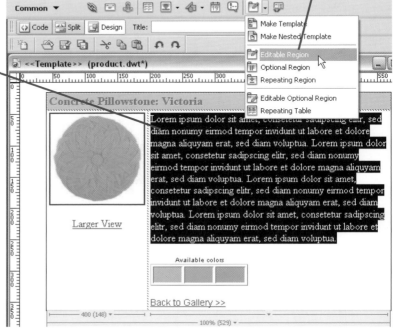

8 When the New Editable Region dialog box appears, select the generic name in the Name text window, type in a more descriptive name, and click OK.

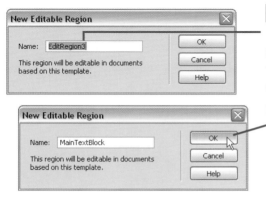

reuse items to save time

9 Your region name will be added to the template page.

10 Continue adding and naming editable regions until you're done.

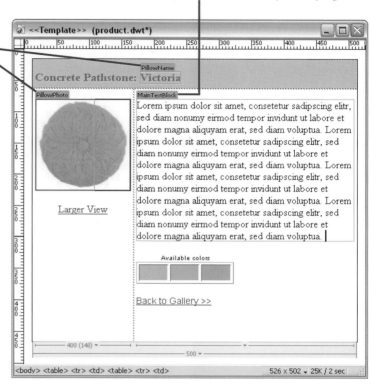

11 Save the template page and its content will appear in the upper half of the Assets tab. You can now start generating pages based on the template.

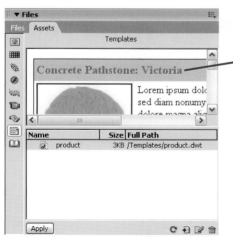

reuse items to save time

use your template

Once you create a template, you can generate as many individual pages as you need based on its design.

Choose File > New and when the New from Template dialog box appears, select the Templates tab.

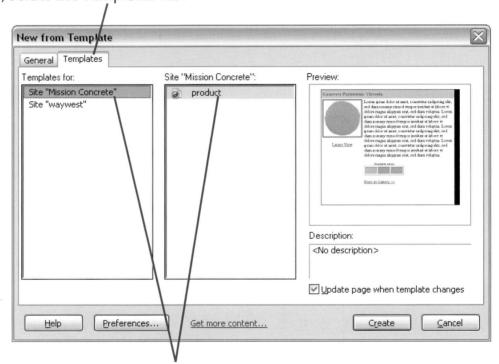

Choose your site in the first column, select the template you just created in the second column, and click Create.

reuse items to save time

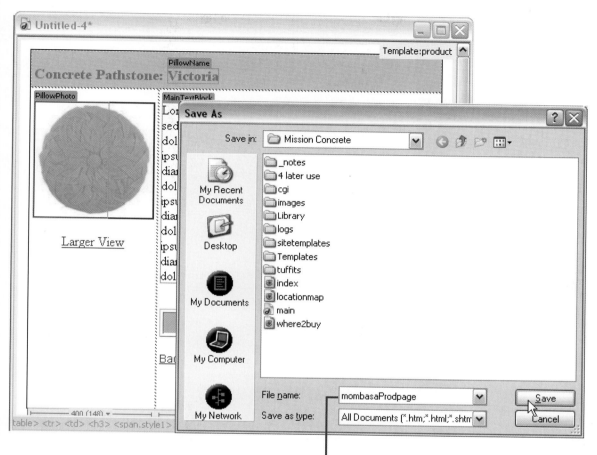

When a new untitled page based on the template appears, save it and give it a new name. (In our example, we've named the page mombasaProdpage to reflect its eventual content.) Be sure to also give the new page a title, which will be blank initially since it's a template-based page.

reuse items to save time

use your template (cont.)

You now can begin to replace the page's editable regions, marked with teal-colored names, with content tailored to the individual page.

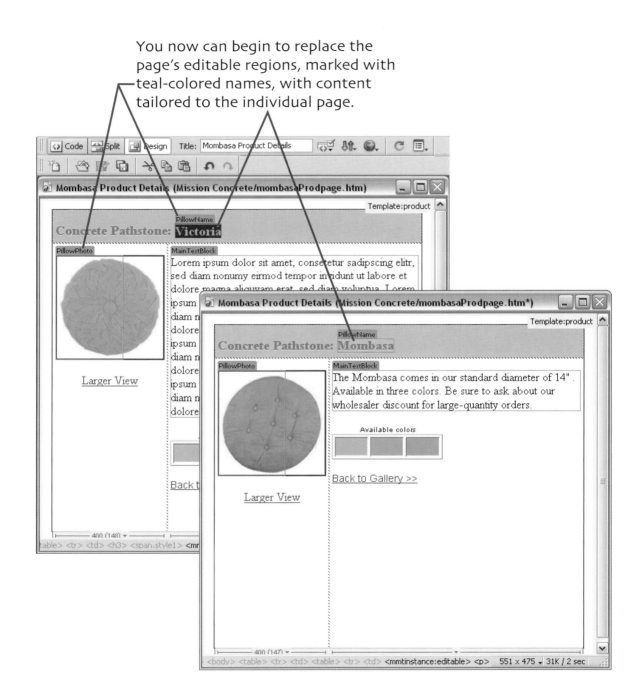

reuse items to save time

edit template

Here's the real payoff for building individual pages based on a template: You can change the template and all the pages will be updated automatically.

Open the template that you need to change by selecting it in the Assets tab and clicking the Edit button.

Once the template opens, make the needed changes. (In our example, we've changed the header to a color more in keeping with the Tuffits pillow palette, using the Property inspector.)

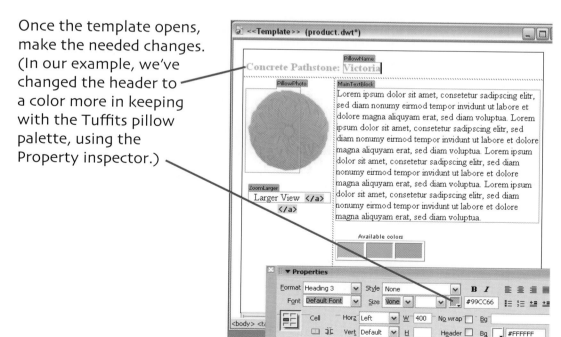

reuse items to save time

edit template (cont.)

Save your changes to the template. Click Update when Dreamweaver asks if you want to change pages based on the template.

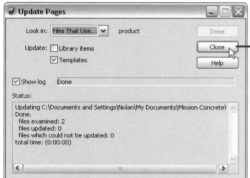

A status dialog box will list the pages updated. Click Close to apply the changes.

If you open any of the pages based on that template, you'll see that they've been updated to reflect the changes.

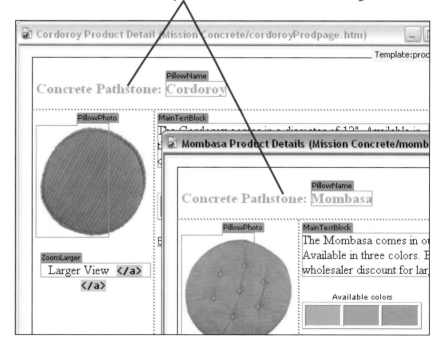

extra bits

create a library item p. 76

- The horizontal rule and copyright notice can be a single library item because they sit next to each other. If they were in two different spots on the page, they'd have to be made into two separate library items.

- While library items contain no styling themselves, they can contain references to style sheets. Use external style sheets to keep library items consistently styled, as explained on page 60.

- Dreamweaver will automatically add the .lbi suffix to a library item file name, designating the file as a library item.

create a template p. 82

- By default, every item on a template is initially locked, that is, not editable. Only the items you specifically mark as editable will be available for changes.

- When you save the template, Dreamweaver automatically adds a .dwt suffix. Dreamweaver sometimes will ask if you want to update any pages using it—even though you haven't built any such pages yet. Just click Yes to close the dialog box.

reuse items to save time

7. add navigation

As your Web site grows in size, visitors need an easy way to move from page to page, or even section to section. By including a navigation bar, often called a Nav-bar, on all your pages, visitors can move around your site without getting lost.

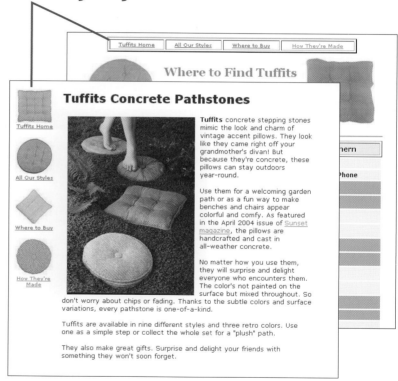

We will start by adding a Nav-bar to your site's home page. (In our example, we're adding it to the tuffits page.) Before we add the Nav-bar, however, we're going to create two layers—one to hold the Nav-bar and one for the main area of the Web page.

add layers

Originally, Web designers were forced to use cumbersome tables or framesets to lay out magazine-style Web pages. But now that most Web browsers support style sheet positioning tags, you can use layers. In Dreamweaver, using layers is a click-and-drag affair.

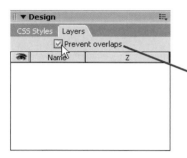

1 Switch the Insert toolbar to Layout using the drop-down menu. Press F2 to open the Layers tab of the Design panel and check Prevent overlaps.

2 Open your site's home page (in our example, the top-level tuffits page). Select the entire page and then cut it (Ctrl X in Windows, Cmd X on the Mac).

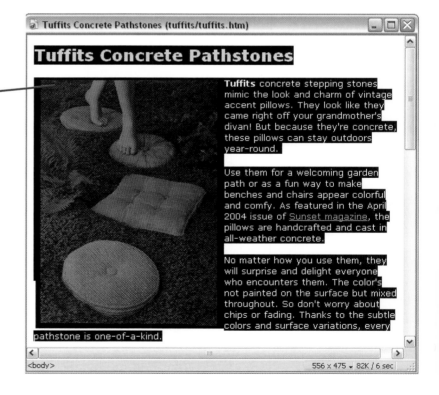

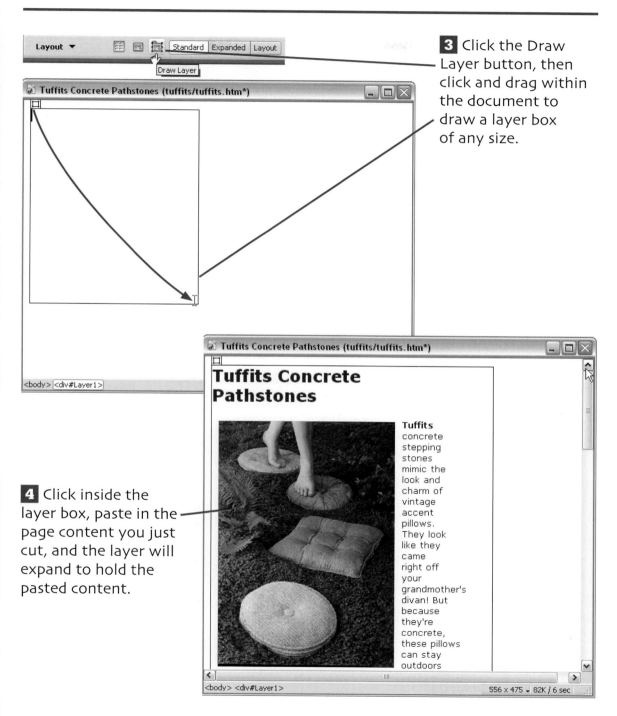

3 Click the Draw Layer button, then click and drag within the document to draw a layer box of any size.

4 Click inside the layer box, paste in the page content you just cut, and the layer will expand to hold the pasted content.

Tuffits Concrete Pathstones

Tuffits concrete stepping stones mimic the look and charm of vintage accent pillows. They look like they came right off your grandmother's divan! But because they're concrete, these pillows can stay outdoors

add navigation

add layers (cont.)

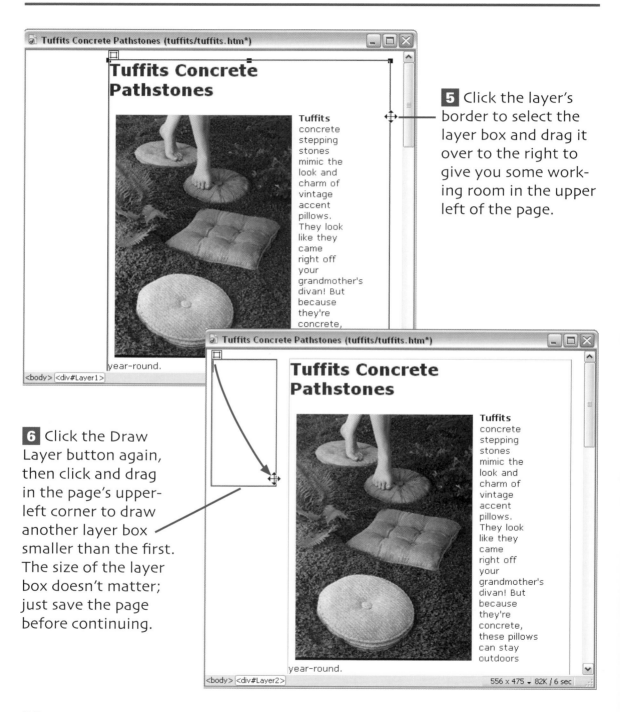

5 Click the layer's border to select the layer box and drag it over to the right to give you some working room in the upper left of the page.

6 Click the Draw Layer button again, then click and drag in the page's upper-left corner to draw another layer box smaller than the first. The size of the layer box doesn't matter; just save the page before continuing.

name layers

We're going to give these layers real names to better distinguish them from one another. (See extra bits on page 110.)

Click the left layer's border to select it and it will be highlighted in the Layers tab.

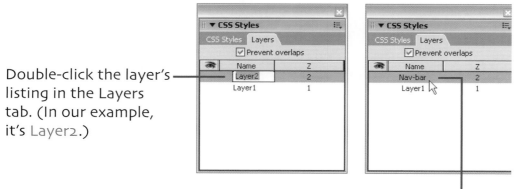

Double-click the layer's listing in the Layers tab. (In our example, it's Layer2.)

Type in a more descriptive name and press [Tab] to apply it. (In our example, we've named it Nav-bar since that's what this will become.) Select the other layer and give it a more descriptive name as well. (We'll use MainBlock.)

position layers

Now we're ready to put the layers exactly where we need them for what will become the Nav-bar. (See extra bits on page 110.)

1 Make sure the Property inspector and rulers are visible. Select the Nav-bar layer and take a look at two of the Property inspector's text windows: L and T, which denote how far in px (pixels) the layer sits from the Left Top corner of the page. (In our example, the layer is 8 pixels to the right and 15 pixels below the top-left corner.)

2 The absolute corner would be L: o and T: o, which is where we want our Nav-bar layer to start. Type in those numbers and press (Tab). The Nav-bar layer will tuck itself into the top-left corner.

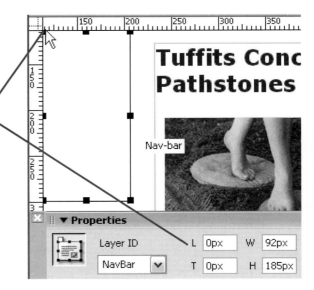

3 The W and H text windows in the Property inspector set the layer's Width and Height. (In our example, we want the Nav-bar to be exactly 100 pixels wide, not 92 as it is on the left, and since we're not sure how high it needs to be, we'll type in 600 to be safe.)

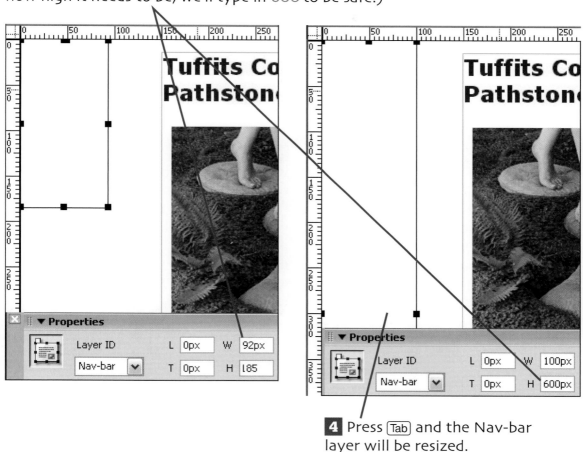

4 Press [Tab] and the Nav-bar layer will be resized.

position layers (cont.)

5 With the Nav-bar layer positioned, we now can put the MainBlock layer exactly where it belongs. The Nav-bar layer's L value is 0 and it's 100 pixels wide, so we'll set the MainBlock's L value at 105 , which gives us a 5-pixel gutter for a bit of breathing room. Press Tab to apply the change and jump to the T text window.

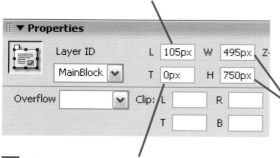

6 Like the Nav-bar layer, the MainBlock's T value should be 0 so that the layers line up across the top of the page. Press Tab to apply the change and jump to the W text window.

7 Finally, we'll set the MainBlock layer width at 495 (100+5+495=600, to easily fit on most monitors). Press Tab to jump to the H text window, where we'll set the height at a generous 750 pixels since Web browsers let viewers scroll down deep windows. Press Tab and you're done. Save your work before continuing.

add navigation

create main nav-bar

With the Nav-bar layer placed where we need it, adding the content is the easy part. (See extra bits on page 110.)

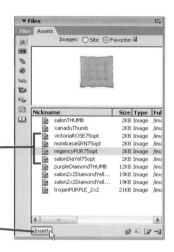

1 If you haven't already, create a series of images small enough to fit inside your new Nav-bar. (In our example, we've taken images of Tuffits pillows, reduced them to 75 pixels wide, and resampled them.)

2 Click in the Nav-bar, and click the Asset tab's Insert button. The selected image will appear in the Nav-bar.

3 Right after the first Nav-bar image, add a line break, type in a short label for what will become your first text link, and then start a new paragraph. Don't bother with styling any of this just yet. Instead, repeat these steps to add the other images and link labels you need for each of your site's main areas of interest.

4 Select the first text label and style it as needed. (In our example, Dreamweaver named it style3, with the text set at 10 pixels so that it will fit better in the narrow Nav-bar.)

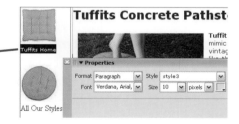

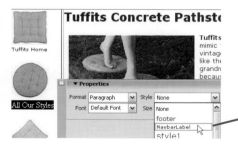

5 Rename the Nav-bar text style. (In our example, we've renamed it NavbarLabel for clarity.) Apply the style to the rest of the Nav-bar text labels.

add navigation   **101**

create main nav-bar (cont.)

6 Use the Property inspector to center all the Nav-bar content.

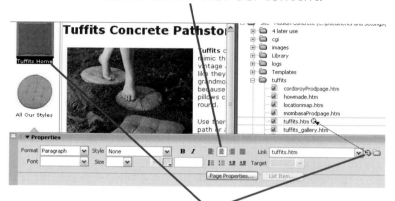

7 Since the Nav-bar's first image and text label will link to the same page, select them both and make the link using the Property inspector. (In our example, we're linking to tuffits.)

8 While the text reflects the link colors we set in our external style sheet (main.css), the linked image shows a big border in the Web browser view that interferes with the Nav-bar's otherwise clean look.

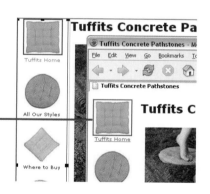

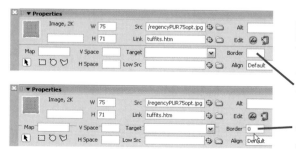

9 Fortunately, the fix is easy: eliminate the border. Select the image and you'll see that the Property inspector's Border setting is blank—the default setting—but not, surprisingly, the same as zero. Type a o (zero) into the Border's text window and press [Tab] to apply the change.

add navigation

10 Save the page and view it in your Web browser. Now the border really is gone!

11 Link the rest of your Nav-bar images and text, set each image border to zero, and your Nav-bar stands ready on your home page to guide visitors through the site.

create small nav-bar

You could place the Nav-bar you just created on every page of the site. But in case you don't want to use that much space on every page for a Nav-bar, we'll create a small, table-based Nav-bar styled much like its home-page cousin. This task pulls together many of the skills you've learned and shows how you can use Dreamweaver to quickly build relatively complex pages.

1 Open your home page, look in the CSS Styles tab, and select the label style you created for the main Nav-bar. (In our example, we've selected NavbarLabel.)

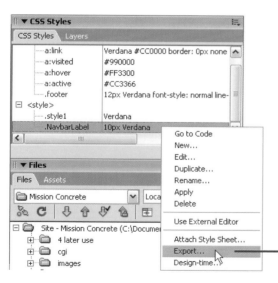

2 Right-click (Windows) or Ctrl-click (Mac) the label style and choose Export from the drop-down menu. When the Export Styles As CSS File dialog box appears, name the exported style nav-barStyle, and click Save.

add navigation

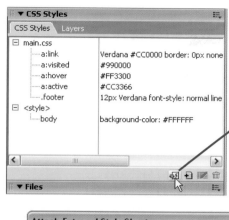

3 Open a page where you want to use a smaller Nav-bar and click the CSS Styles tab's Attach Style Sheet button.

4 Click Browse when the Attach External Style Sheet dialog box appears.

5 When the Select Style Sheet File dialog box appears, select nav-barStyle and click OK to close the dialog box.

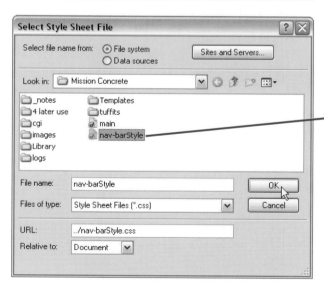

add navigation

create small nav-bar (cont.)

6 When the Attach External Style Sheet dialog box reappears, click OK again to close it as well. The nav-barStyle style sheet now appears in your page's CSS Styles tab.

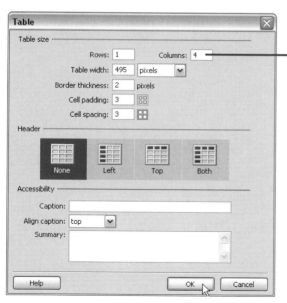

7 Now insert a table at the very top of the page. (In our example, we inserted a 495-pixel wide table with one row and four columns, which will match the number of links in the main nav-bar.)

8 Select and center the table when it appears on the page. In the table's first cell, add the text for your first link. Don't worry when the cell widths shift around as you do this.

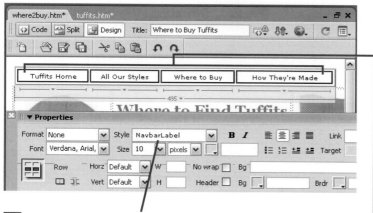

9 Add link text to the rest of the cells, select them all, and in the Property inspector choose the NavbarLabel in the Style drop-down menu.

10 All the selected text will change to that style.

add navigation

create small nav-bar (cont.)

11 Use the Property inspector to link the text in each cell to your site's main pages. ──

12 As you do so, the links will be styled based on the nav-barStyle style sheet you attached to the page. ──

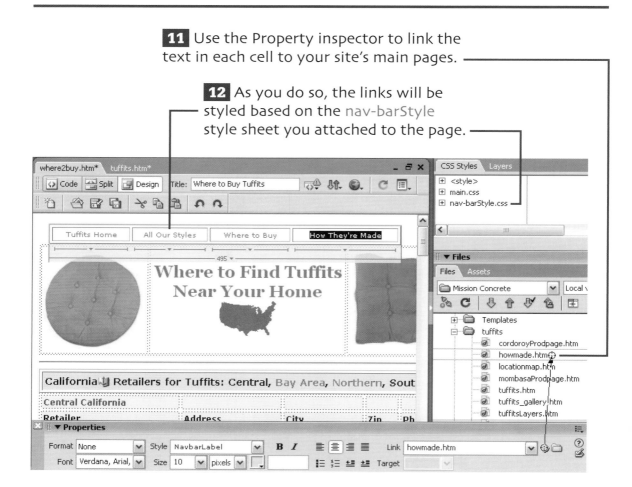

13 After you've linked all the labels in the table, save your work.

14 Select the table, turn it into a library item with a clear name, and you'll be able to add this space-saving Nav-bar to any page that includes the nav-barStyle style sheet.

extra bits

name layers p. 97

- You also can select a layer by clicking its name in the Layers tab.

position layers p. 98

- You also can select a layer and drag it where you want it, but for precise positioning use the Property inspector's text windows.

create main nav-bar p. 101

- While the first link is to the home page itself, that's not really a problem. If visitors viewing the home page click the link, they remain right where they are.

add navigation

8. publish site

Finally, you're ready to put your pages on the Web, a process sometimes called publishing since they'll become available for anyone to read. Dreamweaver's expanded Files panel plays a key role in helping you keep track of which files are where and when they were last changed.

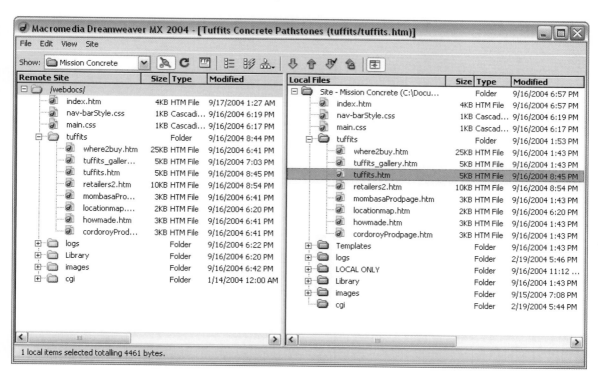

add search terms

Help Web search engines highlight your site by entering a succinct description, along with multiple keywords, in the home page. Dreamweaver places this information in the page's hidden head code. (See extra bits on page 123.)

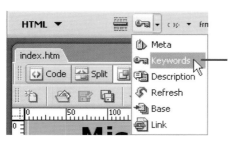

1 Open your home page and switch the Insert toolbar to HTML using the drop-down menu. Click the second button from the left and choose Keywords from its drop-down menu.

2 When the Keywords dialog box appears, type words that you think people might use to search for your site. Once you're done, click OK to close the dialog box.

3 Click the the second button from the left again and choose Description from its drop-down menu.

4 When the Description dialog box appears, type in a short paragraph that sums up the purpose of your Web site and the products it displays. Once you're done, click OK to close the dialog box.

5 If you want to see the otherwise hidden keywords and description, click the Split button. The terms appear as part of the meta data in the page's head code.

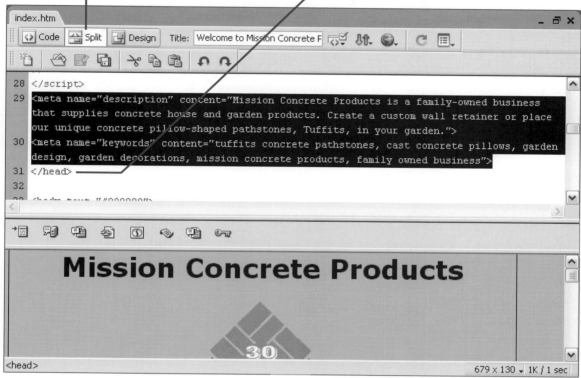

check and fix links

Few things are more frustrating for Web users than broken links. Dreamweaver can check your entire site in seconds and save everyone hours of frustration.

1 Choose Site > Check Links Sitewide and the Results panel will list any pages with broken links. (In our example, Dreamweaver found a link we deliberately mistyped, tuffBREAK.)

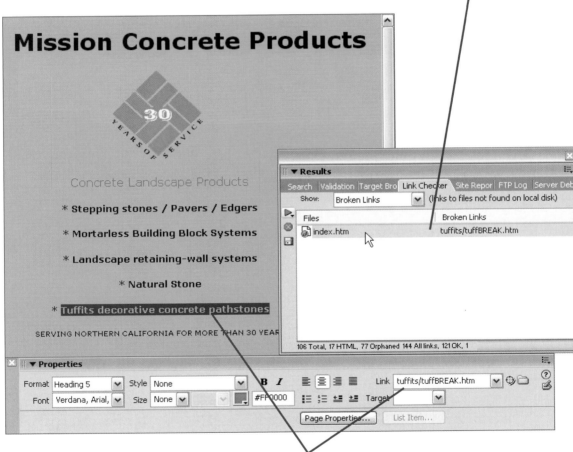

2 Double-click the file listing and Dreamweaver will open the Property inspector, along with the page that contains the broken link.

3 Use the Property inspector's Link window to correct the mistake by typing in the correct link or redrawing the link with the Point-to-File button.

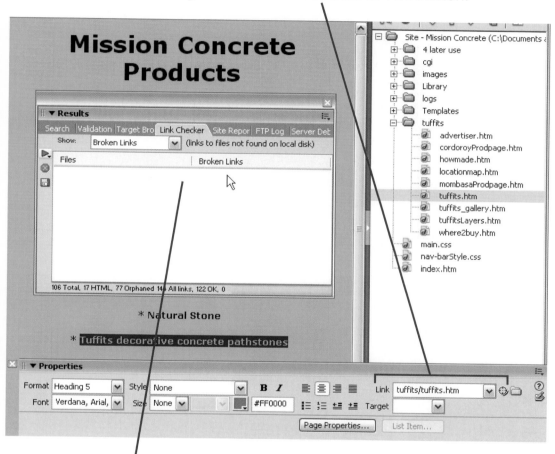

4 Once you make the fix, save the page and the Results panel automatically removes the previously broken link from its list. Repeat until you've fixed all broken links.

explore the files panel

The Files panel serves as your main tool to put files from your local site on to the remote Web site. You also use it to get any of your remote files if, for example, you've accidentally deleted their local site counterparts. (See extra bits on page 123.)

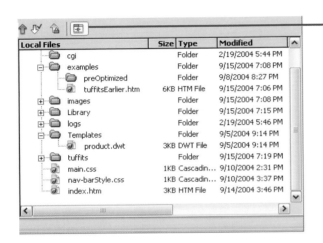

Normally the Files panel only shows your local files. Click the Expand/Collapse button to see them along with your remote Web site's files.

The toolbar running above the file listings contains all the buttons needed to move files between the two locations.

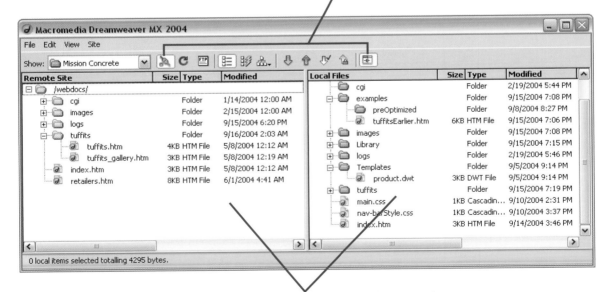

The expanded view of the Files panel shows your remote and local files.

publish site

Click the
Connect/Disconnect
button to open or close
a live connection to the
remote Web site.

Click the Put files
button to move
selected files from
your local site to
the remote site.

Click the Get files
button to move
selected files from
the remote site to
the local site.

Click the Refresh
button after moving
files in either direc-
tion to update the
file listings.

Do not use these two buttons
unless you're working with a
group of people and have
activated Dreamweaver's
check-in/check-out file system.

The Expand/Collapse button
lets you see the remote and
local files, or just the local files.

connect to remote site

After double-checking your files, you're ready to place them on your remote site. Since you already entered the remote site's address details back in Chapter 1, you're ready to connect. (See extra bits on page 123.)

1 Unless you have an always-on connection to the Internet, activate your computer's dial-up connection now.

2 Return to Dreamweaver, make sure the Files panel is visible, and click the Expand/Collapse button.

3 Once the view expands, click the Connect button.

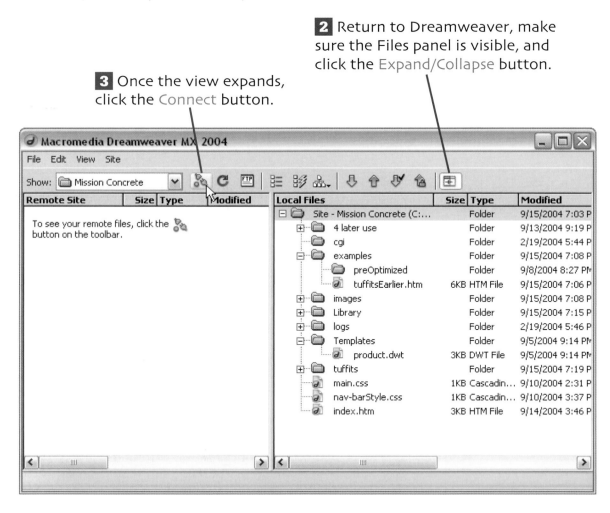

4 The Status dialog box will appear briefly as Dreamweaver negotiates the connection to your Web site.

5 Once the connection is made, the remote site's files will appear in the left side of the Files panel. (In our example, we haven't put any files on the site yet, so all you see is the top-level folder, webdocs, and two don't–touch subfolders, cgi and logs.)

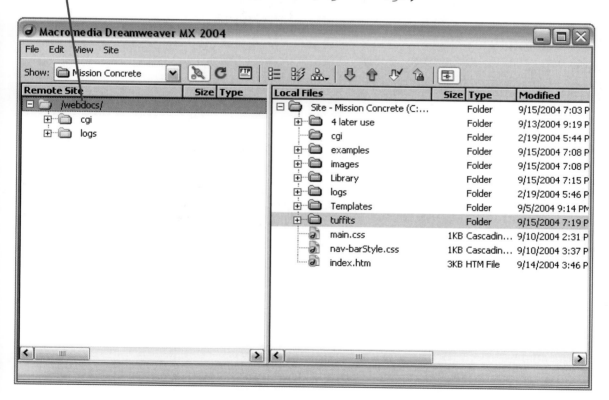

6 You're ready to upload your files.

publish site

upload multiple files

If this is the first upload to your Web site, you'll be publishing multiple files, including all the necessary images for your pages. (See extra bits on page 123.)

1 Select the home page, index, in the Local Files pane and click the Put button to begin the upload.

You also can select individual files or folders by Ctrl-clicking (Windows) or Cmd-clicking (Mac) them in the Local Files pane. Click the Put button to upload them.

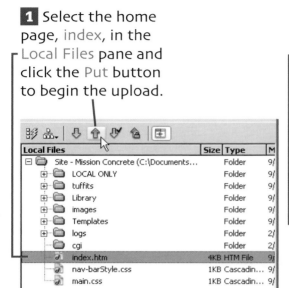

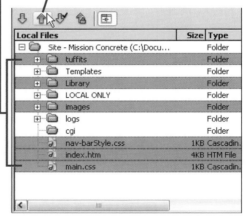

2 When Dreamweaver asks if you want to include dependent files, click Yes. Dependent files include every file and image linked, directly or indirectly, to the selected page(s). (In our example, this would include not only the index page, but also the attached main.css style sheet.)

3 A series of progress dialog boxes will flash by as Dreamweaver uploads the home page and all its dependent files. This may take several minutes to complete, depending on how many files you're uploading and the speed of your Internet connection.

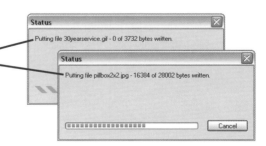

4 When the progress dialog boxes stop appearing, press the Refresh button...

5 ...and then compare names of the Remote Site files to the names of your Local Files.

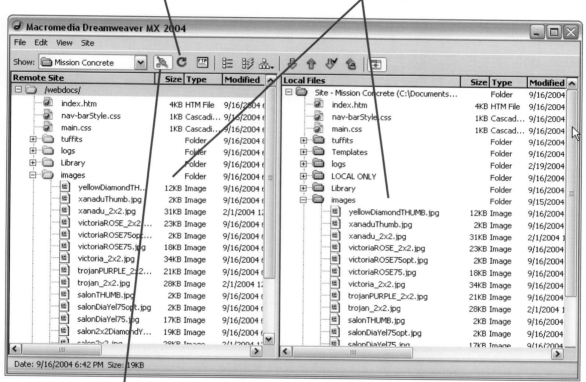

6 Check how the remote site pages look in your Web browser to make sure their appearance matches that of your local files. If you find mismatches, upload the local files again.

7 Once you're done, click the Disconnect button.

upload a single page

Sometimes you'll need to upload only a single page—for example, when you need to update information or fix a mistake. (See extra bits on page 123.)

1 Once you're connected, click the page file in the Local Files pane and drag it to the folder where the older version appears in the Remote Site pane.

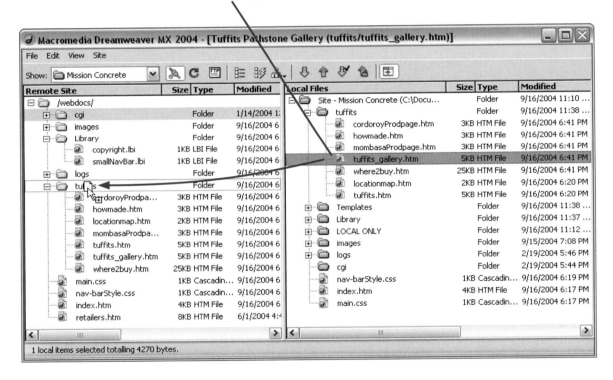

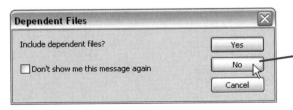

2 When Dreamweaver asks if you want to include dependent files, click No. A single progress dialog box will appear as Dreamweaver uploads the selected page. Use your Web browser to check the page on the remote Web site, and when you're done, click the Disconnect button.

extra bits

add search terms p. 112

- When picking keywords and a description, especially for an uncommon product or service, think of similar products or services and use words people would most likely type in to find them.

explore the files panel p. 116

- If you are working solo, the check-in/check-out system is cumbersome since it forces you to alert yourself that you're using a file.

connect to remote site p. 118

- The local and remote versions of the cgi and logs folders are different since they reflect the specific activities for each set of files. If you try to replace one with the other, Dreamweaver will cancel the transfer.

upload multiple files p. 120

- While you could select your local site's top-level folder (in this case, Mission Concrete) and upload the whole thing, it's not recommended. You run the risk of publishing files you're still working on, not to mention wiping out remote files not found on your local site. Instead, it's best to upload only the local files and folders you specifically select.

upload a single page p. 122

- Since you've only changed the HTML file, there's no need to upload the dependent files that are already on the remote site.

index

index

index

Properties command, 12
Property inspector, 3, 9
   correcting broken links
     with, 115
   image tools, 24
   opening, 12
   positioning layers with,
     98–100
   positioning Nav-bar content
     with, 102
publishing site, 111–123
   adding search terms,
     112–113
   checking links, 114–115
   connecting to Internet,
     118–119
   defined, 111
   uploading files, 120–123
Put button, 117, 120

R

Refresh button, 117, 121
remote site
   connecting to, 117, 118–119
   uploading files to, 120–123
   viewing files on, 116–117
Rename command, 27
Rename Style dialog box, 44
renaming items. See naming
Resample button, 31, 35
robot programs, 71
rollover links, 59
root folder, 26, 35
rule, horizontal, 76, 91
ruler, 2, 38

S

Save As dialog box, 11
saving
   home pages, 11
   images, 26
   Nav-bars, 109
   styles, 44
   templates, 85, 90, 91
scripts, 35

search engines, 112
search terms, 112–113, 123
Select Image Source dialog box,
   26, 40
Select Style Sheet File dialog
   box, 105
Sharpen button, 31
Sharpen slider, 31
Show Grid command, 38
Site Definition window, 6–8
Site radio button, 74
Size menu, 14
Snap To Grid command, 38
Sort Table dialog box, 51, 53
spacing, cell, 46
Split button, 113
Split view, 2
spreadsheet data, 46
Src box, Property inspector, 24
Standard button, 38
Standard toolbar, 2
Start Page, 22
Status dialog box, 119
Studio MX 2004, xiii
Style box, 13–14
Style drop-down menu, 48
style sheets, 22, 60–63, 91
styles
   naming, 48, 101, 104
   saving, 44
   for tables, 46–47, 53
   for text, 13–14, 101
subfolders, 35

T

tab-separated text, 46, 53
table-based Nav-bar, 104–108
Table dialog box, 39
table headers, 39, 42–43, 53
Table size options, Table dialog,
   39, 42
tables, 37–53
   adding images to, 40–41, 53
   adding to Web pages, 38–39
   applying colors to, 50, 53
   applying styles to, 44–45, 53

deleting cells in, 49
editing, 48–49
importing data into,
   46–47, 53
labeling columns/rows in, 39,
   42–43, 53
as page-layout tool, 37
selecting, 53
setting options for, 38–39
sorting, 51–52, 53
turning on grid/ruler for, 38
Tabular Data icon, 46
templates, 82–91
   adding content to, 83
   creating, 82–85, 91
   editing, 89–90
   file suffix for, 91
   generating pages based on,
     86–88
   marking editable regions in,
     84–85
   naming, 82
   opening, 83
   purpose of, 82
   replacing editable regions
     in, 88
   saving, 85, 90, 91
Templates tab, 86
Test Connection option, 7, 8
testing
   links, 57, 58, 70, 114–115
   online connection, 7, 8
text
   adding to Web page, 12–15
   applying styles to, 13–14
   choosing color for, 13
   choosing font for, 12
   linking to, 56–58, 108
   on Mac vs. Windows systems,
     12, 22
   sizing, 14, 22
   wrapping around images,
     24, 32–33, 35
Text Color box, 13
text styles, 22, 101
thumbnails, 30
tiled images, 20

Full-color projects
from the folks
who bring you
Visual QuickStart
Guides...

Visual QuickProject

Creating a Web Site

with *Flash*

**DAVID
MORRIS**

creating
a web site
with flash

Visual QuickProject Guide

by David Morris

**Peachpit
Press**

Visual QuickProject Guide
Creating a Web Site with Flash
David Morris

Peachpit Press
1249 Eighth Street
Berkeley, CA 94710
510/524-2178
800/283-9444
510/524-2221 (fax)

Find us on the Web at www.peachpit.com.
To report errors, please send a note to errata@peachpit.com.
Peachpit Press is a division of Pearson Education.

Copyright © 2005 by David Morris

Editor: Rebecca Gulick
Production Editor: Hilal Sala
Compositor: Owen Wolfson
Indexer: FireCrystal Communications
Interior Design: Elizabeth Castro
Cover Design: The Visual Group with Aren Howell
Cover Production: Owen Wolfson
Cover Photo Credit: Photodisc

Notice of Rights
All rights reserved. No part of this book may be reproduced or transmitted in any form by any means, electronic, mechanical, photocopying, recording, or otherwise, without the prior written permission of the publisher. For information on getting permission for reprints and excerpts, contact permissions@peachpit.com.

Notice of Liability
The information in this book is distributed on an "As Is" basis, without warranty. While every precaution has been taken in the preparation of the book, neither the author nor Peachpit Press shall have any liability to any person or entity with respect to any loss or damage caused or alleged to be caused directly or indirectly by the instructions contained in this book or by the computer software and hardware products described in it.

Trademarks
Visual QuickProject Guide is a registered trademark of Peachpit Press, a division of Pearson Education.
Macromedia is a registered trademark, and Flash and Macromedia Flash are trademarks of Macromedia, Inc., in the United States and/or other countries.

Many of the designations used by manufacturers and sellers to distinguish their products are claimed as trademarks. Where those designations appear in this book, and Peachpit Press was aware of a trademark claim, the designations appear as requested by the owner of the trademark. All other product names and services identified throughout this book are used in editorial fashion only and for the benefit of such companies with no intention of infringement of the trademark. No such use, or the use of any trade name, is intended to convey endorsement or other affiliation with this book.

ISBN 0-321-32125-1

Printed and bound in the United States of America

For Duane,

My endless source of strength, hope, and love.

Special thanks to...

Liz Dobecka and Timeless Blooms, for graciously agreeing to be my design guinea pig. I hope I did justice to your beautiful works.

Leigh Rountree, for providing such a solid base of content for me to lift and mangle.

My editor, Rebecca Gulick, for the hand-holding and for making it all much better than it was.

Nancy Davis, for shepherding this great book series and for giving me this opportunity.

And finally, Marjorie Baer, who remembered me from another life and was such an enthusiastic advocate. Thanks so much. I owe you many dinners.

contents

contents

introduction

The Visual QuickProject Guide that you hold in your hands offers a unique way to learn about new technologies. Instead of drowning you in theoretical possibilities and lengthy explanations, this Visual QuickProject Guide uses big, color illustrations coupled with clear, concise step-by-step instructions to show you how to complete one specific project in a matter of hours.

Our project in this book is to create a beautiful, engaging Web site using Macromedia Flash. Our Web site showcases a small, home-based business, but since the project covers all the basic techniques, you'll be able to use what you learn to create your own Flash-based Web sites—perhaps to promote your own business, showcase a hobby or collection, or provide a site for your neighborhood association.

what you'll create

This is the home page of the Timeless Blooms Web site, the project you'll create. In the process, you'll learn the following useful techniques:

Create interactive buttons for navigation between the different sections of your site.

Draw graphic elements to define your site's look and feel.

Import graphics and images created in other applications.

Animate text to provide interest and a professional quality.

Format text in the font, size, and color of your choice.

Add progress bars to update viewers
about download progress of large movies.

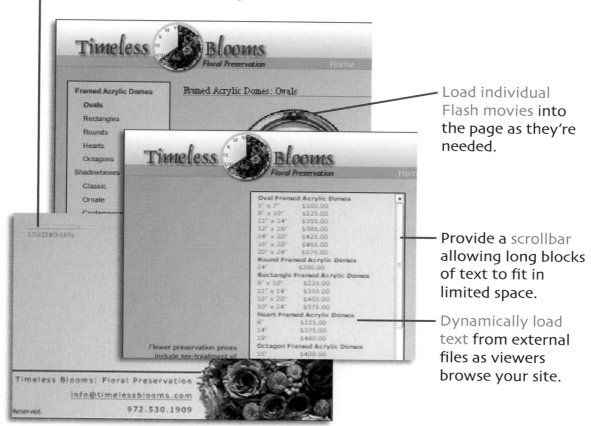

Load individual
Flash movies into
the page as they're
needed.

Provide a scrollbar
allowing long blocks
of text to fit in
limited space.

Dynamically load
text from external
files as viewers
browse your site.

introduction

how this book works

The title of each section explains what is covered in that section.

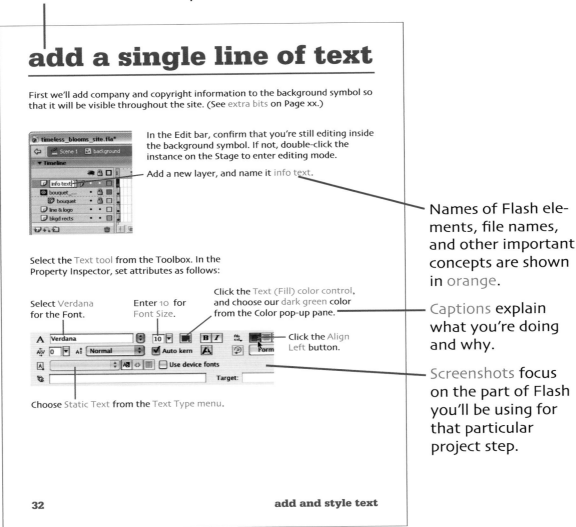

add a single line of text

First we'll add company and copyright information to the background symbol so that it will be visible throughout the site. (See extra bits on Page xx.)

In the Edit bar, confirm that you're still editing inside the background symbol. If not, double-click the instance on the Stage to enter editing mode.

Add a new layer, and name it info text.

Names of Flash elements, file names, and other important concepts are shown in orange.

Select the Text tool from the Toolbox. In the Property Inspector, set attributes as follows:

Select Verdana for the Font.

Enter 10 for Font Size.

Click the Text (Fill) color control, and choose our dark green color from the Color pop-up pane.

Click the Align Left button.

Captions explain what you're doing and why.

Choose Static Text from the Text Type menu.

Screenshots focus on the part of Flash you'll be using for that particular project step.

32   add and style text

The extra bits section at the end of each chapter contains additional tips and tricks that you might like to know but that aren't absolutely necessary for creating the Web page.

extra bits

draw background elements p. 11

- In Flash, when an object is overlapping another, the overlapped section of the existing object is deleted. This makes adjustments such as nudging new objects into place a nightmare. To avoid this, you can either create a new layer for every object you draw or group an object as soon as you draw it. I prefer grouping.

create reusable graphics p. 18

- Using symbols in Flash provides two main benefits: reduced file size and ease of editing.
- When you create a symbol and place instances of that symbol on the Stage, your movie's file size is reduced because no matter how many times you use it, the code required to define it is only included in the file once. Each instance just points to the symbol and describes any modifications to that symbol, such as transparency or size.
- Modifying work later is also much easier. Imagine that you've placed 100 blue squares (not instances of a blue square symbol) throughout your movie, and then you decide

to change the color. You have to find and change all 100 squares. But if you made a symbol of a blue square and placed 100 instances, you only have to change the symbol, and the 100 instances are updated automatically.

edit a symbol p. 19

- When you have an object on the Stage that is a container for other objects (groups, symbols and text boxes) you can just double-click it to "get inside" and edit the contents.
- To exit the editing mode of the container, you can double-click outside the bounds of the container.
- Sometimes when you draw a line in Flash, it isn't placed at the top of the object stacking order like you'd expect it to be. Instead, it is placed behind other objects. Defying the standard convention that a new object is stacked above existing objects on the same layer, Flash stacks lines based on a mysterious formula involving the line's color that only programmers could come up with!

design the layout of your stage

29

The heading for each group of tips matches the section title. (The colors are just for decoration and have no hidden meaning.)

Next to the heading there's a page number that also shows which section the tips belong to.

companion web site

You can find this book's companion site at http://www.peachpit.com/vqj/flash.

In the Support Files section of the site, you'll find all of the files you need to complete the project in this book. You can also download the intermediate files created in each chapter and the files that make up the final project site.

Visit the Project Site section to see a completed example of the site you're building in this book.

You can also find any updated material in the Corrections section of the site.

explore flash

At first glance the Flash interface can be overwhelming with its many panels and controls, but don't be concerned. As you progress through this project, you'll learn how to access the important stuff and how to harness all the power of Flash. When you finish the project, you'll have the knowledge and skills needed to create a professional-quality Web site to suit your business, organization, or personal needs.

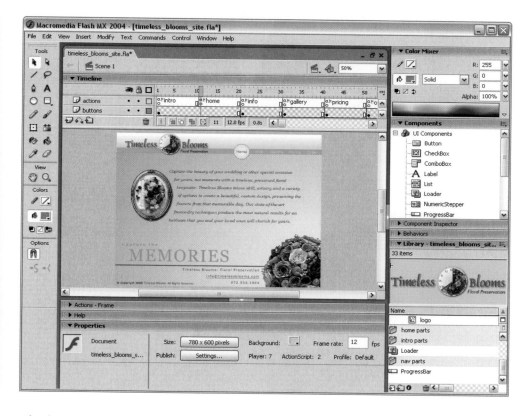

Flash borrows many of its conventions and terms from film production. The presentation you create for viewers is a movie, the distinct parts of the movie are scenes, the players (your content) are on the Stage, and movement through time is accomplished via the Timeline. Thinking about the Flash interface in the context of this film metaphor will help you quickly grasp the way we work in Flash. We are producing a movie that features your content and tells the story you want Web viewers to see. (See extra bits on Page xx.)

explore flash (cont.)

The story you're telling with your movie is presented on the Stage. You'll use it as your workspace to place and arrange the elements of your site. The Stage's rectangular dimensions define the area of your movie that viewers will see.

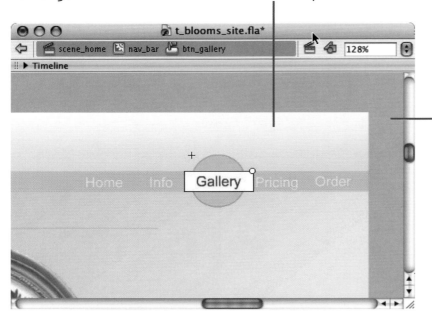

Gray space around the Stage makes up the Work Area, which holds objects that hang off the Stage and animated elements that move onto or off of the Stage. To view or hide objects in the Work Area, choose View > Work Area, or press [Ctrl][Shift][w] (Windows) or [Cmd][Shift][w] (Mac).

In Flash, you'll often find yourself drilled down multiple levels within elements, such as editing text that is inside a button symbol inside a movie placed in a particular scene. The Edit bar at the top of the window displays those levels to help keep you oriented and to let you quickly backtrack when your edit is complete. Additionally, you can use it to navigate between scenes, to locate and modify symbols, and to change view magnification.

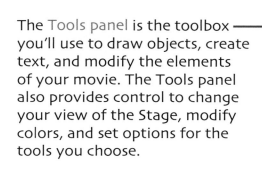

The Tools panel is the toolbox you'll use to draw objects, create text, and modify the elements of your movie. The Tools panel also provides control to change your view of the Stage, modify colors, and set options for the tools you choose.

Review and change the attributes of objects in the Property Inspector. Controls in the Property Inspector change dynamically, displaying the attributes and settings relevant to your current selection. Here you'll be able to modify the attributes of text, graphics, frames, animations, and more.

introduction

explore flash (cont.)

The Timeline controls the order, timing and flow of your movie. The panel contains three primary sections: frames, layers, and the Playhead.

The Playhead indicates the current frame displayed on the Stage.

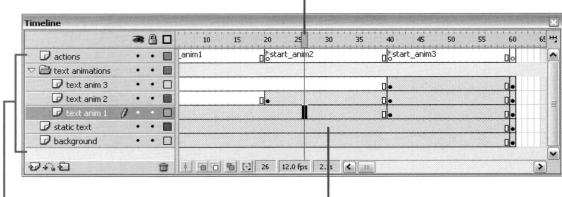

Think of layers as independent strips of film, each containing its own objects, stacked on top of one another, and composited to present a particular frame. In most cases, each layer we create will contain only a few objects, making it easier to keep track of things as the project gets progressively more complex.

Frames in the Timeline represent changes in your content over time. However it's important to think of frames as something more than just for animation; frames also serve an important function as milestones within your site to which you can link other content.

If the elements in your movie are the players, then symbols are the featured stars. Using symbols, which we'll
learn more about later, decreases file size, saves time on
edits, and organizes your file. The symbols in your movie
are stored and accessed from the Library panel.

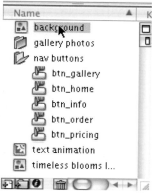

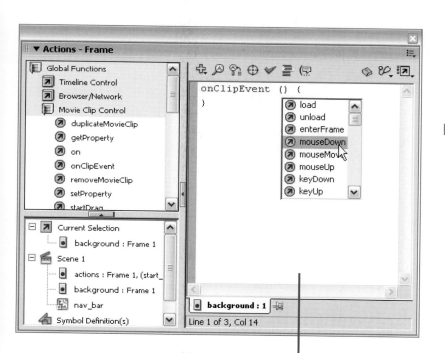

The Actions panel is used for adding ActionScript to your movie. ActionScript is
Flash's scripting language for adding complex interactivity, controlling navigation, and programming many of the advanced functions found in robust Flash
applications. As you can imagine, it can be a daunting task to script a movie, but
don't worry. We'll use the simplified process provided in the Behaviors panel and
have minimal use for the Actions panel in our project.

introduction

explore flash (cont.)

The Behaviors panel provides the power and control of ActionScript without your having to code the script yourself. Behaviors are prepackaged bits of ActionScript presented with interfaces that allow you to easily set up complex interactions that would otherwise require coding.

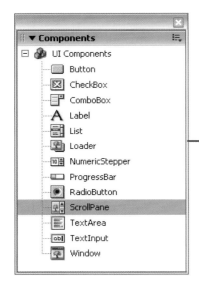

If Behaviors are packages of ActionScript that you apply to objects in your file, components, accessed from the Components panel, are packages of special-purpose objects that include the ActionScript to control their behavior. Components include simple user interface controls, such as buttons and checkboxes, and more complex controls that contain content such as scroll panes and windows.

After you add a component to your file, you'll use the Component Inspector to specify parameters specific to the component type and your particular design requirements.

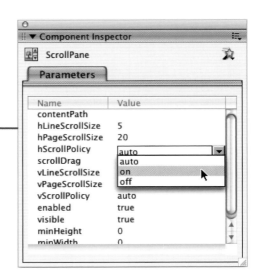

the next step

While this Visual QuickProject Guide teaches you the basics for creating a Web site in Flash, there is much more to learn. If you're curious about Flash development, try Macromedia Flash MX 2004 for Windows and Macintosh: Visual QuickStart Guide, by Katherine Ulrich. It features clear examples, simple step-by-step instructions, and loads of visual aids to cover every aspect of Flash design.

After that, you can take it to the next level with Macromedia Flash MX 2004 Advanced for Windows and Macintosh: Visual QuickPro Guide, by Russell Chun and Joe Garraffo.

extra bits

explore flash p.xiii

- Avoid the temptation to "store" unused objects offstage in the work area; they'll still be exported in the final movie and will add to the file size, prolonging download times.

- Clicking the small triangle-shaped icon in the bottom-right corner of the Property Inspector toggles visibility of the bottom half of the panel, which contains controls that are considered secondary. Hiding these controls is not recommended for the novice so that you don't wasted time hunting around the application when you do need them.

- The Library panel in Flash differs from other panels because you can have multiple instances of it open at the same time—one for each Flash document you have open. While handy, it can also be confusing when you want to access a symbol but are looking at another document's library. For easy identification, the name of the file is appended to the panel title.

- Need a custom user interface element that's not included in Flash installed components? Many custom components can be found on the Macromedia Exchange for you to download and install. The Exchange is located at: http://www.macromedia.com/exchange

1. prepare your site files

Before you begin the design and development of your Web site, it's important to get organized.

In this chapter, we set up a directory structure for all of our files, create and save the Flash file that will be our site movie, and define the color scheme that we'll use throughout the site.

If you haven't already done so, download the asset files for the Timeless Blooms Web site from this book's companion site at www.peachpit.com/vqj/flash.

define folder structure

Before beginning work on our Flash movie, you need to set up a hierarchy of folders and files on your computer's desktop. Within this structure we'll have two discreet folder sets: one for files that we'll use during the development of the site and one for files that will be uploaded to the Web.

From the Windows Explorer or Mac OS's Finder, choose File > New > Folder to create the parent directory. Name the folder timeless_blooms_website.

Open the timeless_blooms_website folder, and create two new folders. Name one site_files and one development_files.

Copy the asset files that you downloaded from this book's companion site into the development_files folder.

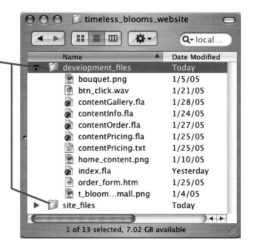

prepare your site files

create your site file

There are two types of Flash files that we'll be working with. A FLA file is the working file you create in Flash and do all of your design and development in. FLA files are opened only with Flash. At the other end of the process, a SWF file is the file you export from Flash and post on the Web. The SWF file is your Flash movie and can be opened by browsers, the Flash Player, and some other applications.

Launch Flash, and choose File > New to create your FLA file.

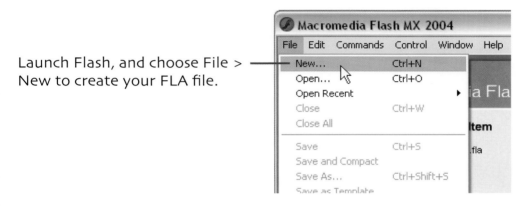

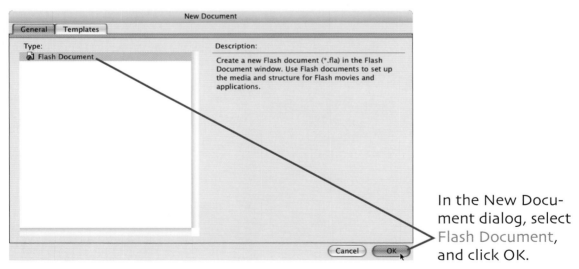

In the New Document dialog, select Flash Document, and click OK.

set canvas properties

Flash defaults to a canvas size of 550 x 400 pixels with a white background. Let's change those settings to fit the needs of our project.

If the Property Inspector is not visible, choose Window > Properties to open it.

In the Property Inspector, click the Document Properties button. This is a bit confusing, since the button is next to a label that reads Size and the text on the button shows the canvas dimensions. Even so, this is the Document Properties button.

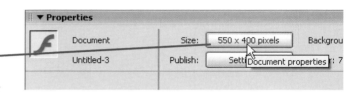

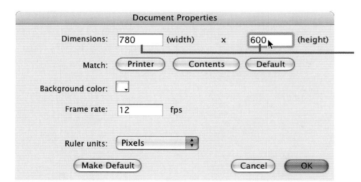

In the Document Properties dialog, enter 780 for the width and 600 for the height.

Next, click the Background Color control to open the Color pop-up pane.

In the Hex Edit text field, select the text #FFFFFF, replace it with # CBE6B2, and press ⏎Enter. Click OK to exit the Document Properties dialog.

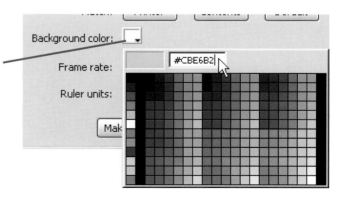

4

save your file

Before going any further, you should save your file. Choose File > Save, or press Ctrl S (Windows) or ⌘ S (Mac).

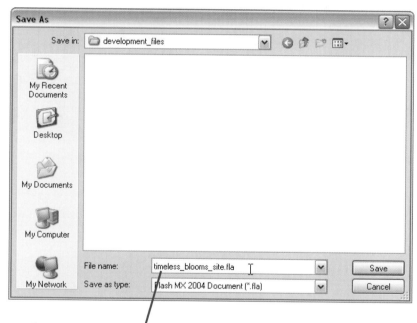

In the Save As dialog, navigate to the development_files folder we created earlier. Enter timeless_blooms_site.fla for the file name, and click Save.

I'll remind you to save your work at the end of each chapter, but you should keep in mind the old edict "Save early and often."

save your color scheme

To make applying our color scheme easier and to speed development, we'll first add the colors for our site to the Color Swatches panel, where they can be easily accessed from any of Flash's color pop-up windows. (See extra bits on Page 8.)

1 If it's not already visible, open the Color Mixer panel (Window > Design Panels > Color Mixer, or press (Shift)(9)). To define the dark green color, enter the hex color value #59803E in the Hex value field at the bottom left of the panel.

2 On the right of the panel's title bar, click the Options menu icon, and choose Add Swatch.

prepare your site files

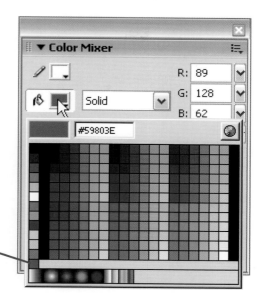

Click one of the color wells in the panel to open the swatches pop-up. Notice that our dark green color has been added to the bottom row of swatches.

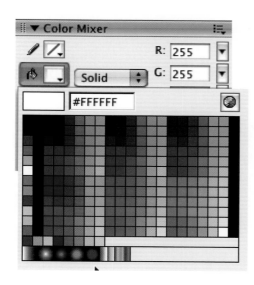

Repeat steps 1 and 2 to add the other colors to the swatches.

Medium Green: #99CC66

Light Green: #CBE6B2

Dark Rose: #94214F

Medium Rose: #CC2C66

Light Rose: #DA7EA1

Dark Yellow: #F1DC95

Light Yellow: #FFE89E

extra bits

save your color scheme p. 6

- Choosing the color scheme for your Web site is an important first step in the design phase of development. Here are a couple tips to keep in mind:

  Limit the number of colors used in your design. Too many colors make the design look chaotic and cluttered.

  Pick two or three main colors, and then use different tints of those colors for highlights, backgrounds, etc.

  If your organization has a color logo or a primary graphic for the home page, pull colors from that existing artwork, or choose colors that are complimentary.

prepare your site files

2. design the layout of your stage

Our first task in Web site development is to design the visual framework within which all of our content will be presented. Think of it as dressing the set of your movie: providing the backdrop, defining different regions, and making it visually attractive. Along the way we'll learn how to use many of Flash's most basic functions. The following are some of the tasks we'll cover:

Import and transform vector artwork.

Save reusable objects, called symbols, for easy modification and smaller movie file size.

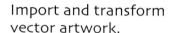

Use drawing tools to create rectangles and lines.

Create and modify special fills, such as linear and radial gradients.

Create layers to organize your file.

Import and mask bitmap images.

set up guides

Using guides in your file helps you define areas of your Stage and eases placement of objects. Let's add some guides before we begin drawing our background.

1 Choose Window > Design Panels > Info to launch the Info panel.

2 Choose View > Rulers to turn on rulers along the left and top of the Stage.

3 Click and drag down a guide from the horizontal (top) ruler. Watch the Info panel; when the cursor location's y value is 60, release the mouse. Drag out two more rules at 80 and 520.

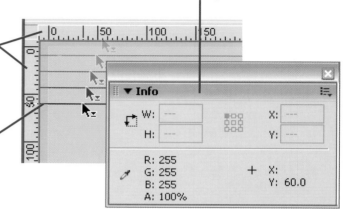

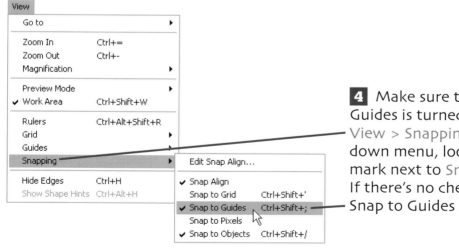

4 Make sure that Snap to Guides is turned on. Choose View > Snapping. In the drop-down menu, look for a check mark next to Snap to Guides. If there's no check mark, click Snap to Guides to turn it on.

design the layout of your stage

draw background

With our Stage divided into different areas, we're ready to begin drawing the objects that will serve as the background for our Web site.

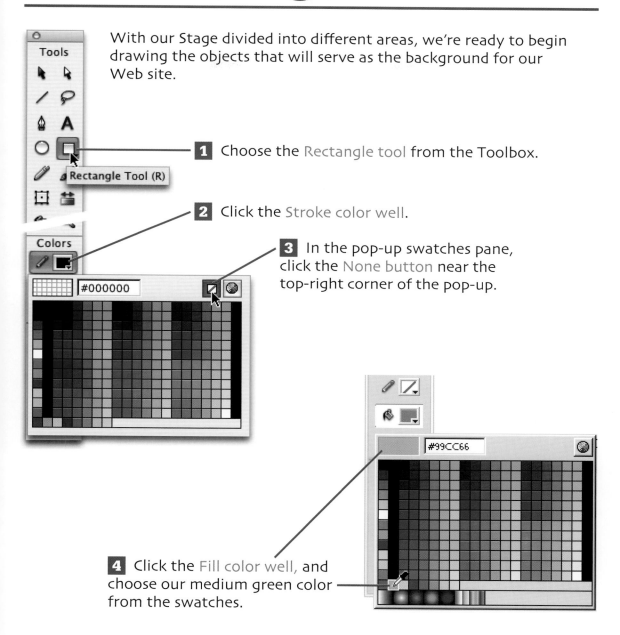

1 Choose the Rectangle tool from the Toolbox.

2 Click the Stroke color well.

3 In the pop-up swatches pane, click the None button near the top-right corner of the pop-up.

4 Click the Fill color well, and choose our medium green color from the swatches.

draw background (cont.)

Position the cursor at the left edge of the Stage on top of the guide you placed at 60. Click and drag out a rectangle to the right edge of the Stage and down to the guide at 80.

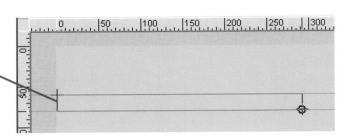

1 You can make adjustments to the rectangle if size or placement is a little off. Choose the Selection tool from the Toolbox, and click the rectangle to select it.

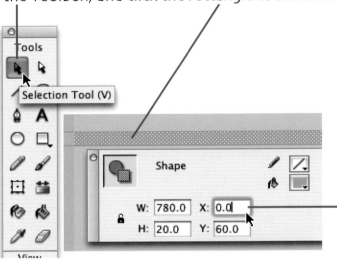

2 In the Property Inspector you can change the values in the width, height, x-position, and y-position text fields. Our rectangle should be 780 x 20 pixels and placed at 0 x-position and 60 y-position.

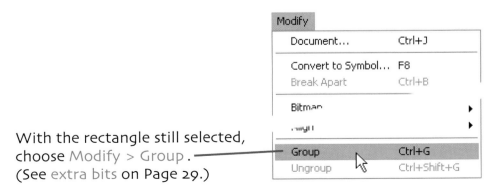

With the rectangle still selected, choose Modify > Group . (See extra bits on Page 29.)

design the layout of your stage

add linear gradient

Next we'll draw some background rectangles with gradient fills to give our Stage some visual interest.

Choose the Rectangle tool. Set the Stroke color well to None, and the Fill color well to any color you choose—we'll change it in a moment.

Click and drag out a rectangle from the top-left corner of the Stage (0,0) to the top of the medium green rectangle and the right edge of the Stage.

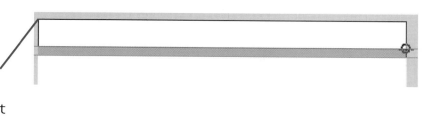

In the Color Mixer, click the Fill Style drop-down menu, and select Linear.

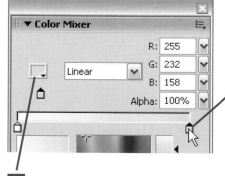

1 You'll see a new control on the panel— a gradient definition bar with pointers below the bar indicating each color in the gradient. Click the pointer on the right end of the gradient definition bar.

2 The color represented by the pointer will now appear in the Color Proxy color well next to the Fill Style menu.

add linear gradient (cont.)

3 Click the Color Proxy color well to open the swatches pop-up. Choose our light green color.

4 The pointer on the left of the gradient definition bar should already be set to white. If it's not, change it now.

5 Choose the Paint Bucket tool, and click on the solid-filled rectangle you drew earlier.

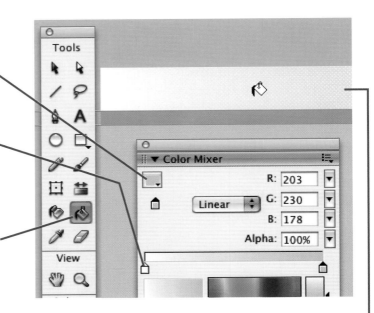

6 Now the rectangle has a white-to-green gradient fill. It's not in the direction we want, so we'll change that next.

edit linear gradient

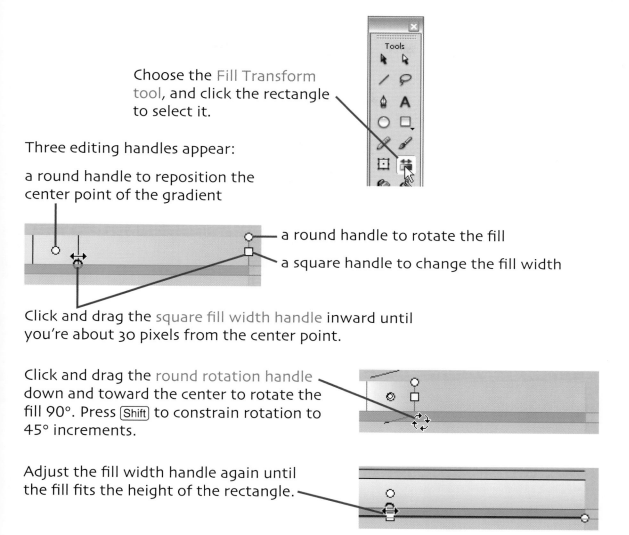

Choose the Fill Transform tool, and click the rectangle to select it.

Three editing handles appear:

a round handle to reposition the center point of the gradient

a round handle to rotate the fill

a square handle to change the fill width

Click and drag the square fill width handle inward until you're about 30 pixels from the center point.

Click and drag the round rotation handle down and toward the center to rotate the fill 90°. Press [Shift] to constrain rotation to 45° increments.

Adjust the fill width handle again until the fill fits the height of the rectangle.

Click and drag the center point handle down a bit to lower the halfway point of the transition, making the rectangle have more white along the top.

Select the rectangle with the Selection tool, and choose Modify > Group .

design the layout of your stage

create radial gradients

Now let's draw the final rectangle, which will make up our Stage's background.

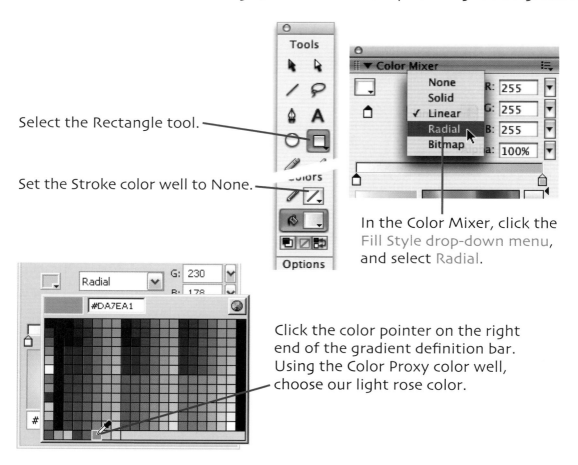

Select the Rectangle tool.

Set the Stroke color well to None.

In the Color Mixer, click the Fill Style drop-down menu, and select Radial.

Click the color pointer on the right end of the gradient definition bar. Using the Color Proxy color well, choose our light rose color.

Now, move the cursor to the left edge of the Stage and the bottom of the solid green rectangle (0,80). Click and drag out a rectangle to the bottom-right corner of the Stage.

Again, the gradient is there, but it's not quite what we want. Let's change it.

In order to see a large part of the Work Area surrounding the Stage, choose View > Magnification > 25%.

Select the Fill Transform tool, and click the rectangle to select it. Four editing handles appear:

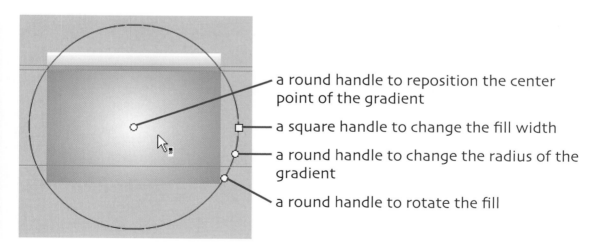

a round handle to reposition the center point of the gradient

a square handle to change the fill width

a round handle to change the radius of the gradient

a round handle to rotate the fill

design the layout of your stage

radial gradients (cont.)

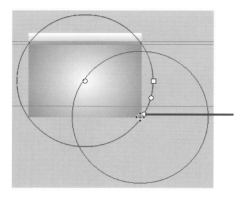

Click and drag the round center point handle to the bottom-right corner of the Stage.

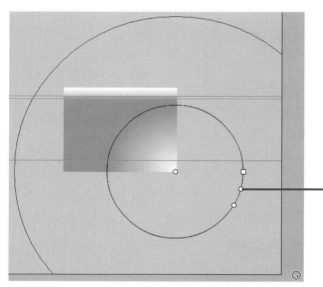

Click and drag the middle round handle, enlarging the circle beyond the top-left corner of the Stage.

Change the view back to the magnification you like to work at.
Select the rectangle, and group it (Modify > Group).

design the layout of your stage

reusable graphics

Since our background is the same throughout our Web site, we can reuse what we've drawn multiple times. To do that, we need to convert our three rectangles into one reusable symbol. When a symbol is used on the Stage, it's called an instance. (See extra bits on Page 29.)

To select the three rectangles, choose Edit > Select All , or press Ctrl A (Windows) or ⌘ A (Mac).

Choose Modify > Convert to Symbol , or press F8 .

Edit	
Undo Group	⌘Z
Repeat Group	⌘Y
Cut	⌘X
Copy	⌘C
Paste in Center	⌘V
Paste in Place	⇧⌘V
Clear	⌫
Duplicate	⌘D
Select All	⌘A
Deselect All	⇧⌘A

Modify	
Document...	Ctrl+J
Convert to Symbol...	F8
Break Apart	Ctrl+B

In the Convert to Symbol dialog, name the symbol background.

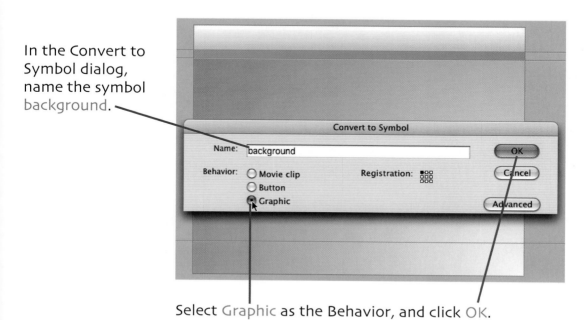

Convert to Symbol

Name: background

Behavior: ○ Movie clip Registration: ▦
○ Button
● Graphic

OK
Cancel
Advanced

Select Graphic as the Behavior, and click OK.

reusable graphics (cont.)

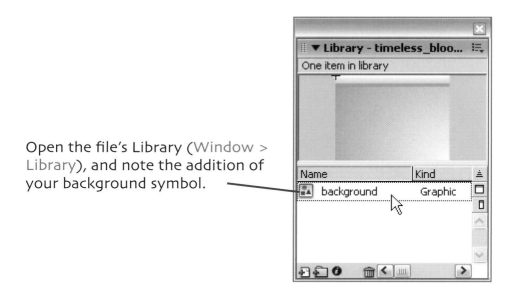

Open the file's Library (Window > Library), and note the addition of your background symbol.

You'll also notice in the Property Inspector that new controls have appeared, reflecting the selection of the symbol instance.

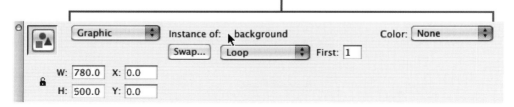

20   **design the layout of your stage**

edit a symbol

Let's edit the symbol to add a line. (See extra bits on Page 30.)

Double-click the symbol to enter symbol-editing mode. The Info bar above the Stage shows what container you're editing.

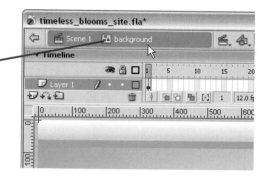

1 From the Toolbox, select the Line tool.

2 In the Property Inspector, click the Stroke color well, and choose our dark rose color.

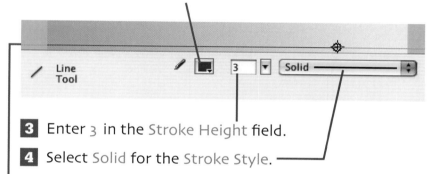

3 Enter 3 in the Stroke Height field.

4 Select Solid for the Stroke Style.

5 Click and drag out a line on the guide we placed at y-location 520 and drag from the left edge of the Stage to the right edge.

Press Ctrl ; (Windows) or ⌘ ; (Mac) to turn off guides.

It appears that the line isn't there, but it is; it's just underneath the rose-gradient rectangle. We'll fix that in the next section.

design the layout of your stage

organize with layers

Layers, as we outlined before, are great organizational tools. They control the stacking order of objects in your movie. We're going to create a new layer above the current one and move our hidden line there.

First, let's rename the current layer to reflect what it contains.

If the Timeline isn't already visible, choose Window > Timeline. In the Layers column, double-click the text Layer 1 to select it. Enter bkgd rects for the layer name, and press (←Enter).

1 Click the Insert Layer button at the bottom of the Layers column. A new layer named Layer 2 appears in the layers list.

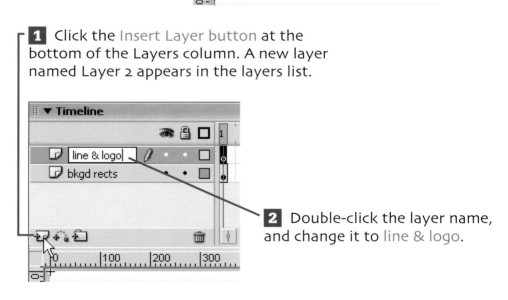

2 Double-click the layer name, and change it to line & logo.

move between layers

Moving objects from one layer to another in Flash works differently than in most drawing applications. Here's how it's done.

With the Selection tool, click in the Work Area to the left of the Stage, and drag a selection marquee around the area where you know your line is. Turn on Show Guides (View > Guides > Show Guides) if you need a visual clue of the line's location.

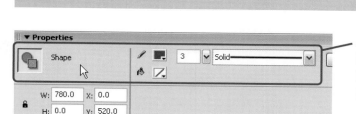

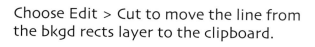

Although you still can't see the line, you'll know it's selected because of the feedback in the Property Inspector.

Choose Edit > Cut to move the line from the bkgd rects layer to the clipboard.

In the Timeline, click the line & logo layer to make it the active layer.

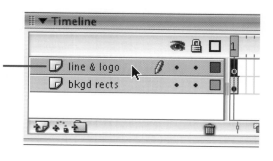

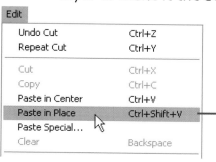

Choose Edit > Paste in Place to paste the line into the exact same location, just on the different layer.

Finally! We can see our line now. It was a lot of effort, but isn't it a beautiful line?

import vector art

Sometimes you'll need to add artwork that has been created in another application or file format to your Flash movie. Here, we're going to import logo artwork that's been provided in a Macromedia Fireworks' PNG file that contains vectors (editable paths) and bitmap objects (images).

Choose File > Import > Import to Library to insert the logo file into your movie as a symbol.

In the Import to Library dialog, locate the file t_blooms logo_small.png, which you downloaded from this book's companion Web site and copied into the site's development_files folder. Select the file, and click Open (Windows) or Import to Library (Mac).

In the Fireworks PNG Import Settings dialog that appears, set the following options:

File Structure: Import as movie clip and retain layers

Objects: Keep all paths editable

Text: Either choice will work in this instance because all the text in the logo has been converted to vector paths to avoid font issues.

Do not check the Import as a single flattened bitmap check box.

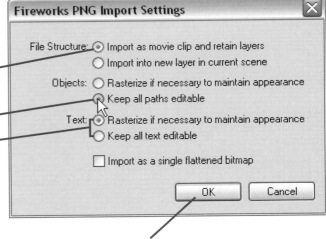

Click OK to close the Fireworks PNG Import Settings dialog. Now the logo has been added to the Library.

design the layout of your stage

organize symbols

If the Library panel for your file is not visible, choose Window > Library . In the Library panel, you'll see three new listings—two bitmaps (which were included in the logo file) and a folder named Fireworks Objects that contains the new logo symbol. Let's take a moment to begin organizing our symbols, which will save us time and headaches later.

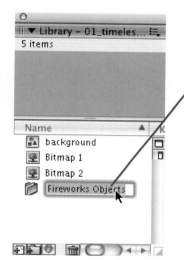

Double-click the folder name to select the text Fireworks Objects. Enter t_blooms logo, and press (←Enter).

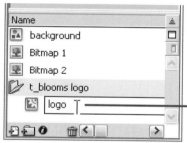

Double-click the folder icon to reveal the folder's contents. Double-click the symbol name to select it. Enter logo, and press (←Enter).

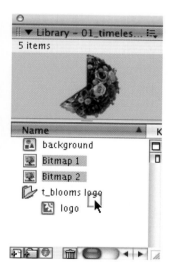

(Shift)-click to select the two bitmap symbols in the Library panel. Click and drag the symbols into the t_blooms logo folder. Double-click the t_blooms logo folder icon to collapse the folder view.

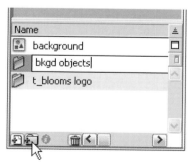

Click the New Folder button at the bottom of the Library panel to add a new folder to the list. Name the folder bkgd objects. Drag the other objects in the list into the new folder.

transform objects

Objects on your Stage, even symbols, can have different transformations applied to them. Transformations such as Scale, Rotate, and Skew are applied with the Free Transform tool. (See extra bits on Page 30.)

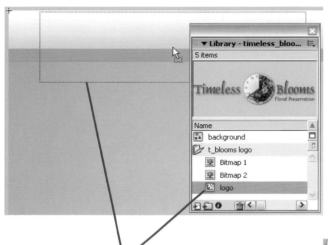

Confirm that you're still editing inside the background symbol. If not, double-click the symbol on the Stage to enter editing mode. Click to select the line & logo layer in the Timeline.

In the Library panel, navigate to the symbol we named logo. Click the symbol, and drag it onto the Stage near the top-left corner.

The logo is a bit bigger than we need, so we'll scale the instance down. With the instance still selected, choose the Free Transform tool. Eight transformation handles appear around the instance's bounding box.

Press and hold [Alt][Shift] (Windows) or [Option][Shift] (Mac). Click and drag the bottom-right transformation handle toward the center of the logo symbol instance. Release the mouse when Floral Preservation is just on top of the solid green background.

Choose the Selection tool to set the transformation.

import bitmap image

With the logo placed and sized, we're going to balance the design by placing an image in the bottom-right corner of the Stage.

In the Timeline, add a new layer to your background symbol. Name the layer bouquet.

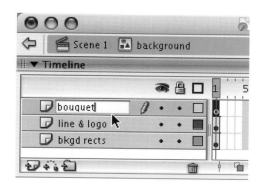

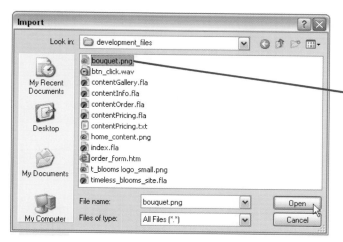

Choose File > Import > Import to Stage. In the Import dialog, navigate to the development_ files folder. Select the file bouquet.png, and click Open.

The bouquet image is placed on the Stage. Drag it to the bottom-right corner until only a little more than one fourth of the image is within the Stage area.

design the layout of your stage

add masking layer

Having the bouquet image hanging off of the Stage won't affect the display of the final exported movie, but it is distracting as we continue developing the site. We'll use a Layer Mask to hide the unused parts.

Add a new layer and name it bouquet_mask.

Select the Rectangle tool. From the right edge of the Stage, above the image, drag out a rectangle that covers the area of the image that is on the Stage.

Right-click (Windows) or Ctrl-click (Mac) the layer bouquet_mask. Choose Mask from the drop-down menu.

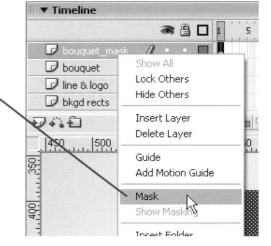

The overhanging part of the image is no longer visible!

Our background framework is complete, and now we're ready to add text. Save your file.

extra bits

draw background p. 12

- In Flash, when an object is over-lapping another, the overlapped section of the existing object is deleted. This makes adjustments such as nudging new objects into place a nightmare. To avoid this, you can either create a new layer for every object you draw or group an object as soon as you draw it. I prefer grouping.

reusable graphics p. 19

- Using symbols in Flash provides two main benefits: reduced file size and ease of editing.

  When you create a symbol and place instances of that symbol on the Stage, your movie's file size is reduced because no matter how many times you use it, the code required to define it is only included in the file once. Each instance just points to the symbol and describes any modifications to that symbol, such as transparency or size.

  Modifying work later is also much easier. Imagine that you've placed 100 blue squares (not instances of a blue square symbol) throughout your movie, and then you decide to change the color. You have to find and change all 100 squares. But if you made a symbol of a blue square and placed 100 instances, you only have to change the symbol, and the 100 instances are updated automatically.

extra bits

edit a symbol p. 21

- When you have an object on the Stage that is a container for other objects (groups, symbols and text boxes) you can just double-click it to "get inside" and edit the contents.

- To exit the editing mode of the container, you can double-click outside the bounds of the container.

- Sometimes when you draw a line in Flash, it isn't placed at the top of the object stacking order like you'd expect it to be. Instead, it is placed behind other objects. Defying the standard convention that a new object is stacked above existing objects on the same layer, Flash stacks lines based on a mysterious formula involving the line's color that only programmers could come up with!

  You can do one of two things to make the line appear where you want it: group the line, which moves it to the top of the stack; or move the line to a layer above the current layer.

transform objects p. 26

- When you're scaling vector objects (those drawn in Flash or imported, as in the logo file) you can increase or decrease the size without negative effect. However, if you're working with a bitmap image, you'll want to avoid enlarging it. An enlarged bitmap has to be resampled and can become distorted or fuzzy. It's best to open the image in an image editor such as Adobe Photoshop or Macromedia Fireworks and scale it to the size you need.

design the layout of your stage

3. add and style text

With the graphic elements of the background in place, we can now add some text. We begin by adding and manipulating static text. (In later chapters we'll do more advanced things with text.) In this chapter we'll do the following:

Use text for graphic appeal.

Add and manipulate fixed-width text boxes.

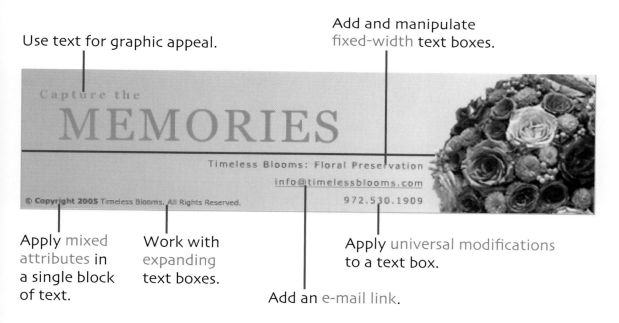

Apply mixed attributes in a single block of text.

Work with expanding text boxes.

Add an e-mail link.

Apply universal modifications to a text box.

add a single line of text

First we'll add company and copyright information to the background symbol so that it will be visible throughout the site.

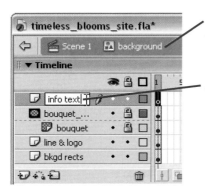

In the Edit bar, confirm that you're still editing inside the background symbol. If not, double-click the instance on the Stage to enter editing mode.

Add a new layer, and name it info text.

Select the Text tool from the Toolbox.

In the Property Inspector, set attributes as follows:

Choose Static Text from the Text Type menu.

Select Verdana for the Font.

Enter 10 for Font Size.

Click the Text (Fill) color control, and choose our dark green color from the Color pop-up pane.

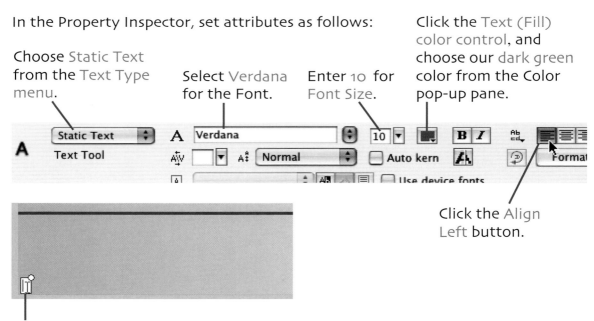

Click the Align Left button.

Click the Text tool in the bottom-left corner of the Stage. An empty text box with a blinking insertion point appears. The round Resize handle denotes that the text box does not have a fixed width and will expand horizontally to hold all the text entered.

Type © Copyright 2005 Timeless Blooms. All Rights Reserved.

Click on the Stage to close the text box.

Let's change the attributes of some of the text in this text box to add emphasis to the copyright notice.

Choose the Selection tool from the Toolbox, and double-click the text box to edit the text inside. To select the text © Copyright 2005, click to the left of the copyright symbol and drag past the 5.

With the text now selected, click the Bold Style button in the Property Inspector.

add and style text

fixed-width text

Click on the Stage to close and deselect the text box. In the Property Inspector, change the Font Size to 12 , and click to deselect the Bold Style button.

With the Text tool selected, click and drag out a text box to the left of the bouquet image and just below the line.

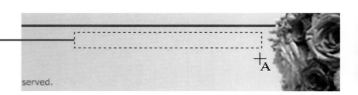

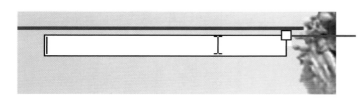

An empty text box appears. The square Resize handle denotes that the box has a fixed width, meaning text will wrap onto new lines rather than stay on one line and stretch the text box.

Enter Timeless Blooms: Floral Preservation. If the text wraps to a second line, click and drag the Resize handle until the text fits on one line.

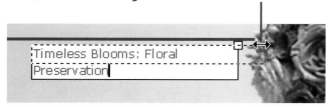

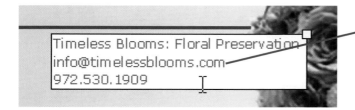

Press ⏎Enter, and type info@timelessblooms.com.

Press ⏎Enter, and type 972.530.1909 .

Choose the Selection tool from the Toolbox to close the text box.

add and style text

change a text box

You can make universal changes to all of the text in a text box by selecting the box and making changes in the Property Inspector.

If the text box is not still selected, click it with the Selection tool. Click the Align Right button in the Property Inspector.

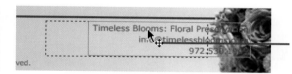

If some of your text is on top of the bouquet image, drag the text box to the left.

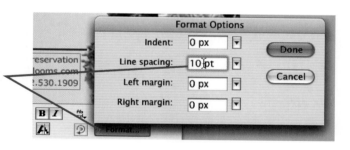

To spread out the lines of text, click the Format button on the Property Inspector. In the Format Options dialog, enter 10 for Line Spacing, and click OK.

Now let's spread the text out a bit. Enter 2 in the Property Inspector's Character Spacing text field.

If the last step caused the text on the first line to wrap, double-click the text box and drag out the Resize handle. Use the Selection tool to reposition the text box away from the bouquet.

add an e-mail link

We want contacting Timeless Blooms to be convenient for viewers of the Web site. Let's add a link to the e-mail address that will automatically launch a new e-mail message in the viewer's e-mail application.

Select the Text tool, and click inside the text box to open the box for editing. Select the text info@timelessblooms. com.

Choose Edit > Copy to copy the e-mail address to the clipboard.

In the Property Inspector's URL Link field type mailto: and then paste the e-mail address into the field. Make sure there is no space between the colon and the pasted address.

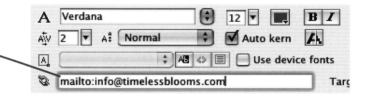

Press ⏎Enter to set the URL attribute.

The standard convention on the Web is that clickable text is underlined. A dashed line appears under the e-mail address, but this is only a visual clue inside the Flash authoring environment that the text has a link; it won't be visible in the exported movie.

We need to add an underline that will display in our movie. Flash doesn't provide an Under-line style for text, so we'll create our own. With the Line tool, draw a line below the address. Set the line height to .25 , and apply the medium green color to it.

add and style text

add graphic text

As our final step in designing the background of our Stage, we need to add a little more text. Unlike the other text we'll have in the site, this text serves a graphic purpose rather than informational—it conveys the theme of the business that this Web site promotes.

Choose the Text tool, and set the following attributes in the Property Inspector:

Color: Light Rose

Font: Georgia   Size: 16   Style: Bold

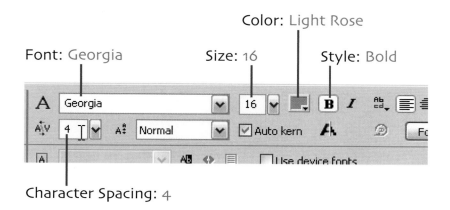

Character Spacing: 4

Click on the Stage, and type Capture the.

Click on the Stage to close and deselect the text box.

In the Property Inspector, set the Font Size to 64. Click the Bold Style button to deselect it.

add graphic text (cont.)

Click the Stage to create another text box and type MEMORIES.

With the Selection tool, position the two text blocks so that they approximate the arrangement shown here.

In the Edit bar above the Stage, click Scene 1 to exit symbol-editing mode.

Save your file.

Our Stage's background is now complete, and we can begin working on the sections and animations in our site.

4. use the timeline to organize your site

As you've probably guessed, the Timeline is used for animation in your Flash movie. But it also serves other purposes.

A frame can represent not only a fluid moment in an animation as an object slides across the Stage, but also a static point in the movie to which we navigate within our movie. In Flash development we use frames for animation, as reference points, and as organizational tools to ease development.

In this chapter, we learn the basics of working with different types of frames, naming frames for easy reference, and controlling frame playback. We'll learn to:

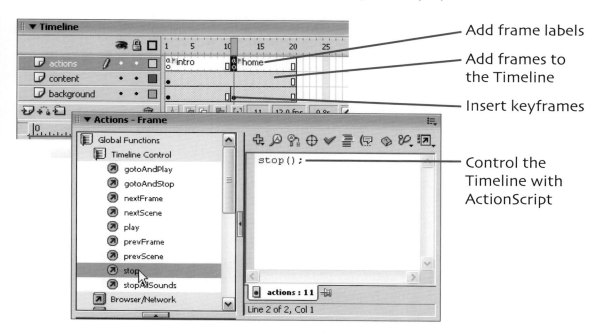

Add frame labels

Add frames to the Timeline

Insert keyframes

Control the Timeline with ActionScript

create the home page

Our home page is looking a little bare. Before we move on to working with frames, let's add some content.

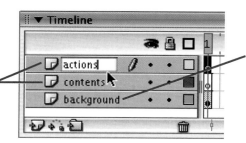

Add one new layer named contents and another layer named actions.

In the Timeline, rename the existing layer background.

From the vertical ruler on the left of the Stage, drag out a guide—lining it up with the 12 o'clock position on the clock in our logo.

Click the contents layer to make it the active layer.

Choose File > Import > Import to Stage . In the Import dialog, navigate to the development_files folder. Select the file home_content.png, and click Open.

In the Fireworks PNG Import Settings dialog that appears, set the following options:

File Structure: Import as movie clip and retain layers

Objects: Keep all paths editable

Text: Either choice will work in this instance because there is no text in the file.

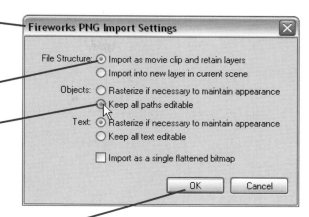

Click OK. The image appears on the Stage.

With the Selection tool, drag the graphic into place, aligning the first line of text with the vertical guide.

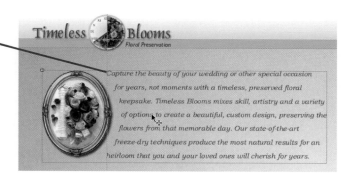

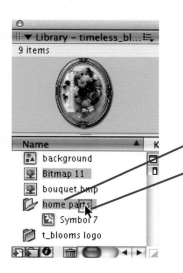

In the Library panel, rename the Fireworks Objects folder home parts. Double-click the folder to expand it.

Drag the bitmap symbol of the framed bouquet into the home parts folder.

Rename the movie clip symbol home content.

To save time and space, I won't instruct you to organize symbols throughout the rest of this book. However, keep in mind the organizing techniques we covered in Chapter 2.

use the timeline to organize your site   **41**

add frames

Currently we have only one frame in our movie. The frames that you see in the Timeline now are available frames, but they're not yet defined. We'll define more frames to help us organize our movie and prepare it for adding animations in the next chapter. (See extra bits on Page 49.)

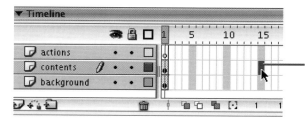

In the Timeline for the contents layer, click the empty cell beneath the 15 marker in the Timeline Header.

Choose Insert > Timeline > Frame , or press F5 .

Notice four things:

The Playhead has moved to display Frame 15.

Flash has automatically created frames 2 through 14.

Our background is not visible.

The contents of the layer's keyframe at Frame 1 are displayed now in Frame 15.

use the timeline to organize your site

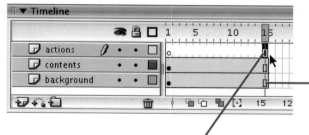

We have no background because Frame 15 has not been defined for the background layer. Add the frame now, repeating the steps you took to create the frame for the contents layer.

Insert Frame 15 for the actions layer.

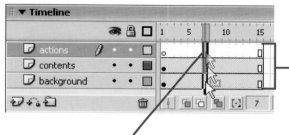

We now have 15 frames in all of our layers. Let's add five more frames to all the layers at once.

In the actions layer, click one of the frames and drag down to the background layer, selecting the frame in all three layers. Choose Insert > Timeline > Frame five times, or press F5 five times.

insert keyframes

Now we're going to add keyframes, which will let us change content from one point in the Timeline to another.

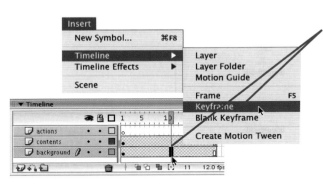

Click Frame 11 in the background layer, and choose Insert > Timeline > Keyframe.

We do this because later we're going to add an animated background that plays when our movie first loads. Keyframe 1 will contain the animated background, and Keyframe 11 will contain the static background we've already created.

In the Library panel, select the symbol background.

On the right of the panel's title bar, click the Options menu icon, and choose Duplicate.

In the Duplicate Symbol dialog that appears, name the symbol animated background.

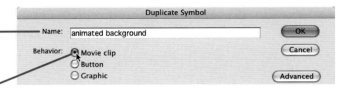

Choose Movie Clip for the Behavior, and click OK.

The animated background will have most of the same objects in the same place as the regular background, so we want the two different symbols to be placed identically. We can ensure this by swapping symbols.

Click Frame 1 in the Timeline Header to move the Playhead to Frame 1, or click and drag the Playhead to Frame 1.

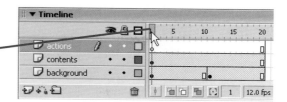

With the Selection tool, click on the Stage to select the background symbol. (Click outside the bounds of the home content symbol so you don't select it by mistake.)

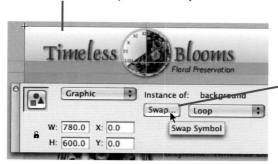

Click the Swap Symbol button in the Property Inspector.

In the Swap Symbol dialog, select animated background, and click OK.

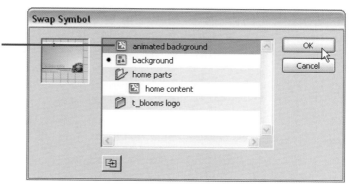

In the Property Inspector, click the Symbol Behavior drop-down menu, and choose Movie Clip.

use the timeline to organize your site

add frame labels

Frame labels let you name frames for logical reference. (See extra bits on Page 50.)

In the Timeline, click Keyframe 1 of the actions layer.

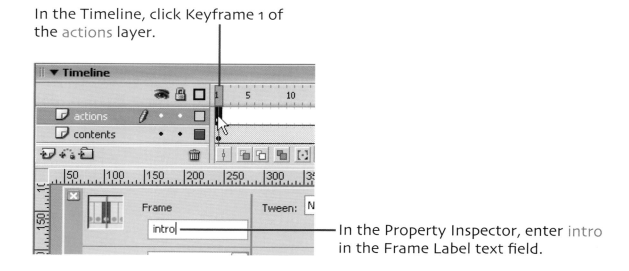

In the Property Inspector, enter intro in the Frame Label text field.

Note that Keyframe 1 in the Timeline now displays a flag signifying that it has a label. Also, because this keyframe has a span of 9 more frames, Flash has room to display the frame label in the Timeline.

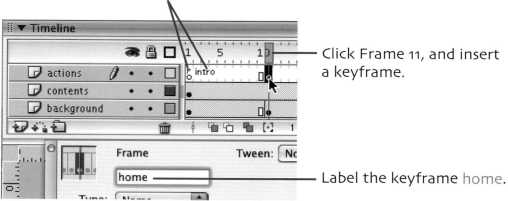

Click Frame 11, and insert a keyframe.

Label the keyframe home.

control the timeline

By default, the Playhead in a Flash movie plays through all the frames in a time-line and loops endlessly unless you tell it otherwise. We use Actions applied to frames and buttons to control the Playhead. (See extra bits on Page 50.)

We'll stop the Playhead in keyframe intro by adding a Stop Action.

If the Actions panel is not visible, choose
Window > Development Panels > Actions .

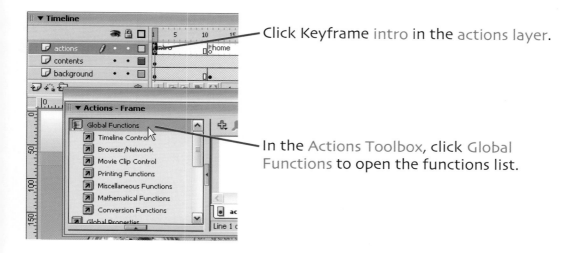

Click Keyframe intro in the actions layer.

In the Actions Toolbox, click Global Functions to open the functions list.

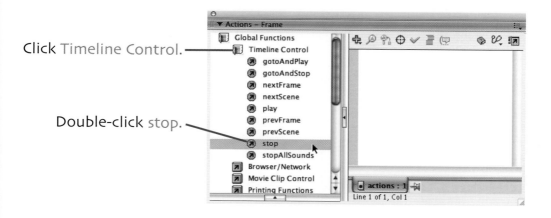

Click Timeline Control.

Double-click stop.

control the timeline (cont.)

Note two things:

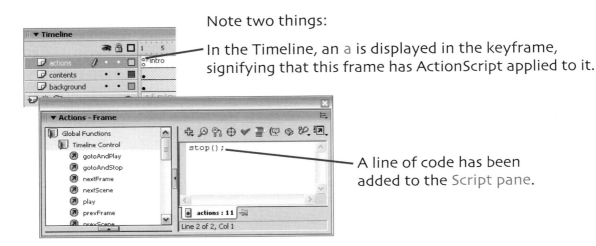

In the Timeline, an a is displayed in the keyframe, signifying that this frame has ActionScript applied to it.

A line of code has been added to the Script pane.

Congratulations! You've just used ActionScript to control your movie!

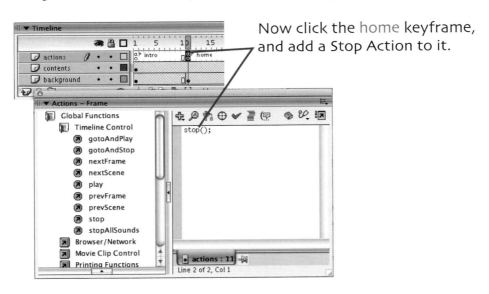

Now click the home keyframe, and add a Stop Action to it.

Save your file.

use the timeline to organize your site

extra bits

add frames p. 42

- Every Flash movie contains multiple timelines. Every scene has a main Timeline, and each symbol has its own independent Timeline, as you saw when editing our background. Within a scene or symbol, each layer also has its own Timeline. In complex Flash movies like the one we're building, it is best to use the scene's main Timeline for organizational and reference purposes only. Use the timelines available inside symbols for animation.

  We define two kinds of frames in a Timeline—basic frames and keyframes. Keyframes are where we do all of our work. Whenever you want to manually change the contents of a frame, you must do it in a keyframe. Basic frames make up what is known as a keyframe's span—the frames between that keyframe and the next. Frames act merely as clones of the preceding keyframe.

- By default, the first frame in any Timeline is a keyframe.

- If you change an object in a frame, you're actually making that change to the keyframe and all frames in its span. It can be incredibly painful to make a change in a particular frame, thinking that you're only changing that frame, and 30 minutes later realize you actually changed 15 frames, so be careful that you are always editing in a keyframe.

- In the Timeline, keyframes are marked with a bullet. A solid bullet signifies that the keyframe has contents, and a hollow bullet signifies an empty keyframe. The final frame in a keyframe span is marked with a hollow rectangle.

use the timeline to organize your site

extra bits

add frame labels p. 46

- When you're working with multiple timelines throughout your movie, moving objects from place to place, and adding or removing frames as you work, it can be difficult to remember what frame number holds an object you're looking for or want to link to from elsewhere in the movie.

  If you have objects on a keyframe at Frame 70 but then add 8 frames to the Timeline, your keyframe is now at 78. If buttons or other movie clips are linking to that keyframe by number, you have to remember to search them out and change the link from 70 to 78. But if you've labeled the keyframe important_frame, that doesn't change, and all the pointers in your movie are still correct.

- It's a common practice in Flash development to add frames after a keyframe just to make enough room to display the frame label, making it easy to locate frames during development. In our Timeline so far, the only frames that will actually be seen by viewers are frames 1 and 11; the other frames will be bypassed. You'll understand this more when we add animations and navigation controlled with ActionScript later in the book.

control the timeline p. 47

- ActionScript is Flash's powerful scripting language that allows developers to control playback, establish complex interactions, and even develop Flash-based applications. While it is considered an easy language to use, those of us who are not programmers don't necessarily think so.

- In this book we'll avoid too much scripting by using very simple Actions (chunks of ActionScript) and Behaviors (prepackaged Actions) to control our timelines and provide navigation.

- To help keep us organized, we add an empty layer named actions to each of our timelines—using the layer only for labeling and Action-Script. This helps us keep the mechanics of our movie separate from the content and lets us visually track frame properties easily.

5. add animation to your web site

By now you might be thinking "Enough with the boring stuff. I want to make things fly across the Stage." If that's the case, then you're going to love this chapter. Here we add the pizzazz to our Web site that separates it from an ordinary HTML-based site. In the following pages we'll do the following:

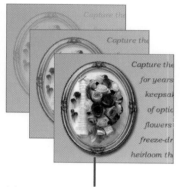

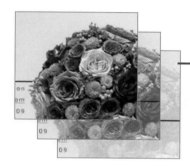

Add a Transition effect to make the bouquet image fade-in slowly at just the right moment

Pause playback of our movie using ActionScript

Add a Behavior to move the Playhead from one frame to another

Use a motion tween for a subtle fade-in of our content

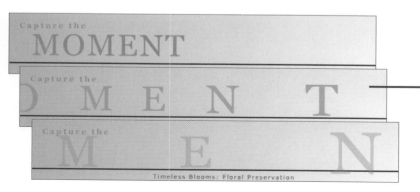

Use Timeline Effects to build a complex animation where text zooms in and out, changing words as it goes

create a motion

We sometimes use animation in subtle ways, rather than hit the viewer over the head with our brilliance. In this step, we'll create a very short fade-in of our home page's content. We do this so that when our movie loads, the content doesn't just pop onto the screen. We see this technique often on web sites and don't even realize there's animation, we just experience a smooth reveal of the contents.

To create the animation, we set up our content's beginning state and ending state, and then instruct Flash to create, or tween, the intermediate frames. (See extra bits on Page 77.)

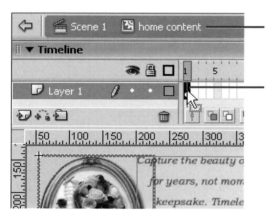

With the Selection tool, double-click the home content symbol to edit it.

In the Timeline, click Keyframe 1 of Layer 1 to select all of its contents—the image and the text. Choose Modify > Convert to Symbol, or press F8.

In the Convert to Symbol dialog, name the symbol fade contents, and choose the Graphic behavior. Click OK.

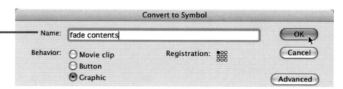

Insert a keyframe in Frame 12 (Insert > Timeline > Keyframe).

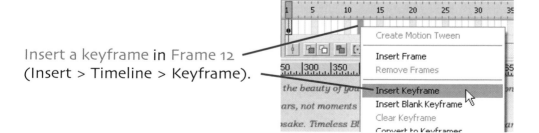

Click to select Keyframe 1.

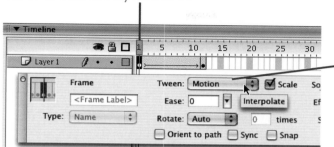

In the Property Inspector, click the Interpolation drop-down menu (labeled Tween), and choose Motion.

Notice in the Timeline that an arrow is displayed from Keyframe 1 to Keyframe 12, signifying an applied tween.

The symbol appears to be selected, but the Property Inspector is displaying the frame properties, not the symbol. Click the symbol to change the contents of the Property Inspector.

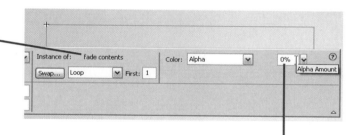

In the Property Inspector, click the Color Styles drop-down menu, and choose Alpha. Set the Alpha Amount to 0%. The symbol is no longer visible.

Move the Playhead to a couple of different frames between 1 and 12 and notice the incremental changes in transparency.

That's it. You just created your first tweened animation.

add animation to your web site

play animation in flash

You can preview an animation inside the Flash application. Let's watch the animation we just created. Choose Control > Play , or press ⏎Enter.

You may think the animation is a bit jerky. This happens when there are too many frames in an animation and the eye is able to distinguish too many of the individual static images. Let's shorten the animation to make that less noticeable.

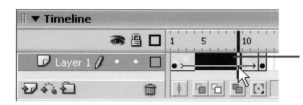

In the Timeline, click a frame and drag to the right—selecting approximately 6 frames. Be sure you don't drag past Frame 11 and select the keyframe.

Choose Edit > Timeline > Remove Frames , or press Shift F5 . The animation is shortened, and Flash re-interpolates the tweened frames.

Press ⏎Enter to view the animation now. You should see an appreciably smoother animation.

Remember that the Playhead loops endlessly unless you tell it otherwise. To make this animation play only once, do the following:

1 Add a new layer to the Timeline, and name it actions.

2 Insert a keyframe at the same frame position as the final keyframe in the animation. If you deleted 6 frames, it will be Frame 6.

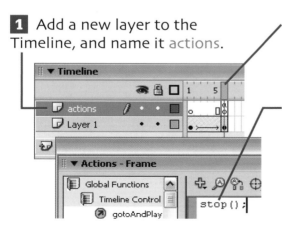

3 In the Actions panel, enter stop(); in the Script pane, or add the action using the steps we used previously.

4 Click Scene 1 in the Edit bar, or double-click the Stage to exit symbol-editing mode.

complex animation

As easy as creating the tweened animation was, Flash goes one major step further. Timeline Effects allow quick and easy creation of some of the most common animation techniques developers want to create.

We'll use a series of Timeline Effects to create an animated introduction in which our graphic text zooms in and out, changing from Capture the Love to Capture the Moment and finally to Capture the Memories. (See extra bits on Page 77.)

In Keyframe 1 of the background layer, double-click the animated background symbol to edit it.

In the Layers column of the Timeline, select the info text layer. Add two new layers. Name the first layer animated text and the second actions.

In Keyframe 1 of the info text layer, select the MEMORIES text box. Choose Edit > Cut to move the text to the clipboard. Select the animated text layer, and choose Edit > Paste in Place .

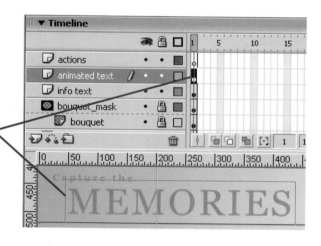

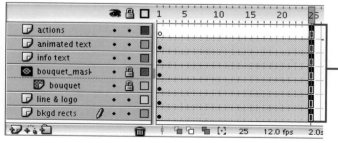

In the actions layer, click Frame 25 , and drag down to layer bkgd rects, selecting the frame in all of the layers. Press F5 to add frames to the layers.

complex animation (cont.)

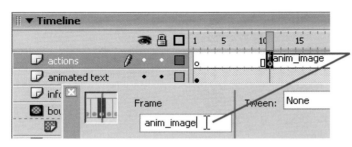

Add a keyframe in Frame 11 of the actions layer, and label the frame anim_image.

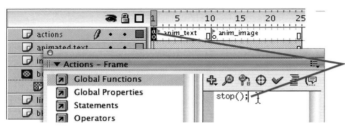

Select Keyframe 1, and enter stop(); in the Actions panel Script pane. In the Property Inspector, label the frame anim_text.

1 In Frame 11 of the animated text layer, add a keyframe.

2 Move the Playhead back to the anim_text keyframe.

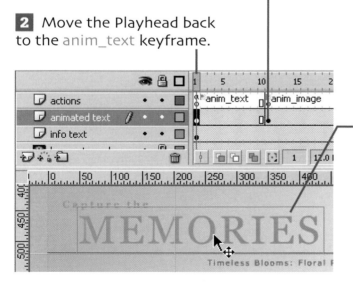

3 Select the MEMORIES text box.

Choose Modify > Convert to Symbol, or press F8. In the Convert to Symbol dialog, name the symbol text animation. Select Movie Clip as the Behavior, and click OK.

add animation to your web site

Double-click the new symbol to edit it. Add three layers to the Timeline. Rename Layer 4 actions. We won't worry about naming the other layers because Flash renames layers when you apply Timeline Effects.

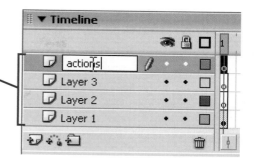

We want a slight delay in our movie before the animation starts. With our movie's frame rate of 12 frames per second, we can create a one second delay by starting our animation on Frame 13.

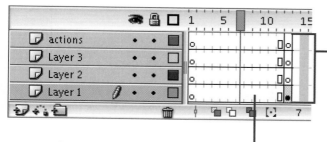

Click Frame 13 in the actions layer, and drag down to Layer 1, selecting the frame in all four layers. Choose Modify > Timeline > Convert to Keyframes, or press F6.

Move the Playhead to any of the previous frames, and delete the MEMORIES text box from Layer 1—deleting it from Keyframe 1's entire span.

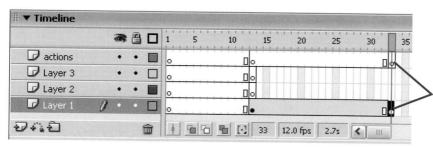

Each segment of our animation is going to be 20 frames long. So let's skip to Frame 33 and insert keyframes in the actions layer and Layer 1 for the start of our second segment.

add animation to your web site

copy and paste frames

Let's copy the text from Layer 1 to the other layers to set up our animation.

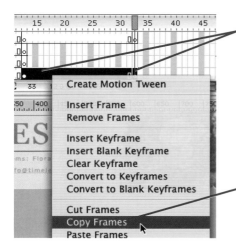

Select Frame 13 in Layer 1. [Shift]-click Frame 33 to select the range of frames.

Right-click (Windows) or [Control]-click (Mac), and choose Copy Frames from the drop-down menu.

Select Frame 13 in Layer 2. Right-click (Windows) or [Control]-click (Mac) and choose Paste Frames. Select Frame 13 in Layer 3, and paste the frames again.

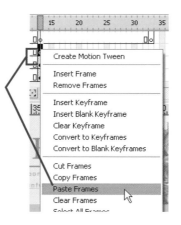

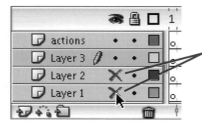

In the Layers column of the Timeline, click in the Eye column in Layer 1 and Layer 2 to hide them. A red X should appear in the column to signify the layers are hidden.

add timeline effects

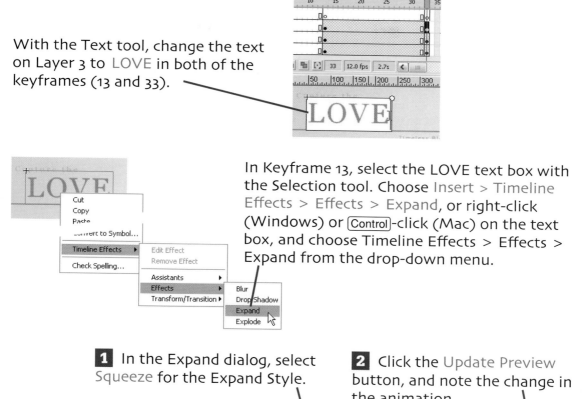

With the Text tool, change the text on Layer 3 to LOVE in both of the keyframes (13 and 33).

In Keyframe 13, select the LOVE text box with the Selection tool. Choose Insert > Timeline Effects > Effects > Expand, or right-click (Windows) or Control-click (Mac) on the text box, and choose Timeline Effects > Effects > Expand from the drop-down menu.

1 In the Expand dialog, select Squeeze for the Expand Style.

2 Click the Update Preview button, and note the change in the animation.

3 Enter 200 for the Fragment Offset value.

4 Set the values for Change Fragment Size by to 120 for Height and 110 for Width.

5 Click OK.

Press ←Enter to preview the animation. It's close to the effect we want, but the letters aren't moving quite far enough.

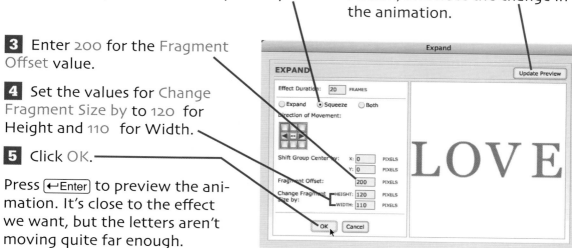

add timeline effects (cont.)

Move the Playhead back to Keyframe 13, and select the symbol that the effect created. (The original text box has been broken up into pieces; that's why we copied it into all of the other keyframes before we started adding the effects.)

In the Property Inspector, click the Edit button to launch the Expand dialog.

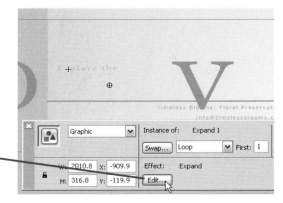

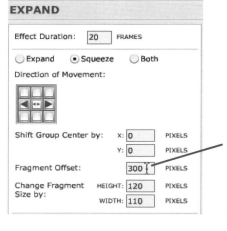

Change the Fragment Offset value to 300, and click OK.

With our animation set to our liking, we're going to add a motion tween of alpha transparency.

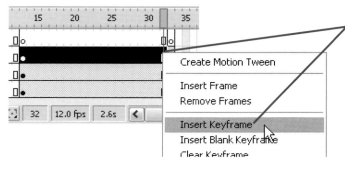

Select Frame 32, and insert a keyframe.

Read the warning dialog that appears, and click OK. We won't be able to make further changes to the animation.

Move the Playhead back to Keyframe 13, and select the symbol. Click the Color Styles drop-down menu and select Alpha. Set the Alpha Amount to 10%.

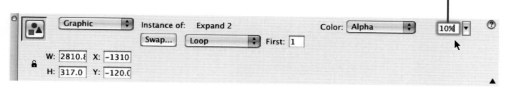

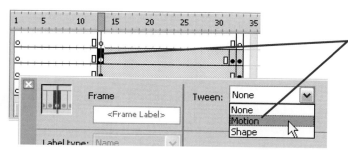

In the Timeline, click Keyframe 13 to select it. In the Property Inspector, click the Interpolation drop-down menu and choose Motion.

Press [←Enter] to preview the animation.

That completes the zoom-in of the text.
Now let's do a reverse, and zoom the text out.

add timeline effects (cont.)

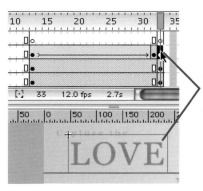

Move the Playhead to Keyframe 33 and select the LOVE text box. Right-click (Windows) or [Control]-click (Mac) on the text box, and choose Timeline Effects > Effects > Expand from the drop-down menu.

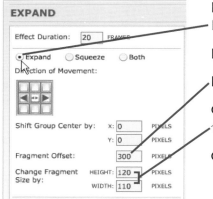

In the Expand dialog, confirm that Expand is selected as the Expand Style.

Enter these settings:

Fragment Offset: 300

Change Fragment Size by:
120 Height and 110 Width

Click OK.

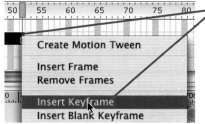

Select Frame 52, and insert a keyframe. Click OK in the warning dialog.

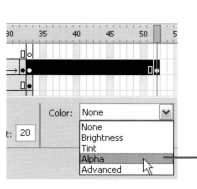

Click to select the symbol. In the Property Inspector, click the Color Styles drop-down menu, and choose Alpha. Set the Alpha Amount to 10%.

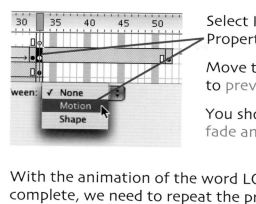

Select Keyframe 33, and set a Motion tween in the Property Inspector.

Move the Playhead to Keyframe 1, and press ⏎Enter to preview the animation.

You should see the text fade and zoom in and then fade and zoom out. If not, review the steps above.

With the animation of the word LOVE complete, we need to repeat the process to create a zoom for our next word: MOMENT.

In the Eye column of the Timeline, click to hide the current layer, and then click to show Layer 2.

Change the text in Layer 2 to MOMENT in keyframes 13 and 33.

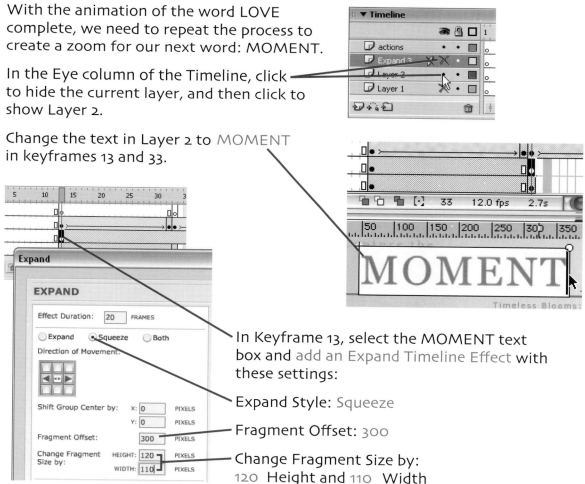

In Keyframe 13, select the MOMENT text box and add an Expand Timeline Effect with these settings:

Expand Style: Squeeze

Fragment Offset: 300

Change Fragment Size by:
120 Height and 110 Width

add animation to your web site

add timeline effects (cont.)

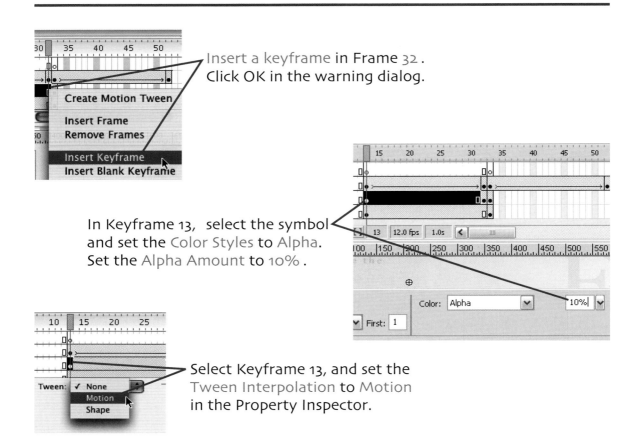

Insert a keyframe in Frame 32.
Click OK in the warning dialog.

In Keyframe 13, select the symbol and set the Color Styles to Alpha.
Set the Alpha Amount to 10%.

Select Keyframe 13, and set the Tween Interpolation to Motion in the Property Inspector.

In Keyframe 33, select the MOMENT text box and add an Expand Timeline Effect with these settings:

Expand Style: Expand

Fragment Offset: 300

Change Fragment Size by:
120 Height and 110 Width

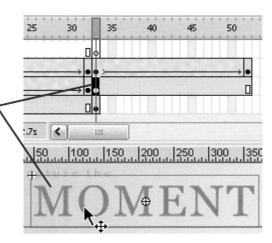

Insert a keyframe in Frame 52.
Click OK in the warning dialog.

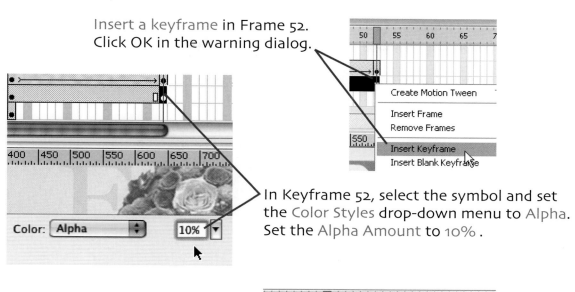

In Keyframe 52, select the symbol and set
the Color Styles drop-down menu to Alpha.
Set the Alpha Amount to 10%.

Select Keyframe 33, and set the
Tween Interpolation to Motion
in the Property Inspector.

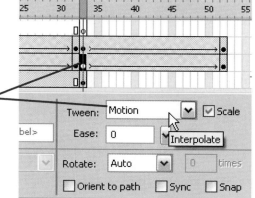

That completes our second segment of animation. Now we just need to add a
zoom in segment for our final word: MEMORIES.

add timeline effects (cont.)

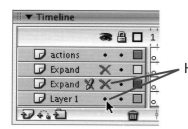

Hide the current layer and make Layer 1 visible .

In Keyframe 13, select the MEMORIES text box, and add an Expand Timeline Effect with these settings:

Expand Style: Squeeze

Fragment Offset: 300

Change Fragment Size by: 120 Height and 110 Width

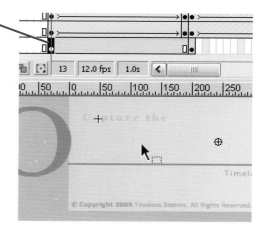

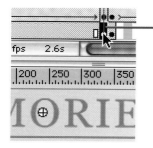

Insert a keyframe in Frame 32 . Click OK in the warning dialog.

In Keyframe 13, select the symbol and set the Color Styles drop-down menu to Alpha. Set the Alpha Amount to 10% .

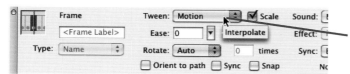

Select Keyframe 13, and set the Tween Interpolation to Motion in the Property Inspector.

move animations

Now all of our animation segments are created, but they're stacked on top of one another, all playing at the same time. We need to spread them out in the Timeline.

The animation for the word LOVE will stay where it is, playing in frames 13 through 52. We want the MOMENT animation to start about one second (12 frames) later, so we'll move its first frame to 64.

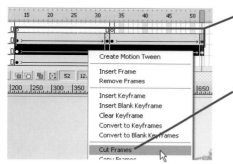

In the layer containing the MOMENT animation, click Keyframe 13. Press [Shift] and click Keyframe 52 to select the range of frames. Right-click (Windows) or [Control]-click (Mac) on the selected frames, and choose Cut Frames from the drop-down menu.

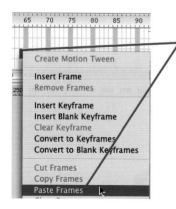

Right-click (Windows) or [Control]-click (Mac) on Frame 64, and choose Paste Frames from the drop-down menu.

Now let's move the MEMO-RIES animation to begin in Frame 115. In the layer containing the MEMORIES animation, select the range of frames from 13 to 33. Right-click (Windows) or [Control]-click (Mac) on the selected frames, and choose Cut Frames from the drop-down menu.

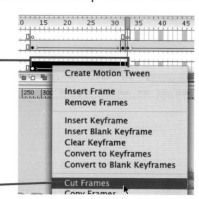

Right-click (Windows) or [Control]-click (Mac) on Frame 115, and choose Paste Frames from the drop-down menu.

Move the Playhead to Keyframe 1, and press [←Enter] to preview our complete animation.

pause an animation

The animation looks great, but it all flies by too fast. We want to add a pause after the text zooms in and before it zooms back out, holding the word in place long enough for it to register with the viewer. (See extra bits on Page 78.)

First we'll pause the word LOVE. Make all of the layers in the symbol visible. In the actions layer, select Frame 32 and, add a keyframe.

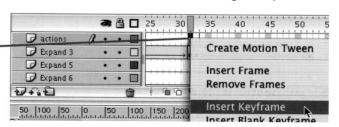

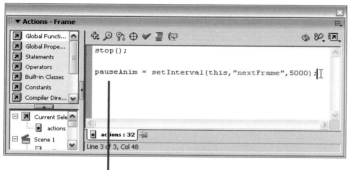

Open the Actions panel, and enter this code in the Script pane:

```
stop();
pauseAnim = setInterval(this,"nextFrame",5000);
```

This code stops the animation, creates a timer, and moves to the next frame after 5 seconds (5000 milliseconds).

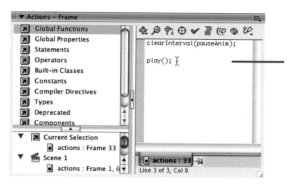

Select Keyframe 33 in the Timeline. Enter this code in the Script pane to delete the timer and play through the rest of the Timeline:

```
clearInterval(pauseAnim);
play();
```

add animation to your web site

Select Frame 34, and choose Insert >
Timeline > Insert Blank Keyframe .
This restricts the ActionScript to
Frame 33 only.

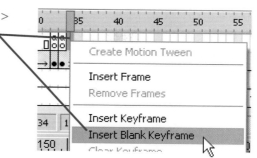

Next we'll pause the word MOMENT using the same ActionScript code.
In the actions layer, click to select Frame 32. [Shift]-click Frame 34 to select
all three keyframes.

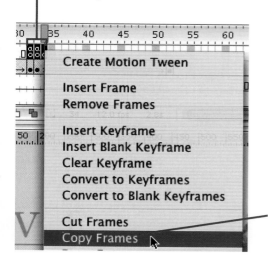

Copy the frames.

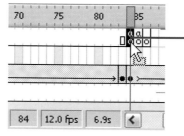

Select Frame 84 and
Paste the frames.

add animation to your web site

preview your movie

Up to this point, we've previewed our animations in the Flash workspace. To preview the effect of the ActionScript pause however, the animation has to be exported as a SWF file and viewed in the Flash Player.

We can do that quickly without going through the export process.

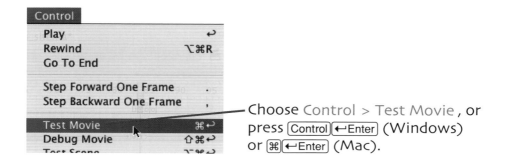

Choose Control > Test Movie , or press (Control)(←Enter) (Windows) or (⌘)(←Enter) (Mac).

Flash quickly exports the SWF, opens a new window, and plays the animation.

Notice the pause on the words LOVE and MOMENT; our ActionScript is working.

The animation loops because we haven't set any ActionScript in the final frame of the Timeline. We'll do that next.

Click the Close button to close the Flash Player window.

control movie clips

Remember that our text animation movie clip is playing in Keyframe 1 of the animated background movie clip. That frame, labeled anim_text, has Action-Script that stopped the Playhead. We're going to move the Playhead forward with ActionScript in the final frame of the text animation movie.

Flash provides easy-to-use, pre-packaged actions called Behaviors. We'll use a Behavior to add the ActionScript we want.

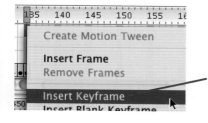

In the actions layer, add a keyframe to Frame 135 .

Open the Behaviors panel (Window > Development Panels > Behaviors). Click the Add Behavior button.

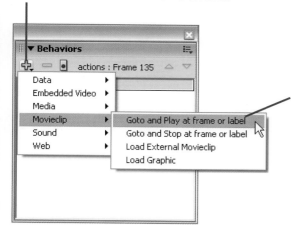

In the drop-down menu, choose Movieclip > Goto and Play at Frame or Label.

control movie clips (cont.)

In the Goto and Play at frame or label dialog, select (animated background) from the list.

Confirm that the button labeled Relative is selected.

In the Frame Number or Frame Label text field, enter anim_image.

Click OK.

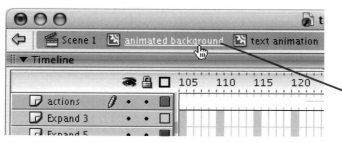

Our text animation is now complete. Click animated background in the Edit Bar to exit symbol-editing mode on the text animation movie clip.

add animation to your web site

add a transition effect

As the final piece in our intro animation, we want the image of the bouquet to appear after the text animation completes. We'll use a Transition effect to fade it in.

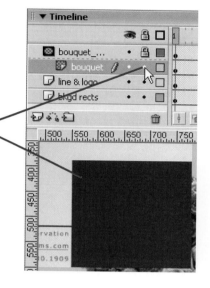

In the Layers column of the Timeline panel, click the Lock icon in the bouquet layer to unlock it. The rectangle we used to mask the bouquet image becomes visible when either layer is unlocked. Ignore it for now. Hide the bouquet_mask layer.

Select the bouquet image. Right-click (Windows) or Control-click (Mac) the image. Choose Timeline Effects > Transform/Transition > Transition in the drop-down menu.

add a transition effect

1 In the Transition dialog, enter a value of 15 frames for the Effect Duration.

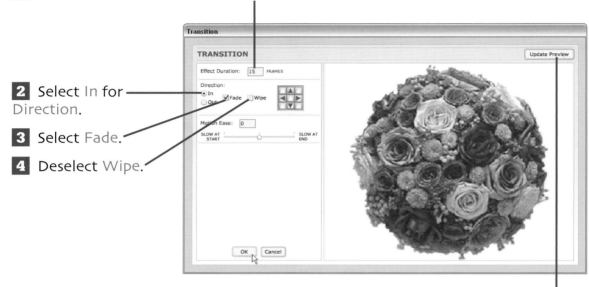

2 Select In for Direction.

3 Select Fade.

4 Deselect Wipe.

5 Click the Update Preview button to preview the changes.

6 Click OK.

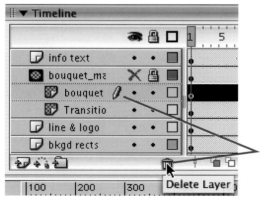

Flash has created a new layer in the Timeline and placed the transition there, leaving the layer bouquet empty. Let's delete it. Select the bouquet layer. Click the Delete Layer button at the bottom-right of the layers column.

Now we need to move the transition so that it begins after the text animation ends. In the transition layer, click any frame between 1 and 15; the range of frames containing the transition is selected.

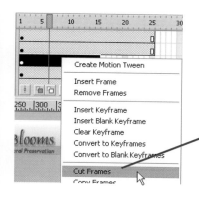

Right-click (Windows) or Control-click (Mac) the selected frames, and choose Cut Frames from the drop-down menu. Click OK in the warning dialog that appears.

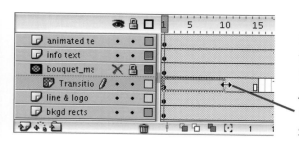

Move the cursor over Frame 15, the final frame in the span from Keyframe 1. Press Ctrl (Windows) or ⌘ (Mac). A bi-directional arrow cursor appears. Click and drag the frame to the left, stopping in Frame 10.

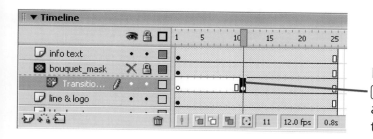

Right-click (Windows) or Control-click (Mac) Frame 11, and choose Paste Frames from the drop-down menu.

add animation to your web site

add a transition effect

Make the bouquet_mask layer visible again. Lock the transition layer.

Our final step in creating the intro animation is to have its last frame move the Playhead in the main Timeline to the frame with the static background.

Add a keyframe in Frame 25 of the actions layer.

Open the Behaviors panel. Click the Add Behavior button.

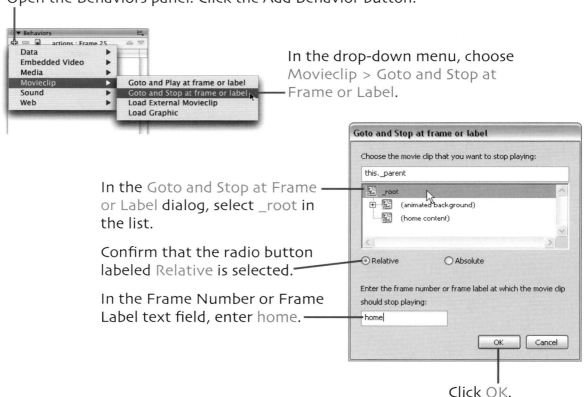

In the drop-down menu, choose Movieclip > Goto and Stop at Frame or Label.

In the Goto and Stop at Frame or Label dialog, select _root in the list.

Confirm that the radio button labeled Relative is selected.

In the Frame Number or Frame Label text field, enter home.

Click OK.

Click Scene 1 in the Edit Bar to exit symbol-editing mode. Save your file.

That's it. Our intro animation is complete. Press ⌜Control⌝⌜←Enter⌝ (Windows) or ⌈⌘⌉⌜←Enter⌝ (Mac) to preview your work in the Flash Player window.

extra bits

create a motion p. 52

- An animation is a series of static images (frames), where objects change incrementally from a beginning point to an end point. In Flash, we can define the beginning and end states with keyframes and let Flash generate the incremental frames. This method of creating the in-between frames is called tweening.

- There are two types of tweens in Flash: motion and shape. Motion tween is a bit of a misnomer, as it can be used to create changes not only in placement (motion) but also in alpha transparency, size, rotation, skew, and color effect. Motion tweens are applied to keyframes in a layer and only work when the layer contains only groups, symbol instances, and/or text blocks.

  Shape tweens work on shapes, not groups, symbols, or text blocks, and are used to change or "morph" the appearance of the shape.

complex animation p. 55

- Ah, the Flash intro to a Web site—probably the most reviled Web phenomenon since the HTML Blink tag. The interminable wait to see the content you came to the site for in the first place and the frantic search for a Skip button, hoping the developer included one, made it all too much to bear and sent many viewers fleeing without ever getting into the site.

  So what will we do? Create an intro, of course! However, we're going to create one that's done the right way—the evolved way. Here are the rules we'll follow to ensure that the animation doesn't irritate our viewers and doesn't get in the way of our content, which is, after all, the reason for having the site. The guidelines and how we're following them are as follows:

  Make it simple and meaningful. Our animation will be elegant while actually furthering Timeless Blooms' marketing message of capturing the emotion of special events.

continues on next page

extra bits

Don't let your intro obscure real content and navigation. Allow users to "get on with it" without waiting for the intro to finish. Our content and navigation buttons will be available from Frame 1, and the animation occurs outside the main content area.

Once viewers have seen the animation, don't make them view it again when navigating back to the home page from other areas of the site. This is why we created two keyframes in our main Timeline and created two background symbols, one for the intro and one for home.

pause an animation p. 68

- You've already seen that you can add time between animations by adding blank frames. We could add frames between the animation segments here, but we want a five second pause, which would require adding 60 blank frames, and our Timeline is already long and unwieldy. Instead, we'll use ActionScript to pause the Timeline.

- As a beginning Flash developer without deep understanding of ActionScript or other programming languages, you can often find code examples to use without understanding the technicalities of what they do.

  There are many resources on the Web that provide such examples. Visit the Macromedia Developer Forums at www.macromedia. com/support/forums/. Also, you can type a question like "how to pause a movie in Flash" in a Web search engine like google.com and get pointers to multiple developer sites offering code help.

- The code we use in this step is very simple. You can copy and paste it into any of your projects to create a pause in animation. To change the amount of time, simply change the number. Time is in milliseconds (1000ths) so 5000 equals 5 seconds.

6. build a navigation system

So far, we've created a great looking home page with an engaging introductory animation. But the site doesn't have any real content yet. It's like a movie with opening credits but no scenes revealing the plot.

In this chapter, we add keyframes to the main Timeline to define the site's sections, and create interactive buttons to navigate between those sections.

create buttons

The Web site has five sections: Home, Info, Gallery, Pricing, and Order. We need to create a button for each section. (See extra bits on Page 100.)

Choose Insert > New Symbol, or press Ctrl F8 (Windows) or ⌘ F8 (Mac).

In the Create New Symbol dialog, enter btn_gallery, and choose Button for the Behavior. Click OK.

Flash creates the new symbol and opens it for editing. Note the special button Timeline with a specially labeled frame for each button state.

Rename Layer 1 background. Add a new layer, and name it text. Leave the text layer selected.

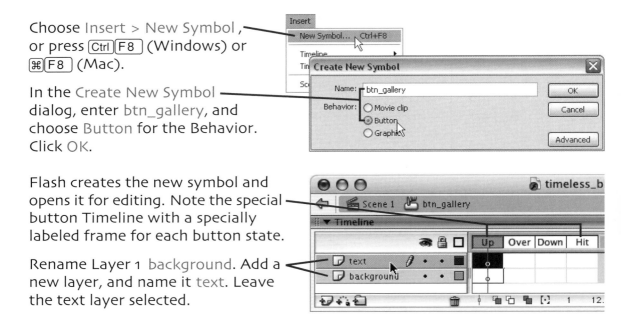

Click the Stage to reset the Property Inspector. Choose the Text tool, and set the following attributes in the Property Inspector:

Character Spacing: 0

Text Type: Static Text

Font: Verdana   Font Size: 14

Text (Fill) color: our light yellow

Alignment: Align Center

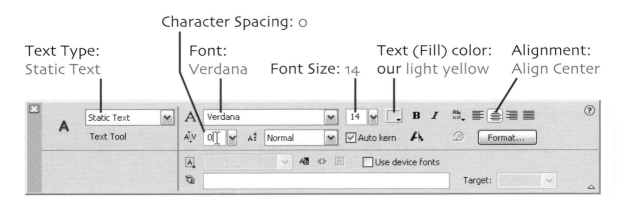

build a navigation system

Click near the Registration Point (+) in the center of the Stage, and type Gallery.

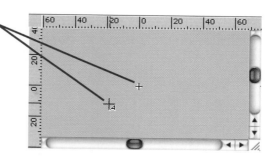

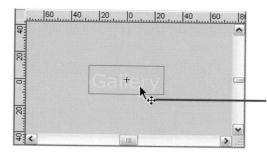

With the Selection tool, position the text box approximating the placement shown here.

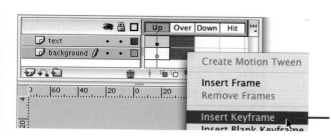

Our buttons won't have a background in the Up state, so we're ready to move on to creating the Over state. In the Timeline, select the Over frame in both layers, and insert a keyframe.

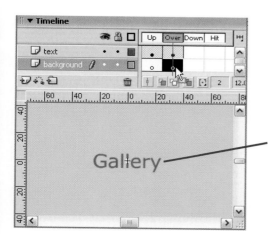

The Gallery text box has been copied into the Over frame. With the Selection tool, select the text box and change the color to our dark green.

Now we'll draw a circle for the background. Select the Over frame in the background layer.

build a navigation system

create buttons (cont.)

In the Tools panel, choose the Oval tool, and select our medium green color for both Stroke and Fill.

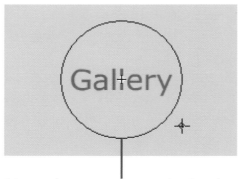

Before your click the Stage to draw the circle, press and hold [Alt] (Windows) or [Option] (Mac) to draw the circle from the middle, and press and hold [Shift] to constrain the oval to a circle.

Move the cursor over the Registration Point in the middle of the Stage. Click and drag out a circle slightly larger than the Gallery text. This completes the Over state.

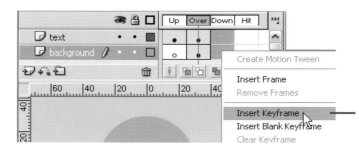

Select the Down frame in both layers, and insert a keyframe.

In the Layers column of the Timeline, click in the Eye column to hide the text layer.

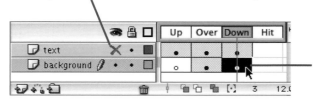

Select the Down frame in the background layer.

Select the Paint Bucket tool.

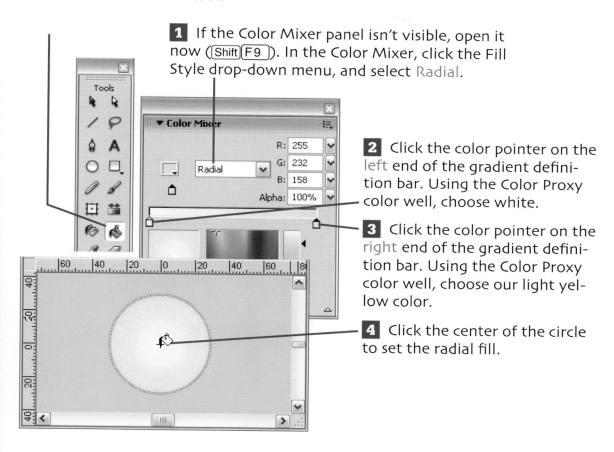

1 If the Color Mixer panel isn't visible, open it now ([Shift][F9]). In the Color Mixer, click the Fill Style drop-down menu, and select Radial.

2 Click the color pointer on the left end of the gradient definition bar. Using the Color Proxy color well, choose white.

3 Click the color pointer on the right end of the gradient definition bar. Using the Color Proxy color well, choose our light yellow color.

4 Click the center of the circle to set the radial fill.

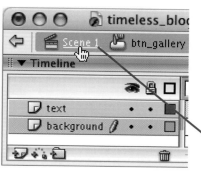

Make the text layer visible again.

The last step in creating a button is defining the Hit state, which defines the area of the button that responds to mouse activity. Before we do that, we're going to place the button on the Stage of our movie and then edit the button symbol in place.

Click Scene 1 in the Edit bar to exit symbol-editing mode.

build a navigation system

create buttons (cont.)

Add a new layer to the Timeline, and name it buttons. Drag the layer to position it between the contents and actions layers.

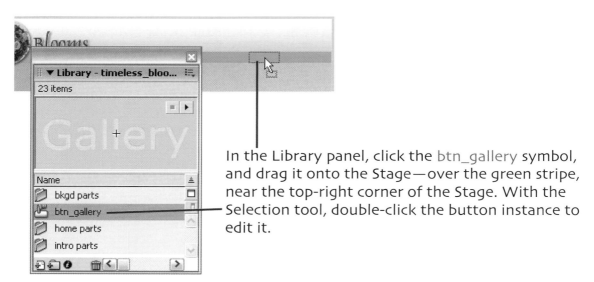

In the Library panel, click the btn_gallery symbol, and drag it onto the Stage—over the green stripe, near the top-right corner of the Stage. With the Selection tool, double-click the button instance to edit it.

Select the Hit frame in the background layer, and insert a keyframe.

The Hit area is defined by the shape of any objects in the frame. We only want a part of the circle to define our Hit area.

With the Selection tool, click and drag out a selection marquee to select the area of the circle that extends above the green stripe. Delete the selection. Repeat this procedure on the bottom section of the circle.

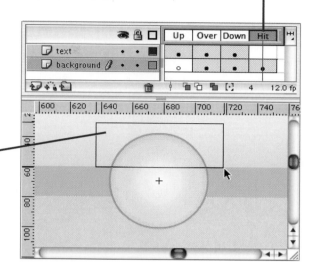

The remaining pieces of the circle now define our Hit area.

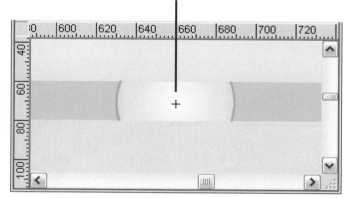

We've now completed a button design.

Click Scene 1 in the Edit bar to exit symbol-editing mode.

preview button actions

We can preview our button actions inside Flash.

Choose Control > Enable Simple Buttons.

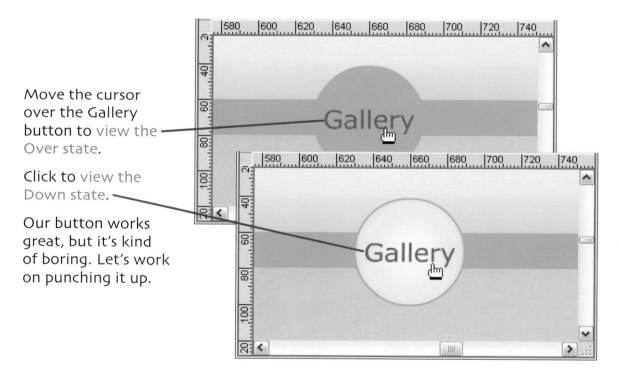

Move the cursor over the Gallery button to view the Over state.

Click to view the Down state.

Our button works great, but it's kind of boring. Let's work on punching it up.

Choose Control > Enable Simple Buttons again to turn off button preview.

build a navigation system

animate a button state

To make our button more interesting, we're going to add a small animation to the Over state and add a slight offset to the Down state.

With the Selection tool, double-click the button instance to edit it.

In the Timeline, click the Down frame of the background layer to select the circle with the gradient fill. Copy the circle to the clipboard.

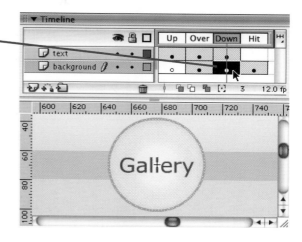

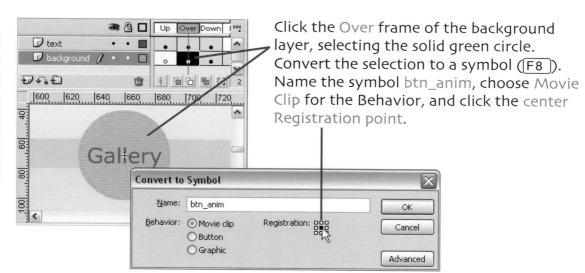

Click the Over frame of the background layer, selecting the solid green circle. Convert the selection to a symbol ((F8)). Name the symbol btn_anim, choose Movie Clip for the Behavior, and click the center Registration point.

animate a button (cont.)

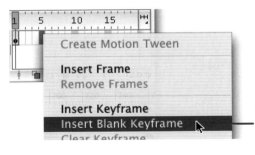

Double-click the new symbol to edit it. Insert a blank keyframe in Frame 5 of the Timeline.

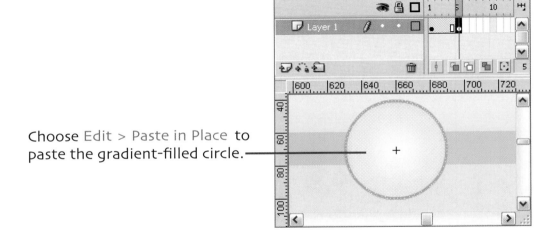

Choose Edit > Paste in Place to paste the gradient-filled circle.

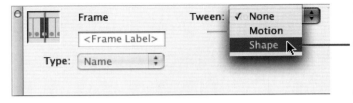

Select Frame 1. In the Property Inspector, set the Interpolate drop-down menu to Shape.

Press ←Enter to preview the animation.

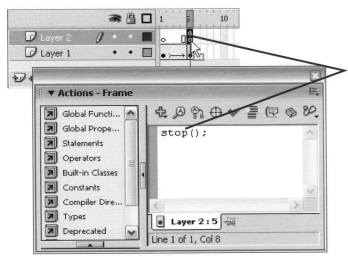

We need to add a Stop Action, or the animation will loop repeatedly when the user's mouse is over the button. Add a new layer. Insert a keyframe in Frame 5. Enter stop(); in the Actions panel.

Click btn_gallery in the Edit bar to exit symbol-editing mode for the movie clip.

For our Down state we want to move the objects down and to the right 1 pixel. Move the Playhead to the Down frame, and choose Edit > Select All to select the text and circle.

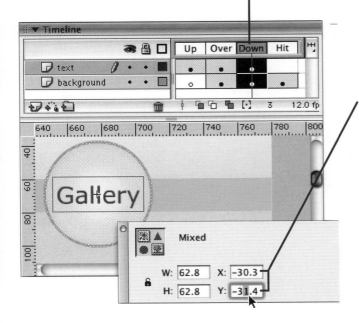

In the Property Inspector, add 1 to the x and y values of the selection. The values are negative, so if x = -31, change it to -30. Do the same for y.

We're done editing the button, so exit symbol-editing mode.

The Enable Simple Buttons feature won't show us the animated Over state, so we'll have to preview our buttons in the Flash Player. Choose Control > Test Movie, or press [Control][←Enter] (Windows) or [⌘][←Enter] (Mac).

add button sound

As the final touch to our button, we're going to add a click sound to the Down state.

Choose File > Import > Import to Library. In the Import to Library dialog, navigate to the development_files folder. Select the file btn_click.wav, and click Open.

Double-click the Gallery button to edit it. Add a new layer, and name it sound. Add a keyframe to the Down frame.

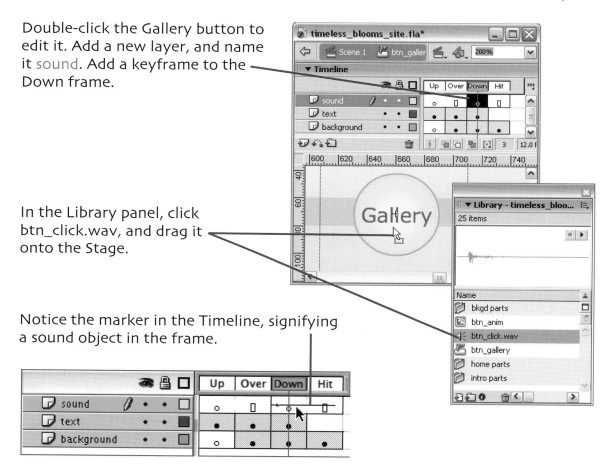

In the Library panel, click btn_click.wav, and drag it onto the Stage.

Notice the marker in the Timeline, signifying a sound object in the frame.

Exit symbol-editing mode.

If you want to test the sound, turn on Enable Simple Buttons.

duplicate buttons

Now that we've completed our button design, we need to make copies for each of the other sections of our site.

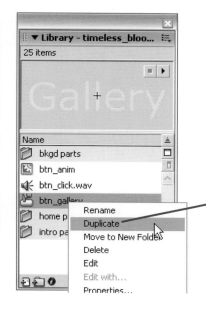

In the Library panel, right-click (Windows) or Control-click (Mac) the btn_gallery symbol, and choose Duplicate from the drop-down menu.

In the Duplicate Symbol dialog, name the symbol btn_home, and click OK.

duplicate buttons (cont.)

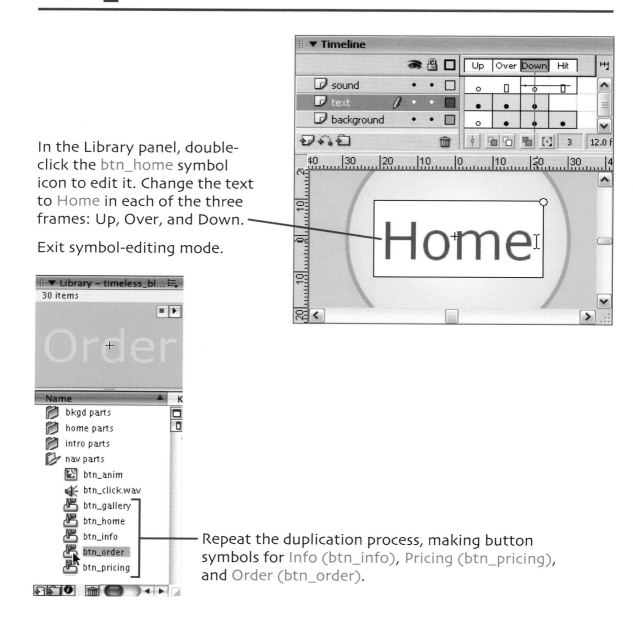

In the Library panel, double-click the btn_home symbol icon to edit it. Change the text to Home in each of the three frames: Up, Over, and Down.

Exit symbol-editing mode.

Repeat the duplication process, making button symbols for Info (btn_info), Pricing (btn_pricing), and Order (btn_order).

layout buttons

With a button for each of our sections complete, we can add them to the layout.

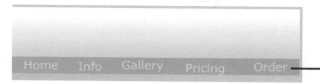

From the Library panel, drag out an instance of each of the buttons into the buttons layer, ordering them as shown here. (Don't worry about spacing or alignment; we'll fix that in a minute.)

With the Selection tool, click outside the Stage, and drag a selection marquee around the buttons to select them all.

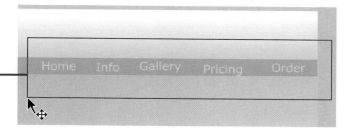

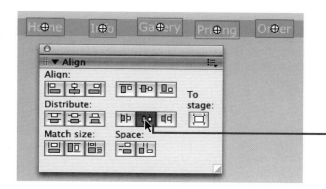

Choose Window > Design Panels > Align to open the Align panel. Click the Distribute Horizontal Center button to evenly space the buttons.

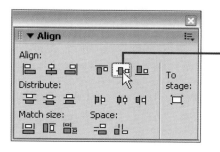

Click the Align Vertical Center button to align the buttons.

add sections to the site

Having buttons in our site is great, but we don't have anywhere for them to point to. We need to add the other sections of our site to the Timeline.

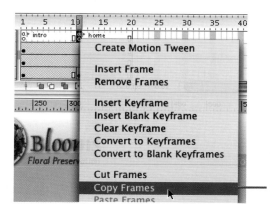

In the Timeline, select keyframe home in the actions layer.

Copy the frame.

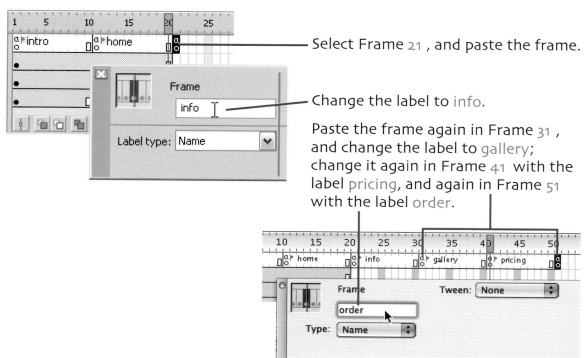

Select Frame 21 , and paste the frame.

Change the label to info.

Paste the frame again in Frame 31 , and change the label to gallery; change it again in Frame 41 with the label pricing, and again in Frame 51 with the label order.

build a navigation system

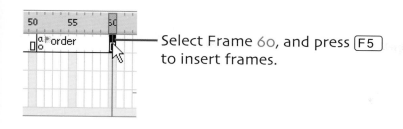

Select Frame 60, and press F5 to insert frames.

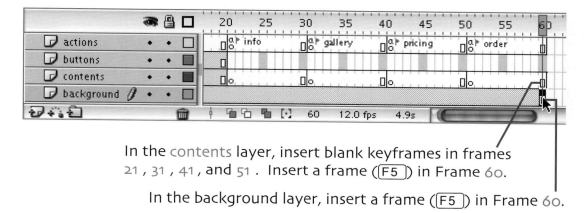

In the contents layer, insert blank keyframes in frames 21 , 31 , 41 , and 51 . Insert a frame (F5) in Frame 60.

In the background layer, insert a frame (F5) in Frame 60.

add actionscript

With our site sections defined, we have places for the buttons to navigate to. Let's add the navigation controls.

Move the Playhead back to Frame 1. Select the Home button.

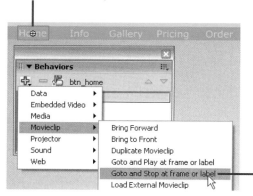

Open the Behaviors panel. Click the Add Behavior button. In the drop-down menu, choose Movieclip > Goto and Stop at frame or label.

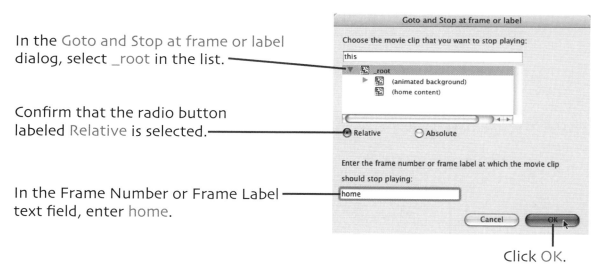

In the Goto and Stop at frame or label dialog, select _root in the list.

Confirm that the radio button labeled Relative is selected.

In the Frame Number or Frame Label text field, enter home.

Click OK.

The behavior is now listed in the panel and can be edited later, if necessary.

Select the Info button. Repeat the steps to add the Goto and Stop at Frame or Label behavior. Enter info in the Frame Number or Frame Label text field.

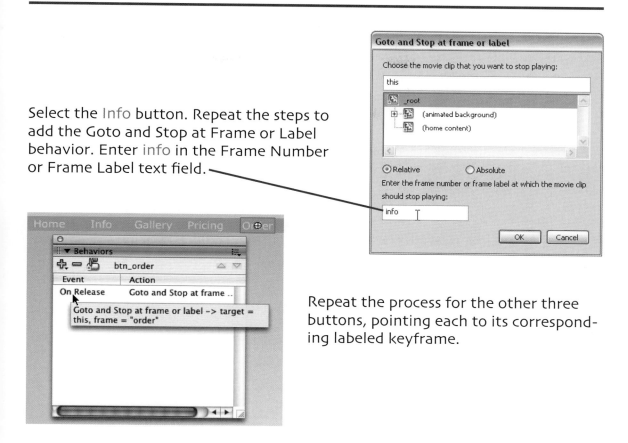

Repeat the process for the other three buttons, pointing each to its corresponding labeled keyframe.

With the behaviors attached, we're ready to copy the buttons to the other sections. In the buttons layer, insert keyframes in frames 21 , 31 , 41 , and 51 .

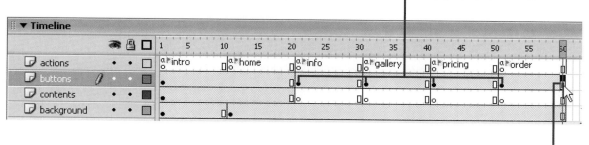

Add a frame (F5) in Frame 60.

alter button behavior

We want to provide viewers with a visual cue of where they are within the Web site. We do that by displaying the Down state of the corresponding button in each section of the site.

We can instruct Flash to treat a button symbol as a graphic, rather than as a button, to disable it and display its Down state.

Move the Playhead to Frame 1, and select the Home button.

In the Property Inspector, click the Symbol Behavior drop-down menu, and choose Graphic.

A dialog appears warning that the ActionScript will be deleted from the button. Click OK.

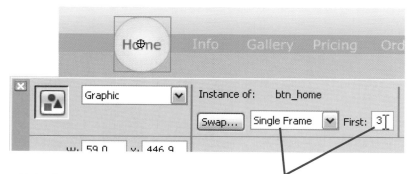

Click the Options for Graphics drop-down, and choose Single Frame. Enter 3 in the First Frame field. The third (Down) frame of the button symbol is displayed.

Move the Playhead to Frame 21 , and select the Info button. In the Property Inspector, set the same attributes that you did for the Home button.

Step through the remaining three sections, repeating the process in each.

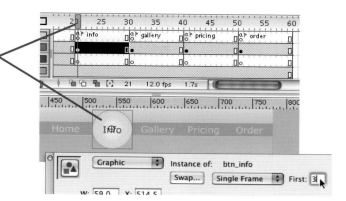

Press ⌈Control⌉⌈←Enter⌉ (Windows) or ⌘⌈←Enter⌉ (Mac) to preview your work and test your button navigation in the Flash Player window.

You've now successfully created a navigation system for your site!

Save your file.

extra bits

create buttons p. 80

- Button symbols provide an easy method for creating the type of interactive, multi-state button we're accustomed to seeing on the Web. Buttons have different images (referred to as states) that display based upon user action. The Up state displays by default; the Over state displays when the user moves the mouse over the button; and the Down state displays when the button is clicked. A fourth state, Hit, is never displayed but is used to define the active area of the button.

- In most cases, you'll use the same graphic elements for all of your buttons. When you're working out the design, work with the text of the longest name you'll need. This ensures that the graphic fits all of your buttons and you won't have to make frustrating fixes later. In our project, we start with the Gallery button because it is just a little bit wider than Pricing.

7. add inside sections of the web site

In this chapter, we work on developing the content for the different sections of our Web site. We'll accomplish the following:

Add a progress bar to update viewers when a large file is downloading.

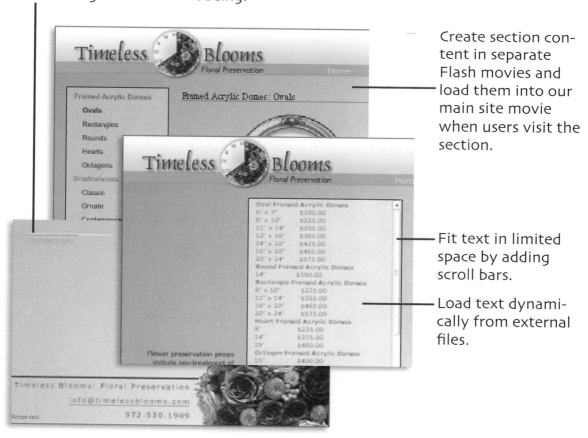

Create section content in separate Flash movies and load them into our main site movie when users visit the section.

Fit text in limited space by adding scroll bars.

Load text dynamically from external files.

build separate movies

If your Flash file takes too long to load when users visit the site, you run the risk of driving them away. One way we reduce that likelihood is by creating content for the site in separate Flash movies that are downloaded into our main movie when they're needed, as the user moves through the site.

For instance, when users go to the Gallery section of the site, they'll be view-ing the Gallery keyframe of our main movie (timeless_blooms_site.swf) with another movie (contentGallery.swf) loaded into the frame.

We'll learn the mechanics of loading movies a little later. First we need to create a movie to load.

add inside sections of the web site

create scrolling text

There is more text for the Info section than will fit within the content area of our layout. To fit the text into the area, we'll create a text box with an attached scroll bar component. (See extra bits on Page 120.)

Choose File > Open . In the Open dialog, locate the file contentInfo.fla that you downloaded from this book's companion site and copied into the site's development_files folder. Select the file, and click Open.

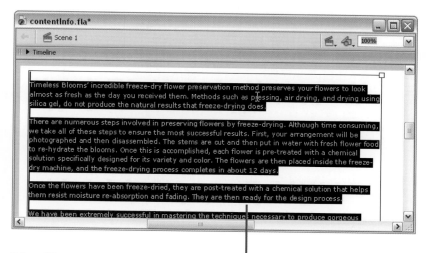

The file contains one large text box with all the copy for the Info section. Double-click the text box, and choose Edit > Select All. Choose Edit > Cut, or press Ctrl X (Windows) or ⌘ X (Mac) to move the text box to the clipboard. We'll paste the text into a special text box later.

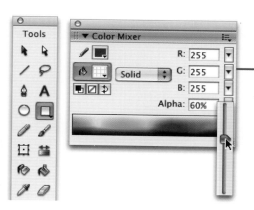

Select the Rectangle tool. In the Color Mixer panel (Window > Design Panels > Color Mixer), click the Stroke color well, and choose our dark rose color from the pop-up swatches pane. Click the Fill color well, and choose white. Change the Alpha value to 60%.

create scrolling text (cont.)

Click the top-left corner of the Stage, and drag out a 640 X 395 pixel rectangle (this matches the dimensions of the usable area in our site design). Check the location and size values in the Property Inspector, and change them if you need to.

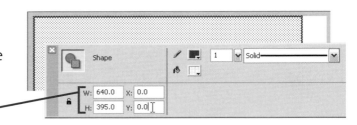

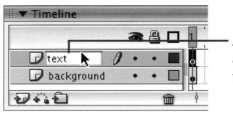

Add a new layer to the Timeline, and name it text. Click on the Stage to reset the Property Inspector.

Select the Text tool, and set the following attributes in the Property Inspector:

Text Type: Dynamic Text

Font: Verdana   Font Size: 11

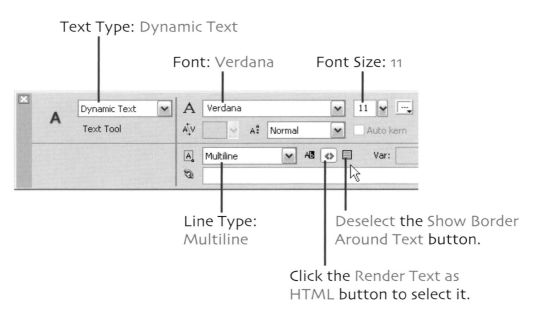

Line Type: Multiline

Deselect the Show Border Around Text button.

Click the Render Text as HTML button to select it.

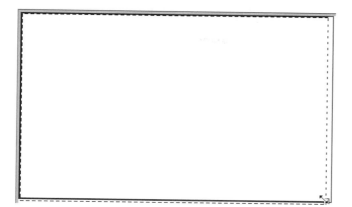

Click the Stage near the top-left corner, and drag out a text box close to the size of the background rectangle.

Choose the Selection tool. Choose Text > Scrollable to make the box accept more text than will fit within its dimensions.

In the Property Inspector, change the Text box placement and size as shown.

Give the text box the Instance Name textInfo.

Double-click the text box to edit it. Paste the text you copied earlier into the text box (Edit > Paste). The text is inserted in the box, and the end of the text is displayed.

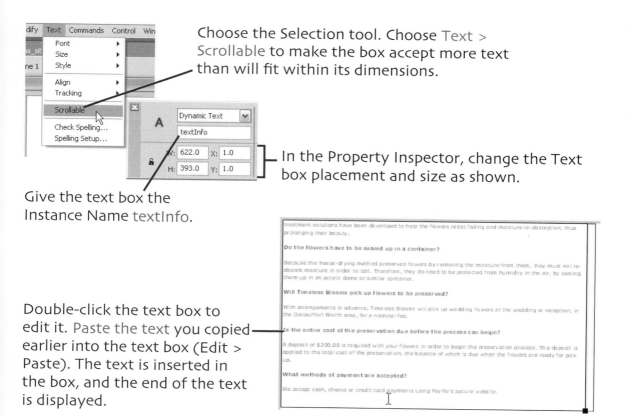

add inside sections of the web site

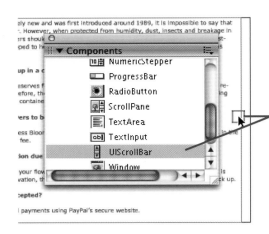

Choose Window > Development Panels > Components to open the Components panel. Click the UIScrollBar component, and drag it onto the Stage, just overlapping the right edge of the text box, and release. The component snaps to the right of the text box and automatically resizes its height to match the box's.

Finally, we need to shrink the Stage to fit our content. Click the Stage to deselect the UIScrollBar component. In the Property Inspector, click the Document Properties button. In the Document Properties dialog, click the Match Contents button to resize the Stage, and click OK.

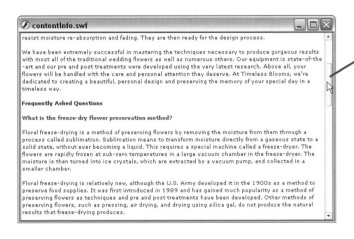

Test the movie, Control ←Enter (Windows) or ⌘ ←Enter (Mac), to view the working scrollbar. Close the Flash Player window.

When we test a movie, Flash exports a SWF movie file to play in the Flash Player, placing it in the same directory as the Flash file. Since we have no special publishing requirements for this movie, we can use that SWF to load into our main movie.

Save and close the Flash file contentInfo.fla.

load external movies

Back in our main Flash file (timeless_blooms_site.fla), we need to set up the file to load the contentInfo.swf movie into the Info section.

Move the Playhead to Frame 21 . The text Capture the MEMORIES looks kind of funny out of the context of the home page content and is taking up valuable Stage area that we could use for content. Let's make another background without the text.

In the Library panel, right-click (Windows) or Control-click (Mac) the background symbol. Choose Duplicate from the drop-down menu. In the Duplicate Symbol dialog, name the symbol background_no_text, and click OK.

Double-click the background_no_text symbol icon in the Library panel to open it for editing.

Select the two text boxes containing the words Capture the Memories, and delete them. Click Scene 1 in the Edit bar to exit symbol-editing mode.

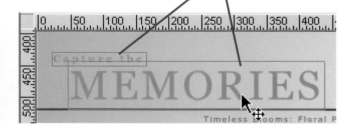

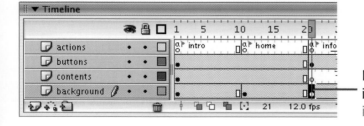

In the Timeline, select Frame 21 in the background layer, and insert a keyframe.

load external movies (cont.)

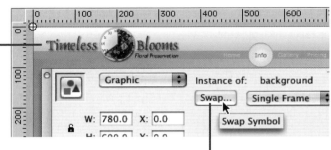

With the Selection tool, click to select the background symbol on the Stage.

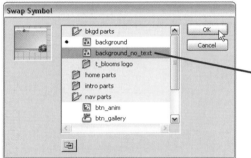

In the Property Inspector, click the Swap button.

In the Swap Symbol dialog, select background_no_text, and click OK.

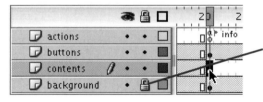

In the Layers column of the Timeline, click in the Lock column of the background layer to lock the layer so we don't accidentally select it as we work on content. Select Frame 21 in the contents layer.

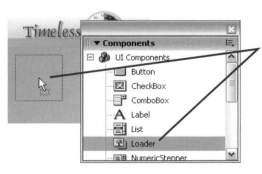

In the Components panel, click the Loader component, and drag it onto the Stage. A Loader Component symbol has been added to the Library, so we'll be able to reuse the symbol in other sections.

Use the Property Inspector to position the Loader symbol at x: 20 and y: 105 . Name the symbol instance loaderInfo.

Component symbols have special properties, parameters that you can set to specify different behaviors. Some of the parameters are displayed in the Parameters tab that is now visible in the Property Inspector, but a more complete set of parameters are displayed in the Component Inspector panel.

Open the Component Inspector panel (Window > Development Panels > Component Inspector). Enter contentInfo.swf in the Value field for the contentPath parameter.

Click in the scaleContent parameter value field, and select false in the drop-down menu. This instructs Flash to display our movie at its actual size, not sizing it to the 100 X 100 dimensions of the Loader symbol.

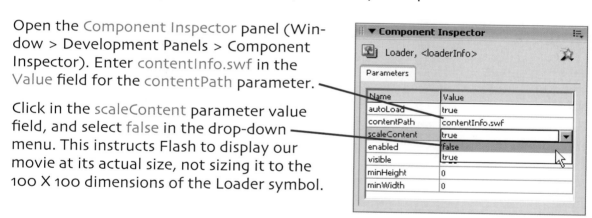

Choose Control > Test Movie , or press ⟨Control⟩⟨←Enter⟩ (Windows) or ⌘⟨←Enter⟩ (Mac). When the movie appears in the Flash Player window, click the Info button.

You see that our contentInfo movie with its scrolling text box is displayed in the content area exactly as we wanted.

Close the Flash Player window.

add inside sections of the web site

load external text

If you have text content for your site that changes on occasion, like a price list, you can put the information in a text (TXT) file with simple HTML formatting and load it into your movie. This makes updating the content much faster and easier—you can update the text file independent of your Flash movie. (See extra bits on Page 120.)

We'll load a text file that contains the Timeless Blooms price list into a movie (contentPricing.swf) that will load into our main movie. First we'll set up the Loader while we're in our main file.

Select the Loader symbol instance that loads the Info content, and copy it to the clipboard. Select Frame 41 in the contents layer, and choose Edit > Paste in Place.

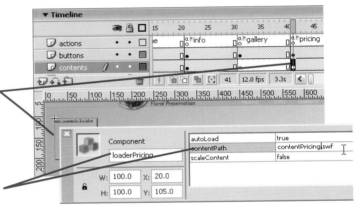

With the Loader symbol selected, change the Instance Name to loaderPricing in the Property Inspector. Change the contentPath value to content-Pricing.swf.

The Loader is ready; now we just have to create the movie. Open the file contentPricing.fla, located in the development_files folder.

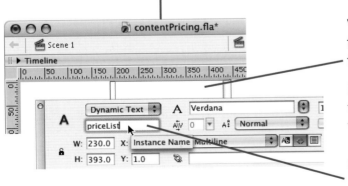

With the Selection tool, select the text box in the middle of the Stage.

In the Property Inspector, note that this text box is already set to Dynamic Text and that the Render Text as HTML button is selected. Change the Instance Name to priceList.

add inside sections of the web site

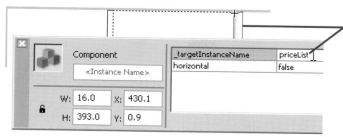

Select the UIScrollBar Component symbol that is attached to the right of the text box. In the Property Inspector, change the _targetInstanceName value to priceList to link the scroll bar to the text box.

Select Frame 1 in the actions layer. In the Actions panel, enter the code exactly as you see it here:

```
loadMyFile = new LoadVars( )
loadMyFile.onLoad = function ( )
{
    priceList.htmlText = this.priceList;
}
loadMyFile.load("contentPricing.txt");
```

Save the file, and minimize the Flash application to view your desktop.

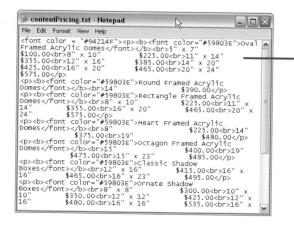

Locate your development_files folder. Inside the folder, locate the file content-Pricing.txt. This is the text file containing our price list information. We need to open it and add some text that identifies it for Flash. Double-click to open the file. The file will open in Notepad (Windows) or TextEdit (Mac).

You'll note that the text file is not formatted in a standard way with carriage returns; this is required to have the text appear correctly when loaded into the dynamic text box in Flash.

add inside sections of the web site

load external text (cont.)

Click to place the insertion point at the beginning of the file, before the text <font.

Enter priceList= . Save and close the file.

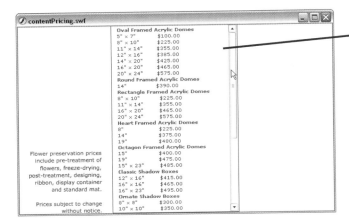

Make the Flash application visible again and test the movie, Control ←Enter (Windows) or ⌘ ←Enter (Mac). You'll see that the text box has been populated with the contents of the text file.

Close the Flash Player window. Save the Flash file content Pricing.fla, and close it.

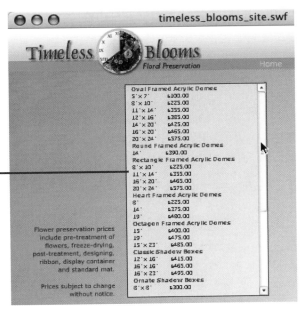

Back in the file timeless_blooms_site. fla, test your movie, Control ←Enter (Windows) or ⌘ ←Enter (Mac). When the movie appears in the Flash Player window, click the Pricing button to see your price list.

Close the Flash Player window.

add inside sections of the web site

link to external pages

We can link to and open external Web pages from within our Flash file. Those pages may be within our site or elsewhere on the Web. In this step, we'll add a link in the Order section movie that opens an HTML file containing an order form.

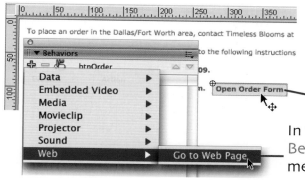

Open the file contentOrder.fla, located in the development_files folder.

With the Selection tool, select the Open Order Form button.

In the Behaviors panel, click the Add Behavior button. In the drop-down menu, choose Web > Go to Web Page.

In the Go to URL dialog, enter order_form. htm (included in the development_files folder) in the URL field. Choose "_blank" from the Open in drop-down menu to open the link in a new browser window.

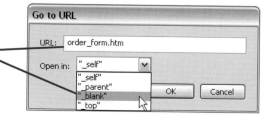

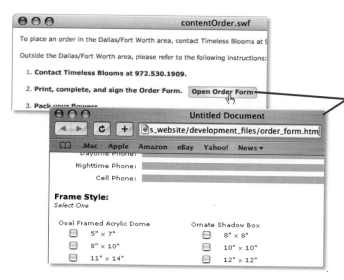

Test the movie, Control ←Enter (Windows) or ⌘ ←Enter (Mac). When the movie appears in the Flash Player window, click the Open Order Form button, and the HTML file should launch into a new browser window.

Close the browser window, and switch back to the Flash application. Close the Flash Player window.

Save and close contentOrder.fla.

add inside sections of the web site

link to external pages

Now we need to place a Loader in the Order section of our main movie to load the contentOrder.swf movie.

In the file timeless_blooms_site.fla, move the Playhead to Frame 41 .

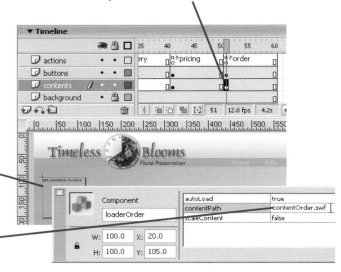

Select the Loader component instance, and copy it to the clipboard. Move the Playhead to Frame 51 , and choose Edit > Paste in Place. Click the symbol to display its properties in the Property Inspector.

Change the Instance Name to loaderOrder. Change the contentPath value to contentOrder.swf.

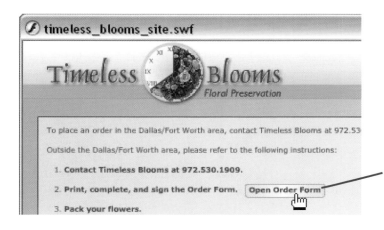

Test the movie, Control ←Enter (Windows) or ⌘ ←Enter (Mac). When the movie appears in the Flash Player window, click the Order button. Click the Open Order Form button to see the HTML file launched into a new browser window.

Close the browser window, and switch back to the Flash application. Close the Flash Player window.

add inside sections of the web site

slide show controls

Finally, a Web site like ours would be incomplete without samples of the beautiful work.

In this step, we open an existing Flash file with images and standard button navigation. We'll add buttons that make it a slide show, moving the Playhead to the next or previous frames in the Timeline.

Open the file contentGallery.fla, located in the development_files folder. Move the Playhead between several frames and note how the file is set up with buttons on the left side.

Select the slide show layer. Open the Library panel for this file and drag out an instance of the btn_prev symbol. Place the symbol instance at the left of the text View Gallery.

In the Property Inspector, enter prev_btn in the Instance Name field.

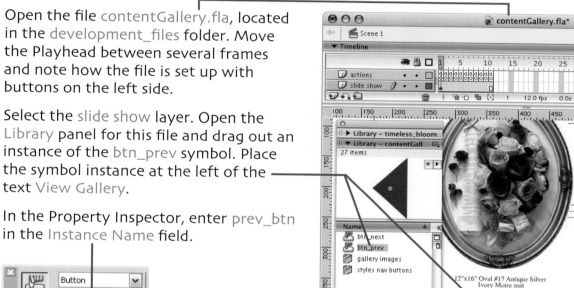

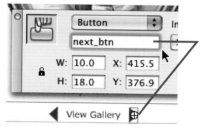

Drag an instance of the btn_next symbol to the right of the View Gallery text. Name the instance next_btn.

slide show controls (cont.)

Select Frame 1 of the actions layer. In the Actions panel, click after stop(); to place the insertion point, and press ⏎Enter twice.

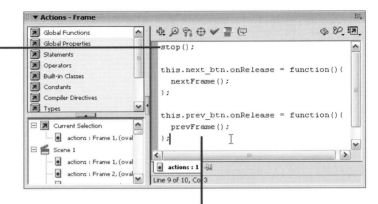

Enter the code shown here exactly as you see it:

```
this.next_btn.onRelease = function( ){
    nextFrame();
};

this.prev_btn.onRelease = function( ){
    prevFrame();
};
```

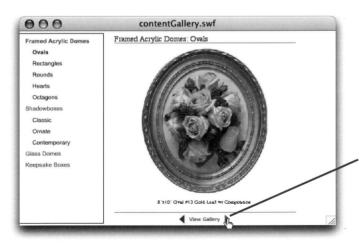

Note the text in the first line of each section that references the Instance Names you assigned to the button symbols.

You've just created slide show controls that you can reuse in your own projects. Test the movie, Control⏎Enter (Windows) or ⌘⏎Enter (Mac), to see the buttons in action.

Close the Flash Player window.

add progress bar

As you might imagine, the number of images in the gallery movie dramatically increase the file size. When you're loading a large file, it's a good idea to provide some feedback for the user to let them know what's happening and how long they can expect it to take.

In this section we'll add a progress bar that appears while the gallery movie loads.

First, we need to set up the Loader for our gallery movie. In the timeless_blooms_site.fla file, select Frame 51 in the contents layer. Select the Loader component instance, and copy it to the clipboard.

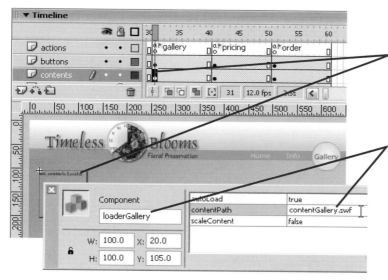

Move the Playhead to Frame 31, and choose Edit > Paste in Place. Click the symbol to display its properties in the Property Inspector. Change the Instance Name to loaderGallery. Change the contentPath value to contentGallery.swf.

In the Components panel, select the ProgressBar component. Drag the component into the center of the Stage.

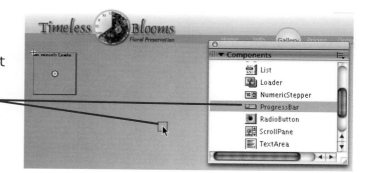

add progress bar (cont.)

The component symbol is added to the Library, and the Parameters tab appears in the Property Inspector. Click the Mode parameter drop-down menu, and choose polled. Enter loaderGallery in the Source parameter field, pointing the progress bar to the loader it will monitor.

With the component still selected, enter this code in the Actions panel to tell the component to disappear when the download completes:

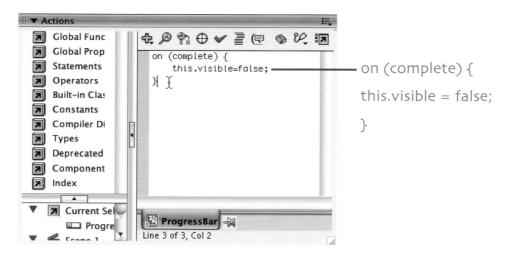

```
on (complete) {
    this.visible = false;
}
```

Test the movie, Control ←Enter (Windows) or ⌘ ←Enter (Mac). When the movie appears in the Flash Player window, click the Gallery button. Because the gallery file is loaded from your hard drive and not over the Internet, it may load too quickly for you to see the progress bar in action.

add inside sections of the web site

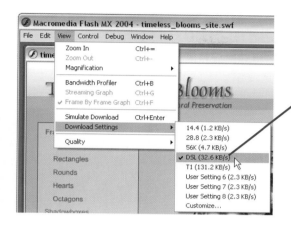

You can simulate a slower network connection with Flash's Simulate Download feature. With the Flash Player window still open, choose View > Download Settings > DSL (32.6 KB/s) .

Choose View > Simulate Download , or press Control ←Enter (Windows) or ⌘ ←Enter (Mac).

When the main movie loads, press the Gallery button and watch your progress bar in action.

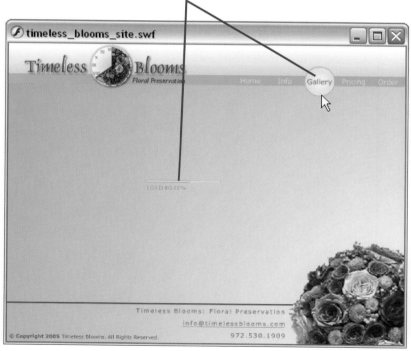

Close the Flash Player window.

All of our site sections are now filled with content. We're ready to prepare our files for upload to the Web.

Save your file.

extra bits

create scrolling text p. 103

- Dynamic text boxes, as the name implies, are designed to serve as containers for text from other sources (typically text loaded at run time). For that reason, you can't format individual text selections inside a dynamic text box. Any changes made via the Property Inspector are applied to all the text in the box. Additionally, dynamic text boxes have limited support for formatting applied to the source text.

  In our exercise, the text was formatted in a standard static text box using only rudimentary formatting options such as Bold and Font Color. If you were to select the static text box and change its setting to Dynamic, all formatting would disappear. To maintain our formatting, we copy or cut the text from the static (formattable) text box to the clipboard, and then paste it into the dynamic text box.

load external text p. 110

- Dynamic text boxes support a small subset of HTML formatting tags in loaded text. Only the following tags are supported:

  <a> anchor

  <a href=" "> hyperlink

  <b> bold

 line break

  <font color> font color

  <font face> font

  <font size> font size

  <i> italic

  <img> image

  <li> list item

  <p> paragraph

  <u> underline

add inside sections of the web site

8. publish your web site

With development of all of our site sections complete, the only thing left to do is to ready our files for upload to the Web.

In this chapter we accomplish the following:

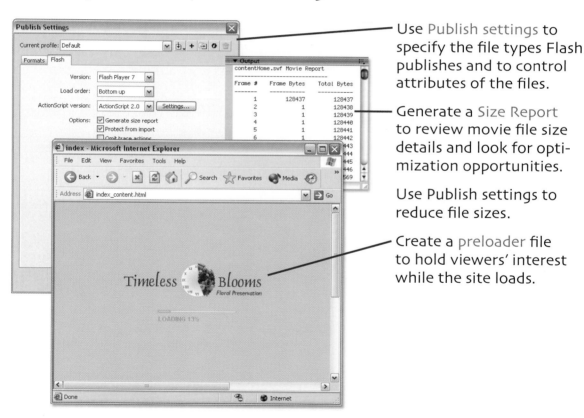

Use Publish settings to specify the file types Flash publishes and to control attributes of the files.

Generate a Size Report to review movie file size details and look for optimization opportunities.

Use Publish settings to reduce file sizes.

Create a preloader file to hold viewers' interest while the site loads.

swf settings

In Flash, we have the opportunity to specify different attributes for the files we're going to publish. In this section, we'll determine the Publish settings for our main site movie.

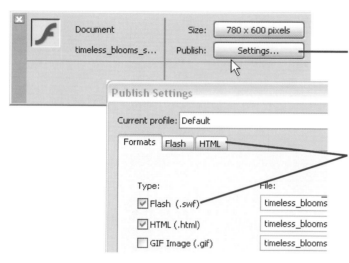

Choose File > Publish Settings, or click the Publish Settings button in the Property Inspector. The Publish Settings dialog appears.

In the Publish Settings dialog, there is one constant tab, Formats, and multiple other tabs that appear based upon the file types you choose in the Formats tab.

For now we only want to publish a SWF file. Choose the Formats tab, and click the checkbox next to HTML (.html) to deselect it. The HTML tab disappears.

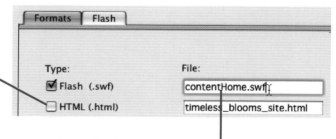

Note that Flash automatically assigns file names based on the name of the Flash file you're editing. Change the SWF Filename to contentHome.swf.

Click the Flash tab. The Version drop-down menu defaults to the Flash Player version associated with the version of Flash you're using. We won't change the setting.

Load Order determines in what order the Flash Player draws layers as the movie loads. Set the Load Order to Bottom up.

Leave the ActionScript version set to the default.

Click to select the Generate Size Report option.

Protect from Import prevents other people from importing your SWF file into Flash—protecting your work from theft. Click to select this option.

Ignore the Omit Trace Actions and Debugging Permitted options, as they are used for more advanced development than we've covered here.

Leave the Compress Movie option selected; it helps to reduce file size.

Leave the Password field blank; it's used in debugging.

Leave the JPEG Quality setting at 80.

Our one sound file was optimized before import, so we don't need to change anything in the Audio settings.

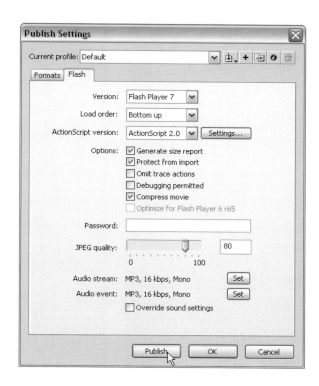

Click Publish. Click OK to close the Publish Settings dialog.

A new window, Output, appears. The window displays the Size Report, which has been generated for the SWF movie you've just published.

optimize file sizes

A Size Report provides a wealth of information about the size of your movie. In fact, the Size Report provides much more information than you need to understand. However, you can review the report to look for unusually large numbers that might lead you to think of ways to decrease file size.

The Total Byte column at Frame 60 (the final frame of the movie) shows that our movie is approximately 130,050 bytes or 130Kb —a bit large for someone on a slower connection. Let's see if we can find an optimization.

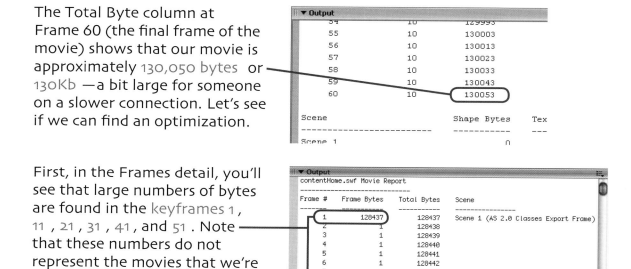

First, in the Frames detail, you'll see that large numbers of bytes are found in the keyframes 1, 11, 21, 31, 41, and 51. Note that these numbers do not represent the movies that we're loading in at run time.

Frame 1 provides the largest size hit because it includes our background components, intro animation, buttons, and all of the ActionScript classes needed to support the Actions throughout the movie.

The two next largest peaks in size are in frames 21 and 31 and can be explained by the addition of the Components we used there. We can't affect their size, so no optimizations are revealed.

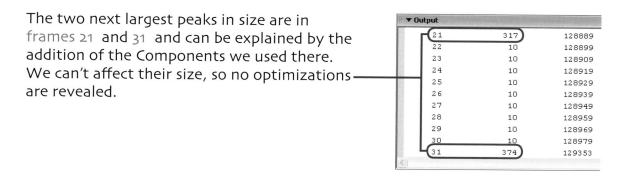

Scroll to the bottom of the document and look at the sizes of the four bitmaps included in our movie. Combined they add 34Kb to the total size. We can probably turn this discovery into an optimization opportunity.

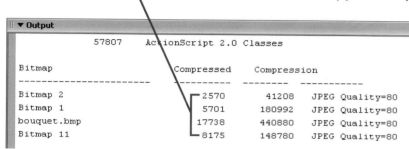

Close the Output window.

Lowering the JPEG Quality setting in the Publish Settings dialog will lower file size. However it's important to remember that there is a trade-off of image quality. The best approach is to try different settings and see if you find the results acceptable.

First let's try a really low number, providing more file size savings but a much lower quality. Open the Publish Settings dialog, and change the JPEG Quality setting to 20.

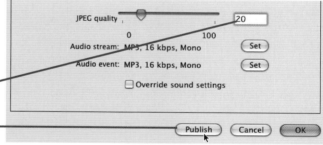

Click Publish. Click OK in the Publish Settings dialog.

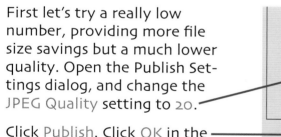

The Size Report shows that we've reduced the file size to just under 104Kb —a reduction of 26Kb. But what about the image quality?

Close the Output window.

optimize file sizes (cont.)

Test the movie, Control ←Enter (Windows) or ⌘←Enter (Mac). The quality of the images has degraded too much; we've set the quality too low. Close the Flash Player window.

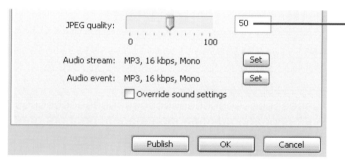

Click the Publish Settings button in the Property Inspector. Change the JPEG Quality setting to 50. Click OK.

Test the movie again. The Size Report shows a file size close to 114Kb (16Kb less than when we started), and the image quality is still good.

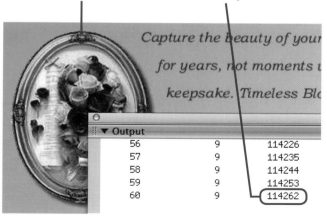

We'll go with these settings; however, we still have a pretty large file that could drive viewers away before it downloads. We'll work next to prevent that from happening.

create a preloader

Preloaders are the short animations and progress bars that play while a movie is loading. You've already created one preloader inside our site movie, the progress bar that plays while the gallery movie loads.

In this step, we create a fast-loading movie that contains only a logo, a Loader component that loads our main movie, and a ProgressBar component that provides download progress feedback to viewers.

When dealing with multiple movies loaded one into another, Flash Player can get confused by references to the Timeline—not understanding to which Timeline the reference points. We need to make one change in our main file to prevent this potential problem.

In the file timeless_blooms_site.fla, move the Playhead to Frame 31 . Select the ProgressBar component.

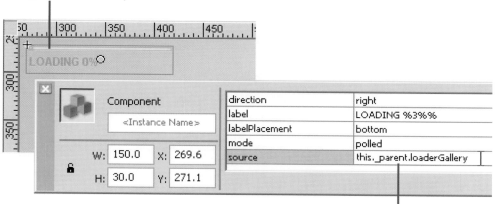

In the Property Inspector, change the source value to this._parent. loaderGallery. This new reference instructs Flash to look in this movie for the Loader component.

Choose File > Publish , or test the movie to generate an updated SWF file.

create a preloader (cont.)

Open the file index.fla, located in the development_files folder. The file has an animated logo symbol in the middle of the Stage.

Select Frame 1 in the loaded movie layer. From the Components panel, drag a Loader component to the top-left corner of the Stage.

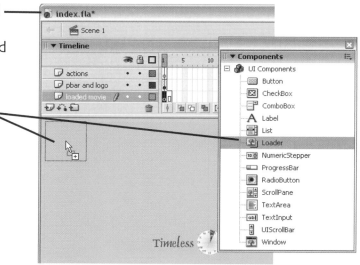

In the Property Inspector, make sure the component is placed at x: 0 and y: 0, and assign an Instance Name of loaderHome.

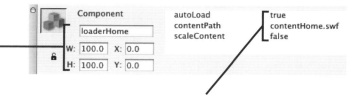

Enter contentHome.swf in the contentPath value field, and set the scaleContent drop-down menu to false.

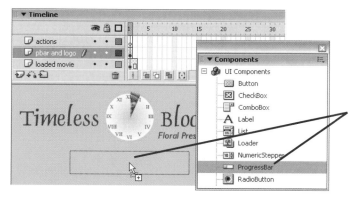

Select Frame 1 of the pbar and logo layer. From the Components panel, drag out a ProgressBar component, and center it just underneath the logo.

publish your web site

In the Property Inspector,
assign an Instance Name of
progressHome. Set the mode
drop-down menu to polled, and
enter this._parent.loaderHome
for the source value to connect
the Progress Bar with the Loader.

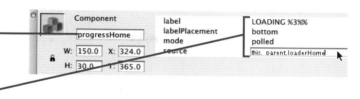

With the ProgressBar component still selected, enter this code in the
Actions panel:

```
on (complete) {
    this._parent.gotoAndStop("2");
}
```

This code instructs Flash to move the Playhead to Frame 2 when the movie is
completely loaded. Note that Frame 2 includes only the loaded movie layer,
so the progress bar and logo will disappear.

Finally, select Frame 1 in the actions
layer, and enter a stop Action (stop();)
in the Actions panel.

Test the movie to watch the preloader in
action. Close the Flash Player window.

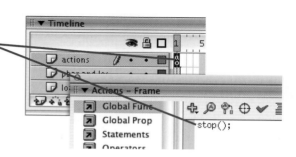

html settings

Flash movies on the Web need to be wrapped in HTML files that provide movie display instructions to the browser. The HTML files can also include code that checks for the presence of the correct Flash Player plug-in and redirects the viewer if it's not there.

Luckily for us, Flash can publish the HTML files we need so we don't have to do the HTML coding ourselves.

In the index.fla file, click the Publish Settings button in the Property Inspector. In the Publish Settings dialog, select the Formats tab. Click the checkbox next to HTML (.html) to select it. An HTML tab appears.

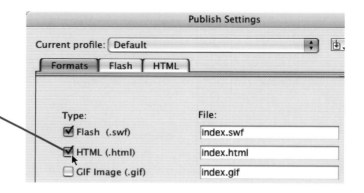

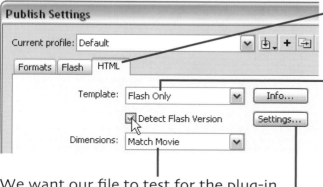

Select the HTML tab.

Flash generates the HTML file from a set of customizable templates designed for different Flash delivery requirements. Choose Flash Only from the Template drop-down menu.

We want our file to test for the plug-in and to provide an alternate HTML file if the plug-in isn't present. Click the check box to select Detect Flash Version.

Click the Settings button.

In the Version Detection Settings dialog, note that Flash will generate three HTML files. The Detection File (index.html) will be our site's first file, the file to which other sites may link and the file that loads when our URL is entered in a browser.

After the browser detection is executed, one of the other files will load—the Content file with our site movie or the Alternate file if the plug-in wasn't detected.

Click OK to close the Version Detection Settings dialog.

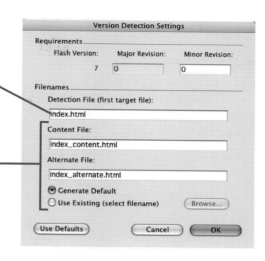

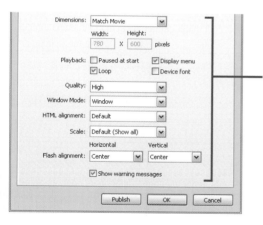

The remaining options in the HTML tab allow users to customize how their movies appear and behave in the browser window. For our purposes the default settings are appropriate, so we won't make any changes.

Select the Flash tab, and select Protect from Import.

Click the Publish button to generate the SWF movie file and the HTML files we've requested. Click OK to close the dialog.

Save and close the files index.fla and timeless_blooms_site.fla. Choose File > Exit (Windows) or Flash > Quit Flash (Mac) to close the Flash application.

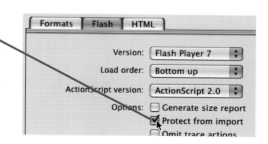

publish your web site   **131**

html settings (cont.)

From your computer's Desktop, navigate to the development_files folder. You'll see that Flash has added the Flash movie (index.swf), the three HTML files (index.html, index_alternate. html, and index_content.html), one movie used in the Flash Player detection (flash_detection. swf) and one graphic file (alternate.gif) that is used in the alternate HTML file.

Before we see our movie working correctly in our HTML files, let's view the alternate file. Double-click index_alternate.html to open the file in the browser. This is what viewers will see if they don't have the correct Flash Player to view our site. You can customize this file using a text or HTML editor, if you want it to reflect the look of your site. Close the browser window and return to the development_files folder.

Double-click the file index.html to open it.

Because you have the correct plug-in (that was installed with the Flash application) you probably won't even be able to tell that the first file loads and executes browser detection before loading the index_content.html file.

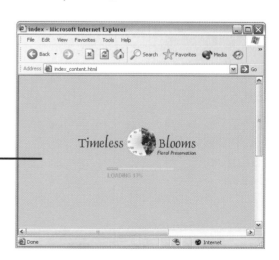

publish your web site

collect files for upload

Our final step is to collect all of the files that will be uploaded to your Web server and copy them into the site_files folder.

The following is a list of the files to copy, along with brief descriptions:

alternate.gif—an image file used in the alternate HTML file

contentGallery.swf—Gallery section movie with samples slide show

contentHome.swf—our main site movie including the Home section, animated intro, and loaders for all the other sections

contentInfo.swf—Info section movie with scrolling text

contentOrder.swf—Order section movie with button that launches the order form into a separate browser window

contentPricing.swf—Pricing section movie with text loaded dynamically from a text file

contentPricing.txt—Text file with HTML formatting that loads into Pricing movie

flash_detection.swf—Movie embedded in index.html file and used for Flash Player detection

index.html—First file loaded when visiting our site; executes Flash Player detection and redirects based on results

index.swf—Preloader movie with progress bar and Loader

index_alternate.html—Page providing Flash Player download option when Player detection fails to find the correct plug-in

index_content.html—Page containing index.swf; our site is displayed in this page

order_form.htm—A Web page containing the Timeless Blooms Order Form; launched from the Order section

collect files for upload

Once you've copied all of these files into the site_files folder, you're ready to upload them using your FTP application and instructions from your Web hosting company or Internet service provider.

When you're done uploading, be sure to view your site via a browser and confirm that everything is working as it should.

That's it! You've successfully created and published a Web site using Flash. Now you have the know-how to create attractive, useful Flash-based Web sites all on your own. Enjoy!

publish your web site

index

index

index

index

index

index

text files, 110, 111
Text (Fill) color control, 32
Text tool
  and e-mail links, 36
  and fixed-width text, 34
  and graphic text, 37
  and scrolling text, 104
  and single lines of text, 32
  and Timeline Effects, 59
Text Type menu, 32
TextEdit, 111
Timeless Blooms Web site
  adding sections to, 94–95,
    101–120
  building navigation system for,
    79–100
  creating home page for, viii–ix,
    40–41
  creating slide show for,
    115–116
  defining folder structure for, 2
  downloading asset files for, 1
  loading external movie into,
    107–109
  loading price list for, 110–112
  preparing files for, 1–8
  publishing, 121–134
  sections of, 80
timeless_blooms_site.fla, 107,
  114, 117, 127
timeless_blooms_website folder, 2
Timeline
  adding layers to, 104
  controlling, 47–48
  how keyframes are marked
    in, 49
  illustrated, xvi
  purpose of, xiii, xvi, 39
  sections of, xvi
  showing, 22
  types of frames in, 49
Timeline Control options, 47
Timeline Effects, 51, 55, 59–66
Tools panel, xv
Total Byte column, 124
transformation handles, 26
transforming objects, 26, 30
Transition dialog, 74

Transition effect, 51, 73–76
transparency, 53, 60
tweening, 52–53, 77
TXT files, 110, 111. See also
  specific files

U

UIScrollBar component, 106, 111
Ulrich, Katherine, xix
underlined text, 36
Up state, 81, 100
Update Preview button, 59
uploading files, 134
URL Link field, 36
user interface elements, xx, 106

V

vector art, 24, 30
Version Detection Settings dialog,
  131
view magnification, xiv, 17
Visual QuickPro Guides, xix
Visual QuickProject Guides, x–xi
Visual QuickStart Guides, xix

W

Web pages, linking to external,
  113–114
Web sites
  adding animation to, 51–78
    (See also animation)
  adding sections to, 94–95,
    101–120
  adding/styling text for, 31–38
  building navigation system for,
    79–100
  choosing color scheme for, 8
  creating home page for, viii–ix,
    40–41
  creating slide show for,
    115–116
  defining folder structure for, 2

designing visual framework
  for, 9
drawing background for, 11–12
Flash intros for, 77–78
linking to external pages from,
  113–114
loading external movies into,
  107–109
loading external text into,
  110–112, 120
Macromedia Exchange, xx
preparing files for, 1–8
publishing, 121–134
saving color scheme for, 6–7
this book's companion, xii
using Timeline to organize,
  39–50
Work Area, xiv, xx
wrapping text, 34, 35

Z

zooming in/out, 55–65